JOB ANALYSIS SERIES OF THE
AMERICAN ASSOCIATION OF
SOCIAL WORKERS

Number Five

VOCATIONAL GUIDANCE IN ACTION

VOCATIONAL GUIDANCE
IN ACTION

BY

JOHN A. FITCH

Published for

THE AMERICAN ASSOCIATION OF SOCIAL WORKERS

BY COLUMBIA UNIVERSITY PRESS

NEW YORK • 1935

PRINTED IN THE UNITED STATES OF AMERICA
COMMONWEALTH PRESS, WORCESTER, MASSACHUSETTS

JOB ANALYSIS COMMITTEE
AMERICAN ASSOCIATION OF SOCIAL WORKERS

Robert K. Atkinson, educational director, Boys' Club Federation

Neva R. Deardorff, director, Research Bureau, the Welfare Council, New York

Ralph G. Hurlin, director, Department of Statistics, Russell Sage Foundation

Albert J. Kennedy, secretary, National Federation of Settlements, and headworker, University Settlement, New York

Louise C. Odencrantz, superintendent, Handicapped Division, New York State Employment Service

Walter W. Pettit, assistant director, The New York School of Social Work

Lillian A. Quinn, director, Joint Vocational Service, Inc.

Frances Taussig, executive director, Jewish Social Service Association, Inc.

Janet Thornton, chairman, director of social service, The Presbyterian Hospital, New York

Walter M. West, executive secretary, American Association of Social Workers

40018

FOREWORD

In publishing this the fifth volume in the Job Analysis Series, the American Association of Social Workers completes an undertaking begun nine years ago. The preceding volumes have presented detailed descriptions of social work practice as it occurs in agencies for the care of the family, in hospital and psychiatric service, in settlements, Y.M.C.A., Boy Scouts, Camp Fire Girls, and other group-work agencies, in child care and protection, and in the treatment and prevention of delinquency and crime. It was the intention of the American Association of Social Workers to study and report on other jobs in social work, such as, for example, that of the visiting teacher and the practitioner-executive in rural and small-town communities who carry a combination load of many social-work specialties. The committee appointed by the Association to carry out this undertaking also considered at one time attempting analysis of jobs in organizations for coördinating and financing the social agencies of communities, such as councils of social agencies and community chests, and in organizations for the promotion, coördination, and standardization of social work in special fields, such as family welfare and child health. For several reasons such a program has not been carried out. The committee became convinced, moreover, that its method of analysis, which had been adapted from that employed in industry, would not yield true understanding of the promoting and coördinating functions, and that for this purpose a different method would have to be developed. In times less disturbed, the attempt to do this might have been made. In the present stress and uncertainty, we have decided to terminate the project with the publication of the study of jobs in the treatment of delinquency and of the present study of vocational counseling and placement.

The studies made have been of great interest and value to those who participated in making them. That they have been of interest to others is attested by the sales of published volumes and by requests for information and assistance from educational, religious, and other groups wishing to undertake similar studies of jobs in their own fields.

The committee recognizes the justice of certain criticisms of its product, as that the repetition of almost identical activities in similar jobs in different fields is tedious and even that the real spirit appertaining to some jobs is misrepresented by the analytical method of depicting them. It remains convinced none the less that the purpose it sought to fulfill was worth fulfilling and that it has in a fair measure been fulfilled. Briefly, this was to discover and describe what social workers in accepted community services were actually doing. Throughout the undertaking it has been our firm intention to hold to the point of view of "a person doing something" rather than that of evaluating things done or of promoting things desired. This is not to say that the evaluating of things done and the envisaging of goals desired is not of great importance, and no doubt of greater importance today in social work than the fact-finding quest we set out upon in 1926. Realization of the great need for resetting goals in social work, it may be said parenthetically, influenced not a little this committee's decision to terminate the present undertaking before many important types of jobs had been analyzed. More than forty jobs have been itemized and the relationships of these jobs within fields of social work displayed. Such value as this method has is well summed up in the comment of one critic: "The method you employed of studying actual situations rather than merely writing up the opinions of experts marks a forward step in the literature of social work."

For conception of the undertaking and for its initiation, credit is chiefly due to Dr. Philip Klein who was the executive secretary of the American Association of Social Workers when this committee began work in May, 1926. For adapting the job analysis method of industry to social work jobs and for analyzing and describing such jobs, credit is due to Miss Louise C. Odencrantz, Miss Margaretta Williamson, and Mr. John A. Fitch. The committee has felt it to be not only a privilege but a great pleasure to work with these able and devoted investigators. As the actual production of these reports would have been impossible without these students of social work so the whole undertaking would have been impossible but for the liberal and sustained support and encouragement of the Russell Sage Foundation. The work has been financed throughout the nine years by this Foundation. The New York School of Social Work coöperated in the financing of the present volume by releasing Mr. Fitch for a considerable part of the time necessary for his field investigations.

It is the committee's earnest hope that these published studies will continue to clarify for many the character and value of social work and will also stimulate further inquiry.

JANET THORNTON, chairman
Job Analysis Committee

NEW YORK CITY
MARCH 4, 1935

PREFACE

This study was first suggested in 1927 by the Committee on Job Analysis of the American Association of Social Workers. The work was tentatively begun in the academic year of 1927-28 when members of a seminar in the New York School of Social Work under the writer's direction made a preliminary study of guidance activities in the public schools and of the work of non-commercial employment offices in New York City.

With this as a background, the writer spent three months in 1928 and another three months in 1929 on field trips which included Boston, Chicago, Cincinnati, Cleveland, Milwaukee, Pittsburgh, Philadelphia, and Rochester, N. Y., for the purpose of making inquiry as to the organization of counseling in the school systems and as to methods employed in junior placement. Providence, R. I., having been unavoidably omitted from the original itinerary, was visited in the spring of 1934. In Milwaukee, owing to limitation of time the study of counseling was restricted to the Vocational School. In each of these cities every possible opportunity was given to observe vocational guidance in practice, including access to records and opportunity to interview counselors and placement workers, to observe the teaching of classes in occupations and to be present at conferences between counselors and pupils and at placement interviews.

In the field study definite schedules were not used. Instead, an outline of topics to be covered was drawn up and used both by the writer and by student assistants as a guide to the study. This method has the advantage of making interviews freer and more likely to elicit full and complete information. It avoids the standardized and routine and makes possible the discovery not only of con-

ventional practices and points of view but of deviations
from them as well. A schedule, like a questionnaire, tends
to limit the information secured to the patterns conceived
of in advance by the investigator.

At the same time it has a disadvantage in that the information thus secured in one place does not correspond in
detail with that obtained elsewhere and consequently does
not make possible tabulation and definite comparison.

It was in the interest of greater definiteness, therefore,
as well as in order that a greater and more representative
area might be covered, that questionnaires were later prepared and sent out widely both to school counselors and
to placement workers.[1]

Throughout the report dependence is upon both methods
to such a degree that it is impossible to separate one from
the other. The questionnaires could not have been drawn
up nor the replies interpreted with assurance had not the
field study preceded them. On the other hand, the returned questionnaires so definitely supplemented and
clarified what had been observed as greatly to add to the
significance of the latter. Because the information emerging from the questionnaires was, in some respects the more
tangible of the two sets of data, much of the report may
seem to be derived from that source alone. This is by no
means as true as may appear and in a sense, for the reason
given above, is not true at all.

As indicated elsewhere, this study is of the practice of
vocational guidance. The writer set out to discover what
workers in this field do, and under what circumstances
their work is performed. In attempting to make a sufficiently clear statement of these things, it has been necessary to refer here and there to the work as carried on in
specific localities. These references are for purposes of

[1] These questionnaires are reproduced in Appendices A and I. The method
used in distributing them is also described.

illustration alone, and with no thought of giving a picture of the organization and practice of guidance in any city. For that, one must look to such studies as that of the Children's Bureau in 1924[2] and of the U. S. Office of Education in 1933.[3] The choice of any particular illustration is made on the basis of availability of material or of the writer's familiarity with it as well as upon its suitability for the purpose at hand.

It follows that in no case is the organization and practice of guidance in any particular city described in full and that many localities where excellent work is being done in this field are not even mentioned. In some cases this is due to limitations of space, in many more it is because of absence of sufficient information.

This report is the result of a study carried on, at intervals, over a six-year period. Analysis of the data gathered and writing the report have been accomplished while carrying on the duties of a full-time teaching position. The work has been started and dropped and started again many times during this period. As a result, while some of the material is as nearly up-to-date as could reasonably be expected, some of it was secured long enough ago to make it reasonably certain that the picture has changed here and there in some of its details. In fact, as will be seen, references are made to activities in areas where they have since been abolished. The report necessarily is burdened by such defects as are made inevitable by its manner of preparation. These are perhaps less serious in a report that aims merely to explain what vocational counselors and placement secretaries do when they are practicing their professions than it would be if we were attempting to give a picture of guidance in any particular locality. The changes

[2] *Vocational Guidance and Junior Placement*, Children's Bureau Publication No. 149.

[3] *Programs of Guidance*. Bulletin, 1932, No. 17. Monograph No. 14. U. S. Office of Education.

that have taken place in five years are in organization and administrative planning rather than in the methods employed by the individual.

After a draft of the report had been prepared in reasonably final form, copies were sent for criticism to a number of leading practitioners in the field. Many helpful suggestions were thus secured, most of which have been adopted and incorporated in this final draft. So many persons in both the counseling and the placement fields have helped to make possible the gathering of the data here presented that it is impossible to enumerate them. The writer is under especially heavy obligations to the following, who read the manuscript in full, though none of them is responsible for statements appearing in the report except when credit is specifically given: Miss Helen Becht, N. Y. State Public Employment Service; Miss Mary Corre, director, Division of Counseling and Occupational Research, Cincinnati Vocation Bureau; Miss Anne Davis, formerly director, Department of Vocational Guidance in Chicago public schools; Miss Susan Ginn, director of Vocational Guidance, Boston public schools; Mrs. Mary H. S. Hayes, director, Vocational Service for Juniors, New York City; Dr. Franklin J. Keller, director, National Occupational Conference, New York City; Miss Louise Odencrantz, superintendent, Handicapped Division, N. Y. State Employment Service; and Miss Dorothea de Schweinitz, U. S. Public Employment Service.

JOHN A. FITCH

NEW YORK
MARCH 18, 1935

CONTENTS

Duties of workers placing the handicapped; Registering the applicant; Referrals to jobs; Follow-up; Finding the job; Visiting places of employment; The agency and conditions of employment.

APPENDICES

Part One: Counseling

Part Two: Placement

Part One

INTRODUCTION

CHAPTER I

WHAT VOCATIONAL GUIDANCE IS

Before entering into a discussion of the field suggested by the title of this book, one must decide whether that field can best be described by the term "vocational guidance" or by the word "guidance" without a qualifying adjective.

In 1908 the late Frank Parsons organized the Vocation Bureau in Boston, and began to give advice to the young people who came to Civic Service House on the choice of and preparation for their vocations, calling his activities "vocational guidance." This is said to be not only the beginning of the use of that term, but the beginning of organized professional service of this sort. Parson's work and his writings influenced the development of work in this field to a marked degree. Private social agencies began to promote the idea and soon there were "Vocation Bureaus" or departments of "Vocational Guidance" in the school systems of several of the larger cities. The National Vocational Guidance Association was formed in 1912 by the workers in this new profession, and in 1921 it adopted a standard definition of vocational guidance. Revised in 1930, this definition now reads: "Vocational guidance is the process of assisting the individual to choose an occupation, prepare for it, enter upon and progress in it."

This definition seems to imply that vocational guidance has to do primarily with the relation of the individual to the economic or occupational world. This was the prevailing concept at the outset, and it is still so in many important centers where guidance work is being done. Indeed there is authoritative support for the idea that the duties of the counselor include not only the giving of information about occupational opportunities, but instruction in the nature of the economic world in which these opportunities lie.[1]

[1] See John M. Brewer, *Education as Guidance*, 1932, pp. 296–300.

In time, however, suggestions began to be made that guidance technique should be extended to a broader field. It was said that the pupil in school needs counsel and advice not alone with respect to the vocational world but on ways of meeting any type of obstacle to living a full and successful life. Hence we began to hear of social guidance, ethical guidance, health guidance—even of life guidance. Vocational guidance began to be thought of as a single phase in a program covering well-nigh the whole of human needs.

Elwood P. Cubberly, then dean of the School of Education, Leland Stanford University, wrote in 1925:

> Beginning with an attempt to direct pupils into the kinds of vocations in which they are likely to succeed, the guidance function has been so expanded, as we have come to understand it better, that today it comprehends educational guidance, health guidance, moral guidance, and social and civic guidance, as well as vocational guidance toward the close of the pupil's school career, proper placement when the training has been completed and some follow-up oversight to see that the youth gets properly established in the work of life.[2]

This idea rapidly caught fire. A movement to change the name of the National Vocational Guidance Association by dropping the word "vocational" was made without success in 1929. An advocate of this change wrote that "life must be considered as a whole and anything that aims to assist individuals in choices that affect life must be considered from the point of view of life rather than from the point of view of some narrow fact of life, however important for the moment this may be."

While this trend is based upon a wholesome underlying idea, it sometimes has the effect of subordinating the vocational aspects of guidance almost to the vanishing

[2] Proctor, *Educational and Vocational Guidance*, editor's Introduction, pp. vii–viii.

point. Thus we find "vocational counselors" in many school systems who have little interest in or knowledge of the occupational world. Their primary function is to direct the pupil through the mazes of the curriculum. Elementary pupils are guided into junior high schools; junior high school students into senior high schools; senior high school pupils into college. This concept of guidance, on the one hand, tends to disregard the interests of those who are unable to go through high school and college, and on the other, seems to assume either that progress through the educational system is, itself, a career, or that prospective college students need no vocational advice. After the question "What are your principal duties?" a "guidance teacher" in a junior high school wrote on her questionnaire, "Since my school is in a neighborhood of highly privileged children, most of my work is educational guidance—acquainting students with local educational opportunities, variety of senior high school and college courses, etc."

Professor Brewer puts the matter in its proper setting:

When vocational guidance became fairly well formulated a few years ago, educators began talking about educational guidance, and later about health guidance, civic guidance, guidance for home relationships, leisure time guidance, and many other kinds. It is quite clear that if the word "guidance" must be given a broad definition, it should seldom be used without a qualifying adjective. Strangely enough, some of the workers in vocational guidance have expressed alarm over the use of the term in connection with the other areas of life activity, and one has voiced the fear that vocational guidance is "in danger of being thrown out of its own house." Another writer states that there is "danger that the movement for guidance will become so broad as to be practically meaningless and dissipate itself into the thin air of general education or of general instruction." Others call the broader concept of guidance "sheer inflation."

But if we who are interested in vocational guidance stick to our definitions when we are dealing with that subject, and if we use our other terms correctly, especially the exactly right qualifying adjectives to designate the several kinds, how can there be the slighest danger to guidance for one area of life by the formulation and exploitation of other forms? Vocational guidance has its definite work to do and need not suffer in the least because educational workers in other fields are also doing their work. It will suffer, however, if we use words in wrong ways, if we expand or restrict our definitions unduly, and especially if we fail to distinguish among the various major kinds of life activity.[3]

The present report has to do with the vocational aspects of guidance. Many of the counselors and others who coöperated in providing data used here represented guidance in its broader aspects. The limitation of our interpretation to the vocational side does not indicate a desire to deprecate or belittle the use of guidance technique in other fields. It merely happens that in this broad field it was vocational guidance in its strict sense that we took as the subject of our study. This alone covers so wide a field that it is extremely difficult to draw a clear and definite line between what is clearly vocational guidance and what is, considered by itself, clearly something else. It seems reasonable, however, to approach the subject with the assumption that the work of vocational guidance is, in the main, that implied by the definition adopted by the National Vocational Guidance Association. This definition with its four objectives—choosing, preparing for, entering, and making progress in an occupation—contemplates three major forms of activity, namely, counseling, placement, and research.

Functions of Vocational Guidance

The process of counseling is obviously essential to all of the four objectives mentioned in the definitions of the National Vocational Guidance Association. It follows that this process is characteristic of vocational guidance through-

[3] John M. Brewer, "Let's All Speak the Same Language," *Occupations—The Vocational Guidance Magazine*, May, 1934.

out, and is practiced in varying degrees in the placement office, in the classroom, and in the office of the counselor. However, it is the counselor, as such, and under whatever name, whose major responsibility is to "assist the individual" with respect to two of the four objectives, namely, choosing and preparing for an occupation. The placement worker is primarily responsible for the other two objectives, those having to do with entering and progressing in an occupation.

The third functionalized activity in vocational guidance is research. The worker in this field is not concerned immediately and directly with any of the four objectives of vocational guidance, but indirectly with all of them. It may be stated in general terms that research which is of service in the field of vocational guidance includes work done in education, mental testing and in the analysis of occupational opportunities.

In practice these three activities (counseling, placement, and research) are sometimes carried on by different individuals, each of whom remains continuously at his own particular task; sometimes the same person carries on two forms of activity and in some cases all three are performed by the same person. Often the counselor does some placement work, even when there is a separate placement office, and in many cases occupational research is a part-time duty of the counselor. The placement secretary does a limited amount of counseling[4] and generally does a good deal of visiting of places of employment. Follow-up is a major duty of the placement office, but it is also a concern of the counselor. The number of persons in the field of vocational guidance throughout the country who are giving all of their time to occupational research is relatively small.

[4] For a discussion of the handicaps to counseling in the placement office see Chapter IX.

Where Vocational Guidance Is Practiced

In the 1930 revision of its statement of principles by the National Vocational Guidance Association the following introductory statement appears: "Vocational guidance is primarily the task of the vocational counselor or the personnel worker in education and industry. The teacher, educational administrator, parent, and social, civic, and religious worker, though engaged chiefly in other forms of individual service, find themselves involved also in vocational guidance activities."

Harry D. Kitson, professor of education, Teachers College, Columbia University, writes that vocational guidance "is not exclusively nor even largely a public school problem. It is not even chiefly an educational problem. It is really a social problem. . . . It appears obvious then that society needs experts who can do vocational guidance *wherever human beings need it*—in elementary and secondary schools, in colleges and professional schools; in business and industrial establishments; and among the masses of the workers."[5]

Nevertheless, it is in the schools that one finds vocational guidance most definitely established. No sufficiently comprehensive survey has yet been made to enable one to reach definite conclusions as to the number of schools having guidance programs, but there is abundant evidence to justify the belief that the work is organized to some extent in the school systems of nearly all of the large cities and frequently, though not in so large a proportion, of the smaller cities.[6] In the schools the program is very much better developed on the counseling than on the placement

[5] *Vocational Guidance Magazine*, February, 1930, pp. 236–37.

[6] The Committee on Vocational Guidance and Child Labor of President Hoover's White House Conference on Child Health and Protection sent out questionnaires to the school authorities in 288 cities. These cities were classified in three groups according to population—those having 25,000 to 50,000, from 50,000 to 100,000 and those having over 100,000 population. Of 150 cities replying, 99, or 66 per cent, said that they had vocational counselors in

side. Counseling is done also in some of the larger social
agencies dealing with families, notably the Association for
Improving the Condition of the Poor in New York and the
Jewish agencies of New York and Chicago. Many colleges
also now have organized personnel or guidance bureaus.

The next most important place to look for vocational
guidance activities is in the noncommercial employment
agencies, public and private. The administrative bodies
supervising the work are the schools, the states, munici-
palities, the Y.M.C.A. and Y.W.C.A., and other social
agencies.

Vocational Guidance as Social Work

Vocational guidance is a logical outgrowth of some of the
major concepts of social work. This is evident, both in its
stated purposes and in its use of social-work technique.
It is evident also in the history of the development of
organized vocational guidance in the various cities. It was
his discovery of the need of vocational advice for young
people gained as a settlement worker in Civic Service
House, Boston, that led Frank Parsons, in 1908, to set up
the Boston Vocation Bureau which he conducted as a
settlement activity. After his death Meyer Bloomfield,
then head worker in the settlement, took over its direction.
This bureau, the first organized movement for vocational
guidance in the United States, worked with the public
school authorities in Boston and influenced the appointment of vocational counselors in elementary and high
schools of the city in 1910. Two years later, a placement
bureau to serve five schools in Roxbury was organized by
the joint efforts of three private organizations, the Women's

---

their schools. This was true of somewhat over half of the 72 small and 42
medium-sized cities and of all but two of the 36 large cities which sent in replies. *Vocational Guidance*, report of Committee on Vocational Guidance and
Child Labor of White House Conference on Child Health and Protection.
The Century Company, 1932, p. 43.

Frequent reference to this report is made on succeeding pages. It is cited
hereafter as "White House Conference Report."

Municipal League, the Girls' Trade Educational League, and the Children's Welfare League of Roxbury—the last an organization which was inspired by the Massachusetts Society for the Prevention of Cruelty to Children. The work of this bureau was soon extended to all the schools of Boston and, though still a private agency, became known as the Boston Placement Bureau. It was gradually absorbed by the Department of Vocational Guidance which was organized as a part of the school system in 1915.

The basis for organized vocational guidance in the Chicago public schools was laid in 1910 by the Department of Social Investigation of the Chicago School of Civics and Philanthropy. In 1910 also, what is now the Vocation Bureau of the Cincinnati public schools had its origin in activities of the Schmidlapp Fund, under its director, Edith Campbell, now the head of the Vocation Bureau, and the National Child Labor Committee. In Philadelphia in 1916 the White-Williams Foundation established a placement bureau and installed visiting teachers in the public schools. The former was shortly taken over by the Board of Education, but the latter service is still being maintained by the Foundation.

Wherever vocational guidance is being effectively practiced there is coöperation at a dozen points between its practitioners and the social agencies of the city. It is, however, in its use of technique that vocational guidance reveals itself most definitely as a phase of social work. Its tools are the interview, the case record, statistics, research, mental and physical measurements, coöperation with social agencies.[7] In the statement of principles of vocational guidance as revised in 1924 by the National Vocational Guidance Association we read that vocational counseling "should include studies by case work methods

---

[7] "The field of social work has contributed much to the guidance movement. The method of the case study in social work has been a very important factor." Allen, *Organization and Supervision of Guidance in Public Education*, pp. 10–11.

of the social life of each child."[8] In the revised statement of principles, adopted by the Association in 1930,[9] "the recognition of individual differences" is laid down as one of the four underlying principles of vocational guidance; the other three being an appreciation of "the complexity of modern occupational life," a recognition "of the right of the individual to make his own choices," and the "realization that the adjustment of an individual to his occupation is an ever-changing situation." In dealing with the subject of individual differences the statement reads,

No two individuals are identical in natural endowment or environmental conditions. Every effort must be made to know the individual, his intelligence, his special abilities, his understanding of work, his health, educational achievement, work experience, temperament, character, interests, and his social and economic situation. These individual differences call for individual attention. To provide equal opportunity for all it becomes necessary to accord separate treatment to each.

In the same statement the following is set forth as representing desirable specialized training for counselors:

Formal courses in vocational guidance at a college or university, preferably as graduate study. These courses should include field work, namely, supervised participation in such activities as counseling, placement, occupational studies, visiting teaching, or other form of social case work, psychological testing, and so forth.

The detailed activities of counselors also correspond very closely to those found in other types of case work, including aiding the individual to adjust himself with respect to health, social environment, economic problems, etc. This becomes strikingly evident in the record of activity of a counselor in a sample week which is presented in Appendix C.

[8] *The Principles of Vocational Guidance*, 1924, Bureau of Vocational Guidance, Harvard University.

[9] *The Principles and Practice of Vocational Guidance*, as formulated in 1921, revised in 1924, and in 1930. Bureau of Vocational Guidance, Harvard University.

CHAPTER II

THE ORGANIZATION OF VOCATIONAL GUIDANCE

As we have already seen, organized vocational guidance had its beginnings in this country under private auspices. In all of the cities studied whose guidance programs go back twenty years or more private enterprise was responsible for launching the project and carrying it forward during its earlier years. In some of the cities mentioned in Chapter I as among those whose activities in this field were launched under social-work auspices, a part of the program is still in private hands. In Cincinnati the Community Chest financed the beginnings of occupational research and still supplies funds to be used for scholarships by the Vocation Bureau. In Atlanta, the placement work is financed by the Community Chest. In New Orleans, a private organization, the High School Scholarship Association, raises a fund for the purpose indicated and pays the salary of a case worker who is on the staff of the Division of Vocational Guidance of the Orleans Parish School Board. Another member of the staff, who is in charge of occupational studies, is maintained by the Community Chest. In New York City, the Vocational Service for Juniors, a private organization, for a number of years directed and paid the salaries of the only full-time counselors in the public schools. At the present time, the Board of Education, having officially recognized counseling as a public-school activity, the Vocational Service for Juniors has curtailed its work somewhat, but it still maintains its scholarship department and operates a placement bureau in one of the continuation schools and a counseling service at its own office. Other private agencies in New York City which are doing work that falls within the legitimate confines of a public-school vocational guidance program are the Vocational Adjustment Bureau, a placement bureau for problem girls, and the Employment Center for the Handicapped, which has recently become the Handicapped Department of the New York State Public Employment Service.

Vocational guidance, having thus received its impetus from outside the school system, is now, however, making its greatest gains from within. While no attempt was made in our study to cover this particular point, the impression gathered was that vocational-guidance activities launched within the last ten years have, in the main, been developed under public auspices.

Vocational guidance has a tendency to grow out of the necessities of the situation within a particular school and without reference to the practice in any other. Without any external impetus or direction from those higher in authority, a principal may become aware of the necessity of giving his own pupils some assistance in planning their future. This may lead him to assign the work to an assistant principal or a dean or to release some of the time of certain teachers, to enable them to carry on a minimum of counseling activities. It is apparently in this manner that nearly every senior and junior high school in New York City has come to have on its staff a teacher, dean, or assistant principal, who devotes a part of his time to counseling, despite the fact that in most schools there is no official arrangement for such service nor has there been, until recently, even the beginning of a centralized organization for counseling. Vocational guidance was introduced into the New York school system in 1908 by a group of teachers who organized themselves into a counseling group, and offered their services in their respective schools without extra pay and on their own time.

At present, in the cities where vocational guidance has become a definite and planned activity two types of organization are to be found, the centralized and the decentralized. Cleveland furnishes an example of the decentralized type. Counseling is carried on to some extent in all of the high schools, but the program in each is worked out independently by the counselor and principal, and consequently wide differences obtain between one school and another. In some of the schools, counseling is done by teachers on a part-time basis; in others there are full-time counselors who are responsible for the whole program, and in one there is a head counselor giving full time, assisted by eleven teachers who give part time to counseling. These counselors maintain an organization for the discussion of problems of mutual interest. Two departments of the public-school system, the Bureau of Educational Research, and the Bureau of Attendance and Placement manifest some interest in vocational guidance, but neither has any control over counselors, who are responsible directly to the principals of their respective schools. Placement work is divided between the counselors, most of whom regard that as a definite part of their obligations, and the Bureau of Attendance and Placement which maintains an employment office at the headquarters of the Board of Education. One worker, devoting full time to occupational research, is attached to the Bureau of Educational Research.

Central organization of vocational guidance involves a central office with a director in charge of guidance activities in the whole school system. With the central planning that an organization of this type implies, a common program is developed with the result that there is a good deal of uniformity in the work done in the different schools.

However, it is impossible to speak of central organization as a type. The plans and methods of central organizations vary widely, influenced in part by the size of the community and its resources, and in part by the purpose of guidance as conceived by those who are in charge. In

Lincoln, Neb., for example, vocational guidance, census, and attendance are the fields covered by the Bureau of Child Welfare under the Board of Education. There is a director and a staff consisting of an attendance worker and a visiting teacher. The counseling, which is under the direction of the head of the Bureau, is carried on in junior high schools by social-science teachers who have a limited amount of time for this purpose and who give occupational information in the civics classes. The work begins in the seventh grade and two hours is devoted to a study of vocations in each semester until 9-A is reached, when twenty hours are devoted to the "Choice of an Occupation." A placement office is conducted by the director.

In La Crosse, Wis., counseling is done by principals, vice-principals, deans of girls, home-room teachers, the teacher of occupations, and the supervisor of guidance. The latter, whose title is Supervisor of Educational Guidance, has no staff, but heads up the work of counseling in the schools, advises teachers, arranges visits to industries, and brings in representatives of many occupations to give vocational talks to the pupils.

The centralized program in Atlanta includes a Director of Guidance and Research who supervises the guidance program for the city through the assistant principals of the various schools. In each of the junior and senior high schools a counselor for each grade group is appointed from among the teaching staff by the principal of the school in consultation with the director of guidance and research. Each counselor continues as counselor for the same group during its stay in the school.

These examples are offered as indications of trends in organization. They are steps in the direction of centralization, but they do not mark the final stage either because of lack of facilities or because of distribution of function or authority. A school system that has gone far toward centralization of guidance activities is that of Cincinnati. The work is carried on by the Vocation Bureau under the Board of Education with a director in charge. The activities of the Bureau fall into five divisions, the duties of which are thus summarized by Mary Corre, director of the Division of Occupational Research and Counseling:

The Psychological Laboratory interprets for the other Bureau Divisions and the schools their important findings regarding the child's mental equipment; the Child Accounting Division through its activities, namely, school census, administration of work certificates and school attendance laws, undertakes to keep all children of compulsory school age in regular attendance at school that they may receive the training that will assist them later in their work, and to protect those who must leave school and go to work by preventing them from entering occupations which might harm them physically or morally; the Scholarship Division administers the scholarship fund provided by the Community Chest and interested organizations and individuals, awards scholarships to superior children (who would otherwise be forced at sixteen years to leave school and go to work) on the basis of intelligence, achievement, and economic need and holds regular conferences with scholarship recipients; the Individual Adjustment Division through its visiting teachers serves the other divisions and the schools in securing and interpreting the social factors relating to the individual children and their problems, and helping in the adjustments necessary to the solution of these problems; the Occupational Research and Counseling Division gathers occupational information, conducts classes in occupations in the junior high schools and counsels with junior high school pupils concerning their vocational plans.[1]

Junior placement in Cincinnati is carried on under the auspices of the city government.

In Boston there is a Department of Vocational Guidance under the Boston School Committee, with a director who

[1] From a paper read before the Schoolmasters Club of Cincinnati in December, 1927. Since that time counseling in the eighth grade in a number of schools and in senior high schools has been added to the duties of the Occupational Research and Counseling Division.

is responsible to the superintendent of schools, and a staff of counselors, five of whom are men, and are called "vocational instructors," and nine of whom are women and are designated "vocational assistants."[2] If the major activities of the Boston Department of Vocational Guidance were organized in subdivisions there would be three in contrast to Cincinnati's five. These three would be designated as the divisions of guidance, placement, and follow-up, only one of which would find a formal counterpart in Cincinnati. There are, however, no subdivisions of this sort in Boston. The staff of the Department of Vocational Guidance carry on all three of the major activities named. Testing is taken care of elsewhere in the school system, as are also administration of school attendance and certification. "Follow-up" (a type of responsibility which we shall discuss later) is definitely practiced to some extent wherever there is competent guidance work, but in Boston it is stressed to a degree not usually encountered.

In Providence, R. I., unlike most of the cities visited, counseling is done in every junior and senior high school in the city. With the exception of one senior high school, each school has a head counselor and a counselor for each grade who remains with the same group of pupils as it makes its way through the school. The guidance program includes testing, program making, individual and group counseling, placement, and follow-up and is under the supervision of an assistant superintendent.

A careful examination of practice in different cities reveals the fact that guidance has become standardized neither in organization, method, nor purpose. In one city it may be that organized guidance is rejected alto-

---

[2] These terms were chosen because, when the Department of Vocational Guidance was organized in 1915 there were already "vocational counselors" in the schools. These were and are teachers who give part time to counseling. The members of the staff of the Department are giving full time to guidance activities.

gether; in another, it may be the keynote of the school system. Where it is accepted and a program is in operation we find one city devoting itself to educational guidance, another to vocational activities, while a third includes both. Furthermore, even in the cities where the vocational aspects of guidance are in the ascendancy, the particular emphasis tends to differ. In one system the specialty is placement, in another follow-up, while another may expend its energies on occupational research and counseling, and ignore placement altogether.

George E. Myers, professor of vocational education and guidance in the University of Michigan, wrote a paper, a few years ago, entitled "Some Tentative Standards for Judging a Comprehensive Guidance Plan."[3] In it he listed the following activities as essential to a complete plan of vocational guidance:

1. Aiding pupils to obtain adequate, reliable, and significant information concerning occupations.
2. Providing try-out, or exploratory, experiences as an aid to pupils in testing their fitness for certain occupations or occupational fields, and as an aid to teachers in discovering pupils' interests and special abilities.
3. Assembling and making available for use pertinent information concerning the abilities, aptitudes, temperaments, and personality characteristics of individual pupils.
4. Individual counseling, or assisting pupils to evaluate occupational information and the results of exploratory experiences in terms of their personal abilities, interests and characteristics, and helping them to plan their vocational preparation.
5. Vocational education, or providing opportunities for pupils to prepare for the occupations which they have chosen.
6. Placement, or aiding pupils to obtain advantageous entry into the occupations chosen.
7. Employment supervision, or assisting the pupil to progress in his occupation if it proves suitable or to change if it proves unsuitable.

[3] Read before the Vocational Guidance section of the American Vocational Association, Louisville, Kentucky, December 4, 1926.

A vocational guidance plan which does not include all of these activities cannot claim to be complete. Its degree of completeness may be judged by the number of these activities which are fostered.

The type of organization that seemed to him important if these activities were to be carried on with effectiveness were outlined in the same paper. He proposed that there should be:

a) An administrative department or bureau concerned solely with the guidance activities listed above, but with *all* of these.
b) That this department or bureau be in charge of a head or director who is responsible directly to the superintendent's office.
c) That expert supervision be provided under the director (the number of supervisors depending on the size of the city) for each of the seven activities.
d) That definite provision be made in the organization for promotion and direction of research.

A factor tending everywhere to interfere with the accomplishment of a completely centralized plan as envisaged by Dr. Myers is the almost irresistible tendency toward divided authority. This tendency is to be found even in the organizations that have gone furthest in the direction of centralization. One of the questions submitted to counselors was this: "To whom in the school system are you responsible?" The answers from 105 counselors ranged as follows:

Superintendent	4
Principal	38
Principal and Superintendent	6
Principal and Assistant Superintendent	9
Principal and Director of Vocational Guidance	24
Principal and Head Counselor	6
Principal and Director of Research	3
Director of Vocational Guidance	9
Director of Vocational Guidance and Dean	1

Head of Research Department 1
Dean of Personnel 1
Director of Vocational School 1
Director of Vocational Education 1
"No one"[4] 1

Apparently, therefore, in thirty-six percent of the cases, the counselor was responsible to the principal alone. In forty-six percent, the principal shared control with another, and altogether the principal participated in the administration of counseling in eighty-two percent of the cases. On the other hand, the director of vocational guidance (assuming that the titles "Head of Research Department," "Dean of Personnel," and "Director of Vocational Education" imply such directorship) had exclusive control in eleven percent of the cases, shared it with others in twenty-seven percent and thus was recognized as a factor in control by only thirty-eight percent of the counselors replying.

In analyzing the replies from counselors no attempt was made to distinguish between those coming from school systems where vocational guidance is centrally organized, and others. However, the impression gained from the preceding is strengthened by reference to the seventeen questionnaires returned by directors of vocational guidance in cities where a central organization exists. In answer to the question, "to whom are counselors administratively responsible?", the replies were as follows:

Director of Vocational Guidance (or similar title) . . . 6
Principal 6
Principal and Assistant Superintendent 2
Principal and Director of Vocational Guidance 3

The field investigation yielded similar evidence. Even where the whole administrative set-up would indicate exclusive authority in the hands of the director, counselors in the schools are generally considered by the principal

[4] This was a principal who did the work of counseling in his school.

as members of his staff and not without reason, since the relation of the counselor to the pupils is as direct as that of the teachers and, in some respects, more personal. The principal necessarily has a direct interest in any activity within the school which affects his pupils and his responsibility is such that all activities must have his approval. The result is that while the director of vocational guidance may have every formal authority for deciding on the scope of the work of his department, he works with the principals and introduces his program only as they are willing to accept it. This is undoubtedly a sound policy, but it is obviously a decentralizing factor.

This chapter has been devoted to organization within the school systems because it is only within the schools that anything like a complete organization for vocational guidance is to be found. It may be well to conclude, therefore, with a somewhat more complete statement about the development of counseling within this area.

The point in the school system at which vocational guidance begins is apt to depend somewhat on the organization of the school. Where the separation between elementary and high school comes at the end of the eighth grade, definite, organized counseling is apt to begin with the ninth. Where the school system is organized on the 6-3-3 basis, counseling begins in junior high school, sometimes as early as the seventh grade. The very organization and purpose of the junior high school, in its fully approved form, provides a guidance program through its exploratory shop courses. "At its best the junior high school may be regarded as one of the most important agencies of vocational guidance. The curriculum itself is a means of discovering to the pupil his particular interests and capacities and of providing the basis for educational and vocational guidance and training."[5] Not all junior high schools offer

[5] *Vocational Guidance and Junior Placement*, United States Children's Bureau Publication, No. 149, p. 2.

a wide range of exploratory courses and some represent nothing more than a convenient administrative arrangement. However, the tendency is to make that division of the school system one in which some opportunity for "try-out" or "exploration" may be afforded. Another type of school in which the curriculum is made to serve a vocational-guidance purpose is the continuation school. Here, as a rule, it may be said the whole purpose of the school is one of guidance. The pupil has already left the regular school and has a job. Having put formal education behind him and having entered the occupational world, he may be presumed to be more keenly alive to the need for information about vocational opportunities than the child who is still in the schoolroom. Both curriculum and pupil attitude,[6] therefore, are such as to facilitate a guidance program.

In most continuation schools the entering group of pupils is ushered first into what is sometimes called a "preparatory" class, in which the organization and purpose of the school are explained. Sometimes the pupils are taken on a tour of the building and given a glimpse into the various classrooms. After this general introduction to the school, each pupil has a personal interview with a teacher who endeavors to discover something of the social history, aptitudes and interests of the pupil as a basis for assigning him to a class in plumbing, wood working, auto mechanics, or what not. This assignment is tentative. If after a few weeks the pupil is dissatisfied, he may come back for reassignment and the process may go on until he finds the trade that is to his liking. Whatever his choice, his teacher is a constant advisor with respect to the trade he is teaching and a constant dispenser of occupational information. The counselor, in the specialized sense of the term, is ordinarily

[6] Though it is to be doubted whether this statement holds true for children of fourteen years of age.

not to be found in the continuation school[7] except as a
placement worker—a form of activity that will be discussed
later.

As the preceding implies, little vocational counseling
takes place in elementary schools. Our study revealed
very few instances where anything of the sort was claimed,
and in these cases it is probable that the counseling was
educational or social in character. The great bulk of the
work of vocational guidance takes place in junior and
senior high schools. Some, but a far smaller amount, takes
place in trade schools, and, as indicated above, the continuation school is in a class by itself.

[7] See, however, Franklin J. Keller, *The Vocational Guidance Task of the
General Continuation School*, Bulletin No. 2, "East Side Continuation School
Series," New York, 1928.

Part Two

COUNSELING

CHAPTER III

DUTIES OF COUNSELORS[1]

Vocational guidance, in the fullest implication of that term, cannot be comprehended within the limits of any specialized and planned activity nor made operative within any definite and exclusive period of life. Influences affecting choice of, preparation for, entrance into, and making progress in a vocation are literally operative from birth. It is not wholly unformed and plastic material that comes into the hands of the vocational counselor, but nervous organisms already conditioned by everything that heredity and environment have provided, including training as well as emotional, social, and economic experience.

The task of the counselor, therefore, is not that of fitting a succession of crafts with automatic steering devices that will guide them unerringly through whatever tempests may be encountered to a predetermined haven. What has happened before the counseling interview and what comes after are matters over which the counselor has no control. Having acquired as complete information as he can concerning the nature and equipment of the individual by whom he is confronted and the occupational world into which that individual is destined to emerge, all that the counselor can do is to assist the individual to make his own plans and to render that assistance with as much wisdom and delicacy as his own native powers, knowledge, and experience make possible.

One of the most vivid impressions received in the course of this study is that counselors tend to subscribe with almost complete unanimity to the foregoing concept of their relationship to pupil or client. No attempt was made in the questionnaires to elicit information on this point,

[1] See also Appendices B, C, D, and F.

but in the field investigation the question was raised in nearly every interview. With but a single exception the counselors stated that their purpose was to help the pupil make his own decisions, and not to force upon him any particular policy or point of view. They said that they tried to make sure that no decisions are made in ignorance of any significant fact, but that the making of the decision is the province of the pupil.

This attitude influences, to some extent, every act performed by the counselor, and it is to be borne in mind as we study the major activities involved in counseling in the schools.

Before turning to a consideration of specific duties performed, it may be noted that the persons referred to throughout this study as "counselors" are often known in their schools by other titles. In the questionnaires a space was left for the name or title of the position occupied by the person answering. As already noted, 105 completed questionnaires were received and on them forty-two different titles appear. In the majority of cases the word "counselor" is used, alone or with a qualifying term. Most of the titles not involving the use of this term, such as "principal," "assistant principal," "dean," etc., doubtless indicate that part time only is given to counseling. The variety of terms used to describe what is obviously the function of counseling is an interesting indication of lack of uniformity. Other terms discovered in the course of the field study were "guidance counselor," "vocational assistant," and "vocational instructor." Following is the list of titles as given by the persons answering the questionnaire:

TITLES OF JOBS

Administrative Positions

Administrative Assistant   1
Dean of Boys   1
Dean of Girls   2

TITLES OF JOBS—Continued

Dean of Personnel 1
Principal 2
Principal, Assistant 2
Principal, Vice 1
Principal, Vice, and Head Counselor[a] 1
Principal, Vice, and Counselor 1

ADVISERS
Adviser and Teacher 1
Boys' Adviser 4
Girls' Adviser 2
Pupil Adviser 1
Student Adviser 1
Vocational Adviser 1

COÖRDINATOR 5

COUNSELOR
Counselor (without qualifying adjective) 32
Counselor and Teacher 3
Girls' Counselor 2
Guidance Counselor and Teacher 1
Head Counselor[a] 1
Individual Counselor 1
Pupil Counselor 1
Student Counselor 2
Teacher Counselor 1
Teaching Counselor 6
Visiting Counselor 1
Vocational Counselor 4
Vocational and Educational Counselor 4
Vocational Counselor and Teacher 2

GUIDANCE, DIRECTOR OF[a] 1

GUIDANCE, VOCATIONAL, DIRECTOR OF[a] 2

GUIDANCE, VOCATIONAL, SUPERVISOR OF[a] 1

GUIDANCE TEACHER 1

INSTRUCTOR IN VOCATIONAL SCHOOLS 2

TEACHER 4

VISITING TEACHER 1

[a] The terms "director of guidance," "head counselor," etc., do not refer here to persons whose primary duties are supervisory. In each case the individual so designated is an active counselor and is included here because his duties correspond in the main to those of the rank and file of counselors.

MISCELLANEOUS

Director, Coöperative Part-Time Classes   1
Director, Juvenile Adjustment Agency   1
Director, Retail Selling School   1
Head, Industrial Department Vocational School . .   1
Secretary, Vocational School   1

Questions 4 to 10, inclusive, of the questionnaire sent to school counselors had to do with duties. Question 4 was general. It read, "What are your principal duties?"

This question was included for the purpose of eliciting, if possible, spontaneous replies giving whatever was uppermost in the counselor's mind. It was assumed that the duties taken most seriously or those requiring the major part of the counselor's time, would be included, rather than a complete catalogue of tasks. That this was a correct inference is indicated by a comparison between the answers to this question and other answers later on in the questionnaire about specific duties. For example, twenty-two of the 105 stated voluntarily that they taught classes in occupations, but when in Question 5 they were asked specifically if they did, thirty-three answered in the affirmative. When answering Question 4 only three mentioned "visiting places of employment," as among their duties, but forty-seven wrote "yes" after Question 8, "Do you make plant visits or occupational surveys?" Twenty mentioned the making of tests as among their duties, but forty-one answering Question 9, said that they administer psychological tests, although this question, through an inadvertence, was omitted from twenty-three of the questionnaires that were returned.

It is probable that the same result would have been obtained if specific questions had been asked with respect to the other duties listed. To take a single example, in answering Question 4, only seven mentioned conferences

with "drop-outs" as among their duties. Yet every counselor personally interviewed during the field study mentioned this as a prominent feature of the work. It is
altogether likely, furthermore, that most of those replying
to the questionnaire had this activity in mind, and merely
failed to use the term "drop-out." Eight used the general
expression "conferences with pupils." Seventeen said
they "interviewed," "adjusted," or otherwise dealt with
"failures," and every questionnaire indicated that "counseling," "conferring," or "interviewing" of some sort
was prominent among the duties performed. A further
indication that the answers to Question 4 were not exhaus-
tive appeared in the reply of one counselor who after putting
down an extensive list added "and a million other things."

The list of "principal duties" which follows, therefore,
should not be taken as all-inclusive, nor should the number
of counselors who mentioned each type of activity be
understood to be the only ones out of 105 replying, who
engaged in it. Rather this is a list of outstanding activities
in which counselors engage, and is offered because of the
evidence it presents of the range of interests and duties
in the field of vocational guidance.

Principal Duties of 105 Counselors

Since all but one of the questionnaires mentioned more than one
duty and since many of the duties were mentioned by several and
some by nearly all, it follows that the total number of "times
mentioned" will greatly exceed the total number of persons
replying.

DUTIES	TIMES MENTIONED
Administrative duties	13
Case work and recording case histories	3
Classifying pupils in ability groups	4
Clerical work	10

TIMES
DUTIES   MENTIONED

Conferences and interviews with:

Duties	Times Mentioned
Teachers	6
Parents	9
Pupils	8
Drop-outs	7
Coöperating with welfare agencies	2
Coördinating	3

Counseling and guidance

Undifferentiated	30
Educational	34
Vocational	27
Moral	4
Social	7
Health	2
Supervision	9

Dealing with

Discipline cases	4
Handicapped pupils	2
Health problems	2

Failures

Adjusting	1
Investigating causes	1
Interviewing	12
Follow-up	3
Follow-up	5

Occupational information

Collecting	9
Disseminating	6
Teaching classes in	22
Supervising classes	5
Placement in jobs	20
Placement of pupils[a]	5
Program planning	27
Programming pupils	6
Record keeping	10
Research	4

Scholarships

Activities in connection with	9

[a] The term placement, as used in the questionnaire and in this report, means the finding of work opportunities. A few of the counselors replying to the questionnaire used the term in the sense of fitting the pupil into the curriculum.

DUTIES	TIMES MENTIONED
Supervision	
Student activities	7
Other activities	3
Teaching	30
Testing	20
Tests, supervising	4
Tests, recording and interpreting	2
Transfer of pupils	4
Visiting	
Homes	7
Plants	3

In addition, the following duties were mentioned once each in individual replies:

DUTIES MENTIONED ONCE

Accounting
Advising teachers
Assisting needy pupils
Coaching plays
Coöperation with other guidance agencies
In charge of building
Interpreting records
Making reports
Organizing home-room activities
Preaching
Registration of students
Studying pupil

The following indicates the number of counselors who, in answer to Question 4, listed the indicated number of duties:

NUMBER DUTIES	NUMBER REPLIES
One duty	1
Two duties	12
Three duties	27
Four duties	22
Five duties	11
Six duties	9
Seven duties	6
Eight duties	5
Nine duties	1
Ten duties	1
Eleven duties	0
Twelve duties	2
No answer	5
Not clear	3
Total	105

Some of the answers to Question 4 did not lend themselves readily to classification. The following three answers
are typical and are given in full because they offer a picture
of the nature and variety of the counselors' duties.

1. Try to assist in meeting problems in the classroom, in the
   home and in social relationships.
2. Supervise student's programs from term to term, general
   supervision of student's school life and many times of his home
   life. Physical, mental, and especially psychological adjustments to his school and out-school environment—sums up
   everything.
3. *a)* To study the pupil
      Health
      Home conditions
      School progress
      Life outside school
   b) To guide the pupil
      Program
      Plan course
      Advise with reference to: health, employment, activities

The following answer deserves quoting because it draws
so careful a distinction between two types of counseling.

EDUCATIONAL COUNSELING	VOCATIONAL COUNSELING
Planning individual programs	Making vocational informa-tion available to pupils, parents and teachers
Making program adjustments	
Explaining educational op-portunities	Arranging group conferences with outside speakers
Collecting data necessary for counseling of individual child	Arranging individual confer-ences with outside men
	Handling placement

An important aspect of vocational guidance is the class
in occupations. The practice varies widely, not only
from city to city, but from school to school. The work is
sometimes a part of a course in civics and is given by the
social-science teachers; sometimes it appears in courses in
English composition—the pupil writing themes on the

occupations that have engaged his interest—and sometimes
it is given as a separate course. The relation of the vocational counselor to the course in occupations also varies
widely. In some schools there is no contact whatever
between the counselor and the teacher of the course. In
others the counselor occupies a supervisory or advisory
relationship; and elsewhere the course is taught by the
counselor.

In answer to Question 5, "Do you teach classes in occupations?", thirty-three replied in the affirmative, sixty-
seven in the negative, and five stated that they supervise
such courses.

The sixth question involved three inquiries: (a) Do you
interview parents? (b) If so, where? (c) What proportion
of all parents do you interview? No attempt was made to
tabulate the answers to the third inquiry, because it soon
became evident that many of the replies were inexact and
many others were couched in general terms such as "Most,"
or "Very few," or "Possibly five to ten percent." Ninety
of the 105 counselors answering the questionnaire stated
without qualification that they have interviews with
parents, twelve that they have such interviews occasionally,[2] leaving only three answering with a negative. As to
the place of conference, fifty-two indicated that conferences are held exclusively in the school; seven, that they
are held exclusively in the home; and thirty-eight mentioned both school and home. One replied "at random,"
one "at office and on phone," and six failed to reply.

Question 7, "To what extent do you have contacts
with social agencies?" did not prove to be a satisfactory
question both because no measuring rod was offered in the
word "extent" and because the word "contact" was
capable of more than one interpretation. It may be, also,
that there was some confusion over the exact meaning of
the term "social agencies." The replies tended to take

[2] One of these replying "not regularly"; another, "if any desire it."

such form as the following: "constant," "very little,"
"occasionally," etc. Rephrasing the question to read,
"Do you have contacts with social agencies?" and grouping
the answers as their form suggests, we have the following:

Yes 15
No 10
"Some" 43
"Very little" 34
No answer 3

Question 8, "Do you make plant visits or occupational
surveys?" In most cases no distinction was made in the
replies between the two types of activity. The separate
returns on occupational surveys were so limited as to
justify rejection. The following, therefore, refers to plant
visits alone:

Yes 47
No 33
Occasionally 19
Not systematically 4
No answer 2

As previously stated, Question 9, "Do you administer
(a) aptitude tests, (b) pyschological tests?" was omitted
from some of the questionnaires sent out. In twenty-three
of the returned questionnaires the question was not included. On the other eighty-two the replies were as
follows:

	YES	NO	OCCA-SIONALLY	NO ANSWER	TOTAL
Aptitude tests . . .	17	61	1	3	82
Psychological tests .	41	38	1	2	82

Question 10 was as follows: "What proportion of your
time is given to

a) Group counseling . . . .
b) Individual counseling . . . .
c) Placement . . . .
d) Obtaining occupational information . . . .
e) Other (specify)" . . . .

A faithful attempt was made by all but thirteen of the 105 counselors replying to answer this question wholly or in part. However, the result was not such as to justify the drawing of any positive conclusions. In the main, counselors do not keep a record of their use of time that is sufficiently exact and complete to enable them to state with certainty just how it is distributed over their many duties. The following is a typical answer to Question 10:

a) Group counseling . . . . . "one-fourth of time"
b) Individual counseling . . . "majority of time"
c) Placement . . . . "only as occasion arises"
d) Obtaining occupational in-
     formation . . . . "one-fourth of time"
e) Other (specify) . . . . . . "assist in building pro-
     gram; make all promotions,
     demotions, and other ad-
     justments."

Obviously, replies such as this could not be tabulated. However, it was possible to determine from the answers to Question 10, whether, and within limits, to what extent, the activities named were engaged in. Using the word "some" to indicate the devotion of any time, however little, to the activity named and up to twenty-five percent of the time; and the term "substantial amount" to indicate twenty-five percent or more of time, we have the following:

TIME DEVOTED BY COUNSELORS TO SPECIFIED ACTIVITIES

	NONE	SOME	SUBSTANTIAL AMOUNT	NO ANSWER	TOTAL ENGAGING IN ACTIVITY TO ANY EXTENT
Group counseling	12	59	19	2	78
Individual counseling	0	23	69	0	92
Placement . . .	33	39	9	11	48
Obtaining occupational information . . .	19	53	3	17	56

Practically all of the activities mentioned in the questionnaires were discovered also through the field study. Since no schedules were used in the field investigation no completely comparable array of data can be presented. However, in some of the cities visited records are kept that show the major activities of the counselors and the time allotted to them. In some of these cities, also, counselors voluntarily kept detailed memoranda of their activities over a definite period, usually a week, and made the record available to the investigator.[3]

[3]See Appendix C.

CHAPTER IV

METHODS OF COUNSELING

Individual and Group Counseling

Counseling may take place either with individuals or with groups. Few schools make use of group counseling alone, but in many of them it is used as a preparation for the individual conference. A class in occupations may very properly be considered a form of group counseling,[1] though in many schools groups are assembled, independently of regular classes, for vocational-guidance purposes.

The information gathered in this study indicates that individual counseling is generally believed to be the more important. All of the ninety-two counselors who answered Question 10[2] said that they do individual counseling, while seventy-eight reported that group counseling is among their duties. Sixty-nine gave a fourth or more of their time to individual counseling, while only nineteen gave that much time to group conferences. Forty-seven stated definitely that they gave more time to individual than to group counseling, while eight put group counseling in first place. The White House questionnaire also covered this point, and replies were received from 108 school systems. Eighty-nine of these mentioned individual counseling as among their activities, and seventy-eight mentioned group counseling.

Nevertheless, there is more group counseling than these figures might indicate. The classes in occupations, as stated, are apt to partake very definitely of the nature of the group conference. The same is true of the meetings in which outsiders explain to interested groups or to the pupils as a whole the advantages or disadvantages of particular occupations. The field study revealed the fact

[1] For a discussion of the class in occupations, see Chapter V.
[2] See p. 37.

that a very common form of the group conference takes place when counselors from junior or senior high school go out to the contributing elementary schools to explain to the graduating classes what the high school has to offer. The practice in this respect is best indicated by excerpts from official statements issued by representative school systems.

BALTIMORE

Junior High School

A group conference with the pupils of 6A classes should be held for a discussion of the value of junior high school and its importance in assisting them in the realization of educational opportunities and vocational aims. A visit of 6A pupils to the junior high school is advised if practicable. When this is not practicable the counselor will visit the 6A grades.

Senior High School

In schools where there is still the old organization of eight grades the counselor should meet all 8A pupils before entering the senior high school. At this conference the counselor should emphasize:
1. The need for training beyond the elementary school.
2. The curricula in the senior high schools and vocational schools and where they lead.
3. Choice of the curriculum with a view to vocational aim.
4. Necessity for good habits of study.

A visit to the senior high school and vocational schools is advised for those pupils and also the 9A junior high school pupils where it is practicable. When this is not practicable the senior high school counselor should visit the 9A grades of the junior high schools.

From *Program of Educational and Vocational Guidance*, Baltimore Public Schools, 1928.

PITTSBURGH

Counseling in the Junior High School

A. Prospective Junior High School Pupils

Group conferences with regularly scheduled classes in elementary schools for a discussion of the value of the high school and its importance in assisting in the realization of individual plans.

B. Junior High School Pupils

7B. Group visitations by regularly scheduled classes to high school departments other than those with which the pupils come in contact for the purpose of developing an appreciation of the opportunities offered by the high school. Group conferences with regularly scheduled classes for the discussion of vocational aims and the filling out of blank form V.G. 1.

Counseling in the Senior High School

A. Prospective senior high school pupils

It shall be the duty of the counselor to meet with all prospective incoming pupils twice before they enter high school When possible one of these meetings should be so planned that parents may be present when the different courses are explained. It shall be the duty of the counselor at this meeting to stress:

a) The need of training beyond the elementary schools.

b) What the Pittsburgh public schools have to offer beyond the elementary schools.

c) Explain the courses offered in the high school and where they are intended to lead.

d) Explain how the home and school can coöperate for the best interest of the pupil.

e) State requirements for place on honor roll or membership in Honor Society.

It shall also be the duty of the counselor at one of these meetings to advise with all prospective pupils regarding their individual programs of studies.

B. Senior High School Pupils

9B. It shall be the duty of the counselor to meet all 9B pupils in regularly scheduled classes or groups during the early part of the semester. At this meeting blank form V.G. 1 will be explained by the counselor and filled out by the pupils. This meeting will offer opportunity for emphasizing the need of vocational information, for encouraging a study of the vocations and for urging a thorough preparation of school tasks. The counselor should also explain his function in the school.

From Pittsburgh Number, *Vocational Guidance Magazine*,
February 1926, pp. 199, 200.

The initial group conference is often a means of preparing for the individual conference. In some schools definite plans are made for individual conferences with every member of a given class. In others such conferences are arranged only when sought by the pupil, or for special cases referred by teachers. In either case the personal record blank is an aid to the counselor's understanding of the pupil to be interviewed.[3]

Personal information called for in these blanks generally cover home conditions, pupil's interests and vocational plans, and other pertinent information. The blanks are usually filled out by the pupil under the careful supervision of the counselor, though some counselors prefer to fill them out themselves in the course of the individual conference. Such blanks were in use in each of the cities studied intensively in our field investigation.

Aids to Individual Counseling

In approaching the individual conference the counselor has access to other sources of information which throw light upon the problems of the particular pupil to be interviewed. In many schools a record of the pupil's achievements is started in the kindergarten or first grade, and added to as he makes progress through the system. A typical cumulative record includes a limited amount of information concerning family conditions or social background, a record of classroom achievement, punctuality and conduct, a physical record made out by doctor or nurse, teacher's observations, pupil's vocational interests, and a report of intelligence and other tests. Such a record, coming into the hands of the counselor assists greatly in understanding the child to be counseled. Where a cumulative record is not available it is usually possible to obtain reports of class standings, results of tests, etc.

[3] Cf. Brewer, *Education as Guidance*, pp. 140–41.

In the larger school systems there are psychological departments which do all the testing required. Seventy-five cities reported to the Committee on Vocational Guidance and Child Labor of the White House Conference that they had a central psychological testing bureau.[4] The present inquiry revealed that of seventy-nine counselors answering the question, eighteen gave aptitude tests and sixty-one did not. Eighty replies were received to the question about psychological tests indicating that forty-two gave them and thirty-eight did not. The following uses to which psychological tests are put were indicated by cities replying to the White House questionnaire:[5]

Classifying pupils 111
Segregation of defectives 132
Recommending special types of training 109
Diagnosis of behavior problems 112
Selection of jobs 43
Choosing scholarship candidates 45

Sometimes these records do not come through as a matter of course and are obtained by the counselor only with great difficulty. In many junior high schools, even where a contrary practice is "supposed" to be in effect, not a scrap of information is available concerning the pupil's record in elementary school.

In addition to this recorded information, necessarily limited in amount and formal in expression, a great reservoir of information is available in the classroom teachers' knowledge of the ability, character, and aptitudes of their pupils. This information is sometimes secured through interviews with teachers. Where, however, it is considered desirable to have the teacher's estimate for every pupil, a more dependable though more formal method is used—the questionnaire. The form used by the Cincinnati Vocation

---

[4] White House Conference Report, p. 31.
[5] *Ibid.*, pp. 25, 26.

Bureau calls for the home-room teacher's impressions as to character traits, quality of work, aptitudes, and relation to others.[6]

Contacts with Parents

Another source of information supplementary to pupil counseling is found in the parents. Ninety of the 105 counselors answering the questionnaire stated without qualification that they have interviews with parents, twelve that they have such interviews occasionally, leaving only three answering with a negative.

The most intensive program of home visiting discovered in the field investigation was that of the Monroe High School in Rochester, New York. There the two counselors have a conference with at least one parent of every 7A pupil. Most of the conferences involve visits to the home though some of the parents come to the school by preference. About the middle of the 7A period (the second semester of the 7th grade) the pupils are asked to fill out a personal record blank, similar to those shown in Appendix E.

This is followed by visits to parents from whom information is secured regarding economic status of family, educational and vocational plans for the child and other pertinent information—all of which is recorded on the back of the pupil's card. About twenty minutes to a family is required.

Many counselors encourage parents to come to the school when individual conferences concerning electives are being held. At the Latimer Junior High School in Pittsburgh such conferences are held in 7A and 8A. Somewhat in advance of the interview the principal writes a letter to the parents of each child, notifying them of the hour set, and inviting them to attend. The result is said to be very nearly one hundred percent attendance by one parent or

[6] See Appendix E for Teacher's Estimate blank.

the other of each child. The counselor does a good deal of home visiting also.

This type of activity tends to overlap somewhat the work of the visiting teacher. The fact that a certain amount of parent interviewing by counselors is practically universal indicates again how impossible it is to set rigid and final boundaries to the vocational guidance field.

Armed with the information thus secured (the personal record filled out by the pupil himself, the school record, results of tests, teacher's estimates, and parents' economic status and plans) the counselor is ready for an individual conference. The importance of this lies in the possibilities afforded for clearing up anything that may be obscure in the record, getting new information by inducing the pupil to talk about himself, and gaining his confidence, so that the counselor may be of the utmost assistance.

The purpose of the vocational guidance interview is, of course, ultimately to assist the pupil to make a wise choice of an occupation. Actually the problem may turn out to be something very much more immediate: whether to leave school and get a job, regardless of ultimate vocational aspirations; how to get a scholarship; what school to enter; whether Latin is essential for college entrance; and personal questions of many kinds. The counselor may discover a physical defect and recommend treatment, or send for the mother and seek to harmonize family difficulties. It is in the individual interview that problems emerge that make the work of the vocational counselor so closely akin to that of the case worker.[7]

A factor in the success of an individual conference is privacy. "Counseling service in many schools is handicapped by the noisy, crowded places in which it is necessary to hold individual conferences. The best results can be expected only when there is an opportunity for the pupil

[7] See record of sample week, Appendix C.

to talk quietly and uninterruptedly with the counselor."[8] In our field investigations we were impressed by the lack of privacy in certain continuation schools. In many cases interviews on personal or family matters are held in the hearing of other pupils waiting their turn. Elsewhere, we found that privacy for the interview was the general rule, although, in many cases, counselors shared their offices with others. This is not necessarily a handicap if the offices are large and the desks far apart, but sometimes the opposite is the case. In the annual report of a vocational guidance bureau a few years ago the necessity for holding conferences on stairway landings was mentioned as a handicap to good counseling. In the field study several counselors were found who had no office other than a stair landing. To the question "Do you have a separate office with privacy for interviewing?" included in the questionnaire, eighty-one of the 105 counselors replying answered yes, twenty-three said they did not, and one wrote "not entirely."

Light on the technique of the counselor in the individual interview as it is practiced in a city where vocational guidance is well organized is to be found in one of the reports of the Occupational Research and Counseling Division of the Cincinnati Vocation Bureau.[9]

In addition to the simple questionnaire filled out by each pupil the following information was collected by the vocational counselor for every child with whom a conference was scheduled and placed in a special folder marked with that child's name:

1. Cumulative record
2. Intelligence test record
3. Teacher's estimate
4. Special information from such sources as social agencies, juvenile court, attendance department, visiting teachers, etc.

In the first conference the vocational counselor tried to secure a comprehensive record of the child, his family background, his

---

[8] White House Conference Report, pp. 60–61.
[9] *Report of Activities*, 1926–27, pp. 3 and 4.

likes and dislikes, his plans for the future. She endeavored to find out whether or not his was a carefully thought out plan, or whether it has been the result of undue persuasion on the part of family or friends. She suggested other occupations which his interests led her to believe he might wish to consider, and told him of ways in which he might prepare for these various occupations. The pupil was encouraged to find out more about the occupations which interested him; to talk with persons employed in the occupations; and to talk with his family concerning the length of time he might be allowed to spend in preparation.

Before the second conference it was usually necessary to secure additional information—from special teachers concerning the child's special abilities, and from persons engaged in occupations not yet listed in the counselor's notebook but concerning which the child wished definite information. In the second conference the child's plans were further developed and often at this time he was ready to make a choice of occupation for which he wished to prepare and the counselor could help him develop his plans for preparing and entering the occupation of his choice. To the child of superior ability the advantages of high school training were stressed and he was encouraged to choose the high school subjects which would permit him to attend college some day should that then seem a wise plan. In the case of those of special ability conferences with parents were sometimes held to urge upon them the importance of further training for these young people and, where necessary, scholarships were recommended. The child with meagre ability was helped to make a plan suited to his needs, and others who were failing in their school work, and who were unable or unwilling to improve, were encouraged and helped to find suitable work. . . .

The general policy of the vocational counselors at all times was not to force their plan upon the child but to lead him to think about his own qualifications and his relationship to various occupations and the training he would need to enter these occupations. Often the child had made a good plan but needed help in developing it—often he was at a loss as to where training might be secured for a definite occupation, perhaps he had never thought of the definite relation between a school course and the world of occupations and frequently he knew little or nothing about occupations and had made no attempt to plan for the future. Occupational facts often persuaded a child to give up a poor plan and to choose one more suited to his needs. (For example, a boy with a low percentile rank who was failing in his work wanted to become a doctor, but when he learned that in order to do so he must graduate with credit from high school and then attend college for six years he was willing to make a plan more suited to his ability.)

From the foregoing it is clear that the counselor needs information on a host of matters when dealing with the problems that arise in the individual conference. In the main these matters fall under two heads: information with respect to the personality of the pupil, and information relating to the vocational world. In the present chapter some of the aids to the securing of the first type of information have been described. The next chapter, while dealing briefly with methods of securing occupational information, is more particularly concerned with its dissemination.

CHAPTER V

THE GATHERING AND DISSEMINATION OF
OCCUPATIONAL INFORMATION

That the vocational counselor needs to know something about occupations is as obvious as it is that a traffic policeman needs to know where the streets are. It is easier to say what is indispensable than it is to set limits to the area with which he should be acquainted.

In the first place, the counselor should have a general knowledge of the occupational world. That is, he should know its chief divisions and something about each division. Brewer lists eighty-seven occupations in which more than 100,000 persons are employed in the United States.[1] These are certain to be the ones about which pupils will desire information and the counselor should know something about each of them.

With respect to the occupations in which experience shows there is the greatest interest, and especially those that offer opportunities in the community in which the school is located, his acquaintance should be detailed. This should include specific information on the following points:

The trend of the occupation or industry toward expansion or contraction

The existence of a shortage or of a surplus of workers in this field and the outlook for the future

The conditions of entrance to the occupation; e.g., training, experience, apprenticeship rules, open or closed shop, etc.

Opportunities for training

Conditions of work—strain, hazards, hours, etc.

Steadiness of employment

Compensation

Opportunities for advancement

Relations between employer and employees

[1] *Education as Guidance*, pp. 311–12.

With respect to the more important positions or those which offer more attractive opportunities he should possess definite job specifications.

One of the ways by which the counselor may advance along the road toward understanding in this field is through the medium of personal experience. The 105 counselors, who reported to us with respect to positions held prior to the present one, mentioned altogether fifty occupational fields or types of activity in which they had had experience. Fourteen of these were academic and thirty-six non-academic.

Obviously another manner of obtaining necessary information is through reading and study of published data. A third method involves the making of field investigations. Forty-seven of the counselors replying to our questionnaire stated that they make plant visits and nineteen more do so "occasionally." Four replied "not systematically," two did not answer. Thus seventy indicated that they give some time to this activity and only thirty-three replied with a definite negative. In answering another question, about distribution of time, fifty-six out of the seventy-five counselors replying stated that they gave some time to the "gathering of occupational information." In the White House Conference questionnaire school systems were asked to state whether counselors make occupational studies. To this question replies were received from 101 cities. Forty-five of them stated that their counselors do make such studies, and fifty-six that they do not.

In some cities it is considered of utmost importance that counselors should become thoroughly familiar with some occupation by making a direct, first-hand study. In Cincinnati, great emphasis is placed on the importance of every counselor preparing at least one occupational survey, before undertaking counseling activities. In 1932–33 the least amount of time given to occupational research by any Cincinnati counselor on full time was twenty-five days. The greatest amount of time was forty-one and one-half days. Altogether 197 days were devoted to occupational research by seven counselors.

Where there is a separate staff for the making of occupational studies the counselor will have at his disposal the findings of the specialists who are delegated to that activity. However, this is a field that has not yet been developed to any very great extent. Of the nine cities covered in our field study only two had such a separate staff. Of the seventeen directors of centralized vocational guidance bureaus who replied to our questionnaire, four stated that they had a separate staff for occupational studies. In one case this consisted of one full-time worker and two on part time; another had two part-time workers; and each of the other two had a part-time worker assigned to this duty.

The gathering of occupational information is a useless procedure unless in some way it is made available for pupils. Where counselors are free to make surveys of occupations and industries, or where there is a separate staff for this purpose, pamphlets are frequently prepared describing the occupation involved. These are usually brief, simply worded statements designed to give the most essential information.[2]

This pamphlet material is usually made accessible through the school library. The counselor interprets it and adds other information through the individual conference and through the medium of classes for the study of occupations which have already been described as a form of group conference.[3] A specialist in this field writes:

[2] The cities that have been most active in the preparation of this pamphlet material are Chicago, Cincinnati, Detroit, Milwaukee, Minneapolis, New Orleans, and Pittsburgh. Ten years ago the Occupational Research Section of the National Vocational Guidance Association was formed to promote better methods in research and in the preparation of material, and the National Occupational Conference, which came into being in 1933 has been active in promoting the gathering of occupational information.

[3] See also Brewer, *Education as Guidance*, pp. 140–41.

If group counseling is not the purpose of the junior course in occupations then the wisdom of adding the subject to the already crowded curriculum may be doubted. The course has social values and is popular with students, but it can be justified chiefly as the first step in vocational guidance. The course usually precedes the first individual interviews with the counselor, and individual counseling is much more effective if the time does not have to be spent in giving information that the student could have received in the classroom. Many of those who come to the interview with hazy or negative ambitions could be helped by the junior occupations course to some intelligent, well-founded, tentative choices, if not to a single, positive choice of vocation. The personal interview could then be given over to a discussion of the best steps to be taken in choice of curriculum or job, and to the discovery of the mental, physical, economic, and social handicaps that should be referred by the counselor to the proper agency of relief.[4]

Courses in occupations were found to be a feature in most of the schools covered in our field study, but no attempt was made to discover how generally this was true. However, one of the questions asked of school systems by the Committee on Vocational Guidance and Child Labor of the White House Conference was this: "Is a special course in occupations given?" Replies were received from 135 school systems, 105 of which, or 78 percent, replied in the affirmative. The distribution of replies was such as to indicate that special classes are much more common in the larger cities than in the smaller ones. Other replies indicated that in the smaller cities there is a tendency to introduce the subject of occupations in other courses, mainly in the courses in civics, though the courses in English and social studies are used for this purpose also.

Courses in occupations are taught either by counselors or by regular teachers. About a third of the counselors interviewed in our field study gave courses in occupations.

[4] May R. Lane, "Relationship between the Counselor and the Occupational Investigator," *Preliminary Report on the First Year Book of the National Vocational Guidance Association*, 1926. (Mimeographed.)

The same fact was apparent from the replies to our questionnaire. Thirty-two of the 105 counselors replying said that they teach such courses, and four that they supervise them. Sixty-nine stated that they do not teach courses in occupations.

From the foregoing it is evident that the counselor may help to make occupational information available to the student through the class in occupations either by teaching it or by assisting others to do so. When the teaching is done by others the counselor may help to plan the course, he may supervise it, or he may supply information for the teacher to use.

An example of the teaching of occupations by classroom teachers under the supervision of the counselor is to be found in the Polytechnic High School of Long Beach, Calif. The work is done by the English teachers. The course is given through a nine-week period in the 11B grade. Jane L. Fox, the counselor, writes of it as follows:

The purposes of the vocational study during nine weeks of composition are set forth in the initial note on the attached green folder. No one is asked to choose a vocation, but each pupil is directed to choose one or more for investigation. There are class discussions about types of work, qualities needed for success. . . . Information is acquired mostly through reading and interviews, though many pupils have had opportunity for observation and experience. We have a growing library of vocational information, including not only books but clippings, pamphlets, and letters. Every pupil is expected to report on an interview with an adult at work in the vocation he is studying. If he cannot get his own interview, one is arranged through my office. I send many pupils directly, with cards of introduction. In addition, perhaps, a hundred a year are provided through coöperation with the vocational guidance committee of the Kiwanis Club.

During this vocational study, I meet most of the junior English classes for an introductory talk, help the teachers and pupils in getting material, and have many individual conferences with pupils. They want to talk about vocations and they want to find out about necessary education.

Many counselors are active in securing pamphlet material, clippings from magazines or newspapers, books, and illustrations for the use of the pupils. Often they coöperate with the school librarian in establishing a vocational-guidance shelf or section in the library.

In Boston in the seventh, eighth, and ninth grades one hour a week is devoted to a course in educational and vocational guidance. A committee representing the Department of Vocational Guidance and the Intermediate Principals' Association has formulated a plan with suggested units for study in each grade. These units include a study of the Boston school system, education and its relation to life, occupational information, and the relation of character and habit to success in school and in making a living. The emphasis placed on different subjects varies in the different grades. For example, the unit on Occupational Information is optional in the seventh grade. In the ninth it is suggested that twelve weeks be given to it.[5]

Another type of course is that offered at the Boston Trade School in the fourth year. The wide range of subjects covered is shown in the following outline.

VOCATIONAL GUIDANCE IV

1. Our courses of study
2. The economics of business
3. The organization of business
4. Personal qualities necessary for success
5. Laws relating to labor
6. Selecting your employer (getting a job; characteristics of a good place)
7. Scientific management
8. Employment management
9. Wages and ways of paying
10. How to avoid unemployment
11. Conditions of work: hours, wages, fatigue, profit-sharing, vacations, etc.
12. Possible work in salesmanship for a person with mechanical ability

[5] The detailed outline of this unit for the ninth grade is given in Appendix G.

VOCATIONAL GUIDANCE IV—Continued

13. The work of the foreman and superintendent
14. Securing promotion
15. Working for others versus establishing a business of one's own—manual skill in addition to business ability
16. Estimating and contracting
17. Importance of capital
18. Credit
19. Prices
20. Keeping fit physically
21. Safety and occupational hygiene
22. Trade papers and keeping up-to-date
23. Correspondence courses and evening schools
24. Unionism
25. Radical labor movements
26. Strikes, arbitration, etc.
27. Coöperative management; shop committee plans, safety committees, employees' representation, etc.
28. Relation of recreation to work
29. Thrift and insurance
30. Housing: the question of renting or owning
31. Relation of your work to your family life
32. What to do in your vacations: how to have a good time
33. Ethics of the occupational world
34. Labor and politics
35. Keeping in touch with the vocational industry

In addition to the method of the interview and the classes in occupations, the counselor may assist the pupil to know the occupational world by arranging visits to plants or other places of employment. In some cities teachers have charge of these excursions, either independently, or with counselors assisting by arranging for the visits and by suggesting things to look for or questions to be asked. The amount of time given to this type of work varies greatly.

In some school systems, also, representatives of occupations are brought in to speak to the pupils about their work. Such plans sometimes culminate in a "Vocational Guidance Week" during which much of the regular schedule gives way to meetings and conferences on vocational subjects.

In Cincinnati the Y.M.C.A. has carried this process further than elsewhere by organizing and training a group of business and professional men who share with boys in senior high schools their specialized knowledge, working in close coöperation with the counseling program of the public schools. The steps in the process are outlined as follows:

(1) The selection and training of interviewers—(men who are specially qualified to interview and advise with boys); (2) a general meeting in the high school with 3rd and 4th year boys; (3) group meetings (in which boys are divided according to their interests, with a specially qualified person answering questions; in one group on engineering, in another on law, etc.); (4) life work emphasis blanks—boys fill out a self-analysis blank—these are accompanied by comments of teachers and intelligence ratings and grades, analyzed and then placed in the hands of man who will interview boy; (5) individual interviews—at the school and later specialized interviews; (6) follow-up—when boy and business man continue to keep in touch with each other. The Y.M.C.A. Employment Bureau advises with employed young men, and conducts classes which enable them to qualify better for their work.[6]

The pupil has access to many other sources of information about occupations, through observation, conversation with parents and others, the newspapers, books, etc. Perhaps the most illuminating source is experience in jobs—after school, on Saturdays, or in summer vacations. The exploratory courses in junior high school offer another valuable opportunity for a glimpse at various methods of earning a living.

[6] Pamphlet, *Some Vocational Guidance Activities in Cincinnati.*

CHAPTER VI

OTHER ACTIVITIES OF THE COUNSELOR

The activities so far discussed are among those that are generally considered indispensable to vocational counseling. There are other activities considered equally indispensable by many vocational guidance authorities, and beyond these are countless others varying according to type of school, methods of supervision, and personality of the counselor. It is obviously impossible to consider all of these in detail, but we may give brief attention to a few of the more outstanding duties not yet discussed. To get the matter in its proper setting let us quote from the White House Report and from one of our questionnaires. Says the White House Report:

Vocational counselors are also educational counselors, for it is usually impossible to help the boy or girl make a satisfactory plan for a future occupation without also considering school courses and electives which may be chosen to give the most adequate preparation for the future vocation. The same is true of social, health and other personal problems, which the vocational counselor considers in the light of the pupil's present educational and future vocational needs. Some vocational counselors attempt to handle a great variety of problems, because special assistance is not available; others, detecting a special health, emotional, or social problem, secure the assistance of the specialist best equipped to take care of the situation.[1]

A high school counselor in California in answering the question, "What are your principal duties?", wrote:

Advisement and enrollment of new 10-B pupils from our six junior high schools, program-planning for students of all grades (10-12), program adjustments (for maladjusted pupils), advisement about length of schooling, information about colleges and trade schools, supervision of occupational study in junior English Composition, sponsoring vocational talks and interviews, col-

[1] White House Conference Report, pp. 40-41.

lecting and dispensing vocational information, interpretation of records to pupils, parents and teachers, case records kept for use of administrators and teachers, coöperation with all other guidance agencies, conferences with parents, share in curriculum making, administrative duties.

From both of these quotations, therefore, as well as from evidence presented earlier, it is clear that educational counseling is a part of the work of the vocational counselor. Our study has revealed two major reasons for this fact. One is the opportunity it gives for making contacts with the pupils. When the vocational counselor meets the incoming pupils in a group to explain junior or senior high school courses and then assists in making up individual programs, he is establishing a relationship that will aid in forming a basis for his future activities in the vocational field. A second reason is the obvious fact that advice about the choice of a calling would in many cases be futile if it were not accompanied by information relative to the necessary precedent training.

It may not be equally obvious that a counselor should work with maladjusted or problem pupils or with those who are failing. It is difficult to avoid the suspicion that in these matters, as well as in many others that frequently engage the counselors' attention, the principal is making use of the counselor as a general-utility, or handy, man.[2]

[2] On reading this statement one of the most discriminating and thoughtful counselors we know, made the following comment: "It seems to me that in certain cases it is quite justifiable for a counselor to work with failing, maladjusted or problem pupils for often it is by interesting these pupils in vocational and educational plans that the best adjustment can be made. The counselor should be able to recommend a course for a failing child that he will be able to do satisfactorily and may win his consent to the change by helping to interest him in certain vocations to which the new course may lead. I believe that every counselor should work some with failing, maladjusted and problem pupils, but it is a great mistake for her to work with these to the exclusion of the large group of normal pupils as may sometimes be the case. Our plan, of course, is that special problems shall be referred to the worker best equipped to handle that particular type of problem and that we shall merely supplement such specialized work by giving the vocational information and guidance that is needed."

Scholarships

One of the important duties of counselors is to confer with prospective "drop-outs"—that is, with pupils who have indicated that they are considering leaving school to go to work. Promising pupils are urged to stay in school. Where the difficulty is financial the counselor often endeavors to find some way of meeting the situation just as he would do if it were a health problem or any other matter calling for adjustment. Sometimes the apparent necessity for leaving school arises out of the unemployment of the father. One counselor encountered in our field study told of her efforts in such a case to obtain employment for the father and thus make it possible for the child to continue in school. Other counselors have interviewed parents with a view to assisting them to budget their resources more effectively. Others refer the family to a social agency for advice or relief.

A direct and logical method of dealing with such cases is to provide a scholarship for the child, as a full or partial substitute for what he could contribute to family support if he were at work. In most of the cities visited in our field study, scholarship funds of one sort or another were available, mostly under private auspices. The White House Conference Report revealed that 80 of the 142 school systems reporting stated that scholarships are granted in their schools.[3] Most of the funds appear to have been contributed by private individuals, and many of them are administered by private organizations.

The relation of the school counselor to scholarships depends somewhat upon their origin and administration. When the fund is administered by the school system, the counselor may decide on the child who is to receive the grant. When it is administered by a private

[3] White House Conference Report, p. 78.

agency, the counselor merely recommends a child for a scholarship award. In either case, the counselor may be called upon to keep in close touch with the scholarship pupil, to report on his progress from time to time, and to follow up his career for a time after leaving school.

These duties fall upon the school counselor when there is no one else whose definite and exclusive task it is. However, with the development of scholarship funds on a large scale, there has come into being a specialized type of counselor known as scholarship counselor. For this purpose, according to the White House Report, the scholarship committees that are doing the best work "engage counselors who have training in social case work; a knowledge of mental hygiene and an understanding of vocational guidance and employment problems, since the scholarship counselor is called upon to deal with every phase of the lives of the boys and girls who come to see her. It is only, however, in a few cities that scholarship work is carried on by trained counselors."[4]

The work of such a counselor is described in the White House Report. First, the procedure followed when a child is referred for a scholarship includes:

A visit to the home to determine the parents' inability to keep the child in school without assistance; to learn the parents' attitude in regard to education and to be assured of their coöperation. The amount of the scholarship is usually based on the family income and the standard budget in use by social agencies in the community.

A visit to the school to find out the child's progress in school and to learn something of his interest and abilities from his teachers.

An interview with the agencies in the community who are acquainted with the family, as shown by clearance with the local central registration office in order that all may be working for best results in the interest of the child.

An interview with the child to find out whether he himself is ambitious to continue his schooling and what plans he has for the

[4] White House Conference Report, p. 79.

future. In the offices where some of the best work is done he is given a physical examination and achievement and aptitude tests to assist the counselor in giving him proper guidance. A record is kept of all information concerning the child, the home, and his scholarship in school. All later interviews are noted and plans and progress recorded.[5]

Scholarship committees and social agencies dealing with families are likely, at times, to find themselves interested in the same family or individual. Commenting on this the White House Report says:

Scholarship committees in all cities urge relief-giving agencies to make no appreciable change in their grant to a family when a scholarship is given to one of the children. In several places the scholarship committees and the relief agency have worked in coöperation, the scholarship organization usually having all contacts with the student, but no responsibility for family problems. This is very satisfactory when the workers can keep in fairly constant touch with each other. It has a value for the adolescent child in making him feel more responsibility and more faith in himself. If the family has never been to a relief agency and needs financial assistance while the scholarship is being administered, the counselor after winning the family's consent, refers it to the proper agency, coöperating with the relief worker. When only a slight service is needed which may involve the student receiving the scholarship, the counselor handles it herself, using it as an opportunity to help the child realize his responsibility to the rest of the family, especially the younger brothers and sisters.[6]

Follow-Up

The term "follow-up" is used to describe any method of checking up on a pupil after he has left school. It has two main objectives. First, to find out whether the counselor can be of any further assistance; and, second, to obtain a measure of the validity of the counseling methods used. So far as the field of counseling is concerned, follow-up is most actively practiced by the scholarship counselor.

[5] *Ibid.*, p. 83.   [6] *Ibid.*, p. 82.

Outside this special interest, follow-up is practiced mainly by the placement worker and will be discussed in Part III of this report. However, a certain amount of follow-up is done by the school counselor. In the main this is limited to invitations to pupils to come back for further assistance whenever they feel the need of it, or to write letters describing their progress. Of the cities visited in our field study, follow-up was practiced by counselors most actively in Boston, where most of the counselors give a definite and substantial part of their time to placement, and in Providence where all follow-up is done by the counselors.

The two chief aims of follow-up in Boston are said to be "first, an attempt to solve the individual problem of the boy who is in employment; second, the use of follow-up for research purposes." All persons registered or placed are invited to come for conference to an evening office hour held once a week. Each year also, several months after graduation letters and questionnaires are sent out to each graduate or attempts are made to reach him through telephone or home visits. In the belief that the information thus secured will be helpful in planning courses of study, a report is sent to each school principal, giving him detailed information on each graduate, including the name of the school or college which the pupil is attending, the names of employers who have employed him, the nature of the occupations engaged in, and the wages or salaries received. Summaries are made up showing also the proportion of graduates of each school who are attending colleges and other schools and the proportion who are at work, and who are taking evening-school courses.

The department has completed a five-year and a ten-year follow-up study[7] of the boys who were graduated from high schools of the city in the years 1920, 1921, 1922, and a five-year study of the girls who were graduated in 1924.

[7] See Appendix L.

The Providence follow-up program is deserving of emphasis since it is more complete and thoroughgoing than that of any other guidance organization of which we have information. In both junior and senior high schools in Providence, there is a counselor for each grade who continues with the same group of pupils as long as they are in the school. Each high school counselor makes a follow-up study of his own classes one year, three years, and five years after graduation. This gives each counselor one new class to be responsible for each third year and after the sixth year involves one follow-up study each year. The method is as follows:

A counselor makes no follow-up study in his first three years, while he is conducting his first class through the school, nor yet in his fourth year, while class number one is acquiring its first year's experience beyond high school. In his fifth year, however, he makes a one-year follow-up study of this class, in his seventh year a three year follow-up and in his ninth year a final five year follow-up of the same class. Meanwhile he has been counseling class number two which graduates at the end of his sixth year and class number three which graduates at the end of his ninth year. These classes are similarly studied with the result that after his sixth year the counselor swings into his stride and does one follow-up study with a different class each year, in the regular order of one-year follow-up, five-year follow-up, three-year follow-up, etc.[8]

Placement

The counselors who have nothing whatever to do with placement are few. The practice varies from that of the Boston Vocational Guidance Department where the functions of counseling and placement are combined in the same persons, to that recently obtaining in Chicago where

[8] See Appendix L.

there was a separate placement division in the Vocational Bureau, with counselors giving full time to it, but where, nevertheless, advisers in the schools were responsible for finding part-time or vacation jobs for pupils in their own schools. In cities where there is no junior placement bureau the counselors naturally do more placement work.

Ninety-two counselors answered our question about proportion of time given to designated activities. Of these, thirty-nine indicated that they did some placement work and nine more that they gave a substantial amount of time to it.

Record Keeping

Much of the value of counseling may depend upon the records which the counselor has kept of the pupil's family and home situation; school grades, past and current; mental ratings and estimates of teachers. Equally important is the record made after the conference with the child, of points in the discussion that have a bearing on the child's problems and his plans for the future.

There are several types of records kept by counselors. The more detailed and comprehensive ones, similar to those of the trained case worker, note chronologically the results of conferences and events, and make available in systematic form all related information concerning the child. On the other hand, some counselors use a simpler system of card forms with spaces for checking and writing in a few words after various items. Still others keep no records but trust to their memories or informal notes to recall the many facts that must be kept in mind about each child.[9]

[9] White House Conference Report, pp. 58–59.

CHAPTER VII

QUALIFICATIONS OF COUNSELORS

Vocational guidance is a process that enlists the activities of many more persons in the school system than is indicated by their titles. The assistant principal, as we have already seen, is frequently a counselor. Others who play a rôle of greater or less importance, according to the nature of the guidance organization in a particular school system, include home-room teachers, visiting teachers, teachers of social science courses, teachers of English, deans, psychologists, and attendance officers. In the smaller schools the classroom teacher is an important factor in guidance. "In the small rural high school, as in the one-room elementary school, whatever is done in the matter of educational and vocational guidance must be done by the members of the teaching staff including always the principal."[1]

In most school systems guidance work is done in the beginning by teachers, often with no allowance of time from their other duties for the purpose. As the work and its value become better understood, the teacher is allowed a period or two a day, free from other duties. Later the time is extended until finally full time is allowed for counseling and other forms of guidance. When this stage has been reached, other persons may be brought in as full-time counselors who have not previously taught—in the same school system at any rate—but who have received special training in vocational guidance.

Of ninety-eight cities replying on this point to the White House questionnaire, "21 school systems indicated that their counselors were specially trained people appointed exclusively for counseling; 33 that they were teachers

[1] Proctor, *Educational and Vocational Guidance*, p. 317.

assigned full time to counseling; and 74 that they were teachers assigned part time to counseling."[2]

One might naturally infer, therefore, that from the standpoint of training, there are two types of counselors in the schools—those with the background and qualifications of a teacher and those with specialized training in the field of vocational guidance.

Let us look at the matter of qualifications from three angles: first, from the point of view of what workers in the field of vocational guidance consider desirable; second, required qualifications as indicated from official sources; and third, the qualifications actually possessed by counselors who are on the job as stated by themselves.

Qualifications as Outlined by the Profession

Dr. L. A. Wilson of the New York Department of Education writes:

A program of vocational and educational guidance in the schools can be carried out satisfactorily only by teachers trained for this particular work. Such teachers must be prepared to make case studies and occupational studies; to counsel with pupils, parents and other teachers regarding guidance problems; to do placement and follow-up work; to teach life career and try-out classes; to secure the coöperation of interested agencies; to keep good general and statistical records and to make intelligence, achievement and aptitude tests. Much of this work is technical in character. Those who are to do it should be thoroughly grounded in every aspect of the theory and technic of guidance. The opportunity for service which teachers have, who have been so prepared, should be a challenge to the ambition of every man and woman who follows the profession of teaching because he or she finds joy in the work of setting the feet of young people on the road to somewhere.[3]

[2] White House Conference Report, p. 44. The total of the figures given above is greater than the number of school systems replying, since some of the cities have two or more of the three types of counselors.

[3] University of the State of New York, *Vocational and Educational Guidance in Junior and Senior High Schools*, 1927, p. 5. Bulletin 887.

Dorothea de Schweinitz, writing in 1926 as president of the National Vocational Guidance Association, indicated in part by questions the general field in which, in her opinion, the counselor should have training:

The problem of training for the counselor looms up as a real consideration in educational and vocational guidance. So much of this work has crept into our educational institutions by the back door. A teacher released from some other classroom duties, without title, with little recognition, with no training, is expected to convince the faculty and the students of the efficacy of the new and mysterious activity. Has he had field work in a vocational guidance department in some other city? Has he been given oportunity to visit cities where experiments are under way or where results have been shown? Has he had a course in vocational guidance? What should such a course include? What should be the prerequisites of such a course? What should the counselor know about labor problems, the industrial structure, the field of industrial research? Similar questions arise in connection with the general field of education, psychology, mental hygiene, social case work. Is the counselor equipped at least to know when to make use of a specialist from another field? How much background in these related fields should the counselor have for a suitable approach to his own work?[4]

Proctor suggests the following as essential qualifications of the counselor:

Three important characteristics should at least be mentioned.

a) Social. The successful counselor will usually be a person in whom the social instincts have been highly cultivated. . . . It is not the dominating type of social leadership that is wanted. Rather, it is the sympathetic, tactful type of person with the capacity for insight into the possibilities of boys and girls and the ability to inspire them to the kind of effort necessary to measure up to their true endowment. . . . This requires sympathy—ability to enter into other people's point of view and to understand their problems; insight—capacity to get quickly at the heart of another person's difficulty; and tact—skill in hand-

[4] "Some Outstanding Problems in School Counseling" in *Preliminary Report on the First Year Book of the National Vocational Guidance Association.* (Mimeographed copy, 1926, pp. 5–6.)

ling people so that they will do the things necessary for their own best interest. . . .

b) Education. For the classroom teacher in the elementary school the minimum of training should be two years of normal-school work beyond a four year high school course. In order to exercise the guidance function effectively, she should have had in the normal school a course in principles of educational and vocational guidance as well as at least a course in educational tests and measurements. The full or part-time counselor in the high school should have had at least an A.B. degree and should have had courses in economics, sociology, psychology and education in addition to the courses in guidance and measurements suggested above for the elementary school counselor. The Director of Research and Guidance should have a Master's or a Doctor's degree with specific training along the lines suggested below.

c) Experience. . . . The person going directly into counseling from college or normal school needs to avail himself of every possible opportunity to become familiar with the world's work and its workers. (Valuable experience includes summer vacation experiences in a variety of occupations . . . wide acquaintance with business and industrial enterprises gained through visitation . . . actual practice under supervision in giving counsel to elementary or high school pupils. . . . Directors should have had teaching experience.[5]

Edwin A. Lee, professor of education in the University of California, writes:

The guidance worker's training should rest, of course, upon a broad cultural foundation. I do not mean simply the completion of a liberal arts course in a recognized university; I mean that deeper something which we sometimes recognize in individuals as being representative of fineness of intellect, keenness of understanding, fineness of perception of moral and ethical values; those things which are hard to define but are nevertheless recognizable immediately you come into the presence of the cultured person. The guidance worker should possess that culture.

The guidance worker should in addition have training in specific branches of knowledge. He should have training in the field of sociology, because the guidance worker is a sociologist; in the field of economics, because the guidance worker is an economist and must be acquainted with the science of economics; in the field of

[5] Proctor, *Educational and Vocational Guidance*, pp. 320–22.

psychology the guidance worker must be thoroughly prepared, must understand and be proficient in the technique of psychology, because he is a psychologist at work in a definite field. He is also an educator and must accordingly have training in the science and art of education, with particular reference to his part as a guidance worker in the whole field. I am demanding an interesting and unusual individual. He doesn't exist very much in our general scheme of things. Yet the training I am laying down for him is not heavy as compared with the training of a physician or surgeon, or a lawyer, or any other of the great professions.

The worker in the field of guidance must have, in addition to this specific training in the fields of knowledge, specialized training in the theory and practice of vocational counseling, which is more and more coming to have a dependable body of knowledge and technique. He must have specific experience in the teaching of occupational classes and in the construction of courses of study in terms of occupations, which in turn are based upon perception and understanding of occupational surveys. He should have experience in social case work, not alone having read about sociology, but actually having participated in the social case work of the social worker. And it is desirable, if possible, that he shall have had actual industrial and commercial experience as an employment manager or in an employment manager's office.[6]

Official Requirements

STATE REQUIREMENTS

In two states, standards of experience and education have been worked out by the departments of education, and constitute minimum requirements for the state as a whole. These are New York and Pennsylvania.

A summary of these requirements follows:[7]

New York

Qualifications of vocational and educational guidance counselors

1. Personality and maturity

Wide range in personality specified. Entrance limits of 30 and 45 years suggested

[6] "The Professionalization of the Guidance Worker," in Allen, *Principles and Problems of Vocational Guidance*, 1927, pp. 26–27.

[7] *State Guidance Programs*, Pamphlet No. 35, U.S. Office of Education, Department of the Interior. Jan., 1933.

2. Experience
   Suggested fields of experience other than teaching
3. Education and special training
   Completion of four-year high school course and a permanent certificate to teach; completion of the following general courses, totaling 12 credit hours:
   Educational psychology (psychology of adolescence preferred)
   Educational measurements
   Principles of secondary education
   Principles of teaching
   Sociology
   Economics
   Completion of special courses with a total of 14 hours credit in
   Educational and vocational guidance (advanced)
   Methods of counseling and placement
   Studies and research in occupational and educational opportunities
   Principles and problems in vocational education (advanced)
   Labor problems, legislation, and employment conditions
   Psychological tests in guidance

Pennsylvania

Certification of guidance teachers and guidance counselors

This state has two forms of guidance certificates, one validated for group guidance (teaching) in the field of school opportunities and occupations, which is required, and a counselor's certificate which is not yet mandatory. The following is a partial summary:

A. Requirements in common for both certificates—
   1. The completion of an approved four-year high school curriculum
   2. The possession of a valid certificate to teach, which includes the equivalent of a minimum of two years of post high-school work
B. Requirements in addition to A above for group guidance (teaching) in school opportunities and occupations

Eighteen semester hours in the field of guidance. Six of these to be in occupations, general introduction to guidance, and labor and personnel problems, and twelve in related subjects

C. Requirements in addition to A above for the guidance counseling certificate not now mandatory

Eighteen semester hours in courses that may be credited under the following:

MINIMUM
SEMESTER HOURS

General introduction to guidance 2
Specialized techniques in guidance 6
Field studies and applications 6
Organization and administration of guidance . 4

State control of minimum standards is assured in New York by a law authorizing the Commissioner of Education to apportion state funds toward the payment of the salaries of vocational counselors whose qualifications he approves to the extent of $1,000 for each counselor.[8]

CITY REQUIREMENTS

As examples of requirements set up by city school systems, those of Boston and Chicago are presented below:

Boston

For the vocational instructor and vocational assistant in day high schools certificate: The degree of Master of Education, Master of Arts, or equivalent degree, from a college or university approved by the Board of Superintendents; evidence of satisfactory completion of a course of not less than 300 hours in the theory and practice of vocational guidance, or the equivalent thereof, approved by the Board of Superintendents; and evidence of two years' approved experience in teaching or in vocational guidance work in day high or day intermediate schools.

The examination consists of one major subject and two minor subjects.

[8] See Appendix H for a full statement of qualifications.

	POINTS
The major subject counts	300
Each minor subject (2 required) counts 150	300
Amount, quality, and character of experience counts .	400
Total	1,000

MAJOR SUBJECTS

1. Vocational guidance (to include applied psychology, and an examination in the theory and methods of vocational guidance)

FIRST MINOR
SUBJECT

2. Statistics

SECOND MINOR
SUBJECT (SELECT ONE)

3. Economics
3. Sociology
3. Business organization

Chicago[9]

Candidates for certificates as assistants in the Department of Vocational Guidance must present in advance credentials showing:

a) Graduation from an accredited college; and in addition thereto,

b) Two years of full-time, paid work with successful experience in any of the fields covered by the work of the Vocational Guidance Department; or in allied fields such as: industrial or sociological investigation with an organization of recognized standing; or case work with recognized social agencies; personnel administration; such experience to be approved by the Board of Examiners, or

b1) One year's specialized training in sociology, economics, and related subjects, in a college or university of recognized standing, and one year of successful experience as outlined in paragraph (b) above, or

b2) One year of successful experience as outlined in paragraph (b) above, and 2 years of successful experience as teacher in graded schools.

[9] Requirements in effect when the Department of Vocational Guidance was abolished in 1933.

They will be examined in the subjects named below:

Major:
1. History and literature of vocational guidance
2. Occupations and industries
3. Social legislation related to minors in industry and related school law

Minors:
1. English
2. Professional study
3. Economics

Further information as to formal requirements was obtained from directors of vocational guidance to whom questionnaires were sent. The request for information on this point was as follows: "Qualifications required for counselors: education; experience; other."

Seventeen replies were received from heads of organized vocational guidance systems in as many different cities. As to educational requirements, sixteen said that they required a college degree and one an M.A. degree. Three said that "special courses" were required in addition, two specifically mentioned training in vocational guidance, and one, courses in testing.

Eleven of the seventeen said that teaching experience is required, one of whom specified an "outstanding record" in the schools of the same system. Four did not mention any type of experience. The one remaining questionnaire stated, under this head, that "experience and training are taken into account." Other types of experience were social work, named by three directors, and business, mentioned by two.

Under the heading "other," three directors mentioned "personality," and one "mature years." Other replies included these items: "principal's rating of excellent on personality, vigor, willingness to study, agreement to follow a study program on psychology, statistics, etc.";

"one or more years in this institution"; and "acquaintance with vocations in this community."

Qualifications Actually Possessed by Counselors

Finally, we come to the statements made by the counselors themselves with respect to their own training and experience.   Three of the questions included in the questionnaire sent to counselors covered the matter of educational preparation.

Question 14 asked "What schools (high school, college, normal school, university) have you attended?   (Please indicate year of graduation and degrees.)"

Completed questionnaires indicated that the 105 counselors should be grouped as follows:

```
Attended normal school (but did not graduate) . . . .   2
Graduated from normal school . . . . . . . . . .   3
Attended college (but did not graduate) . . . . . . .  16
Received bachelors degree . . . . . . . . . . . .  54
Received masters degree . . . . . . . . . . . . .  28
Received doctors degree . . . . . . . . . . . . .   2
```

Question 15 was as follows: "Name any specific courses that have contributed to your understanding of your present position."

This question was answered by ninety counselors.   The following is a list of the courses, arranged according to the number of times they were mentioned:

Courses in Guidance and Counseling

```
Vocational Guidance . . . . . . . . . . . . . .  55
Undifferentiated Guidance . . . . . . . . . . .  25
Educational Guidance . . . . . . . . . . . . .  15
Occupational Research . . . . . . . . . . . .  13
Administration of Vocational Guidance . . . . . .   6
Educational and Vocational Guidance . . . . . . .   5
Personnel Administration . . . . . . . . . . . .   4
Job Analysis . . . . . . . . . . . . . . . . .   3
Placement . . . . . . . . . . . . . . . . . .   3
Advising . . . . . . . . . . . . . . . . . . .   2
Research in Vocational Guidance . . . . . . . . .   2
Personnel Guidance . . . . . . . . . . . . . .   1
```

Courses in Psychology

General	39
Tests and Measurements	39
Educational	12
Mental Hygiene	11
Abnormal	9
Child	7
Vocational	6
Clinical	3
Of Administration	1
Experimental	1
Individual Differences	1
Social	1

Courses in Social Sciences

Sociology and Social Problems	31
Economics	12
Statistics	9
Labor Problems	7
Political Science	1

Courses in Education

Administration	29
Principles	20
Vocational	13
Philosophy of	4
Civic	2
Child Health, Behavior, Welfare, etc.	19
Courses for deans	5
Case work	3
Biology	2
Philosophy	2
Physiology	2
Research	2

Each of the following subjects was mentioned once: Accounting; Advertising; Anatomy; Appreciation of Music; Business Organization; Color and Design; Ethics; Eugenics; Heredity; History of Art; Industrial Geography; Industrial History; Neurology; Orthogenics; Public Health; Shop Courses; Textile Analysis; and Trade Analysis.

In the belief that certain fields of study might reasonably

be of particular value to counselors a specific question was asked about five types of courses. Question 16 read, "In which of the following fields have you had courses? Economics; Sociology; Psychology; Labor Problems; Vocational Guidance."

The White House Conference Report comments on these five subjects as follows:

Psychology is important because it gives knowledge concerning the child's mental and emotional make-up. Sociology contributes to the understanding of the child in relation to his social environment and often includes special courses relating to the family, poverty, and social case work technique. Economics gives familiarity with the underlying principles of the business world and its problems, and the study of labor problems helps in understanding the special phase of economics that applies to the employe in his relation to his employer and the public. Vocational guidance courses are needed to acquaint the counselor with the principles, problems, methods, and special technique of his profession.[10]

The following indicates the number of counselors who stated in their replies that they had taken each type of course:

Psychology 103
Sociology 94
Vocational Guidance 90
Economics 80
Labor Problems 50

It is interesting to note that all but two of the counselors replying, or 98 percent, had had courses in psychology. Ninety percent had taken some course in sociology, 86 percent had had special courses in vocational guidance, 76 percent had had courses in economics, and 48 percent courses in labor problems.

The answers to Questions 15 and 16 taken together present an interesting contrast. If a faithful effort was made to give what was asked for in Question 15, the

[10] White House Conference Report, p. 65.

answers should provide a selected list of the courses found in practice to be most valuable to the counselor. At the same time, the five fields listed in Question 16 are, presumably, of special interest to the workers in the field of vocational guidance.

The answers to Questions 15 and 16 with respect to these five fields when placed side by side present an opportunity for comparison.

SUBJECT	NUMBER TAKING COURSES	NUMBER CONSIDERING THESE COURSES OF SPECIAL VALUE
	Answers to Question 16	*Answers to Question 15*
Psychology	103	80
Sociology	94	31
Vocational Guidance	90	134
Economics	80	12
Labor Problems	50	7

The best case, as one might anticipate, is made for courses in vocational guidance. The number 134 is obtained by counting every course mentioned. Since some of those replying had taken more than one course, the total is greater than the number replying. The same is true of psychology and sociology. In the case of economics and labor problems, however, no reply indicated more than one type of course. The numbers twelve and seven are therefore the exact number of counselors who mentioned these courses as having value. In making comparisons allowance must be made for the fact that 105 counselors answered Question 16 and only ninety answered Question 15. However, it is significant that while 76 percent of those replying to Question 16 (105) had had a course in economics, only 13 percent of those answering Question 15 (90) found it an aid in vocational guidance. It is possible that some inferences could be drawn at this point about the teaching of economics.

Another element in the equipment of counselors is

experience. Professor Brewer states that he has "always suspected that such teachers as are drawn into counseling are likely to be people who have sought and had a greater variety of experience than could be registered by a similar body of workers in any other profession."

In order to verify this belief, he asked students in the Harvard Summer School of 1928 who were engaged in guidance work "to state the occupational experience, aside from educational work, which they had had, with the time of each experience specified."

The results are given below, separately for sixteen men and twenty women.

VOCATIONAL COUNSELORS: MEN

1. Surveying, 9 mos.; Civil engineer, 3 yrs.; air pilot, 1 yr.; flight instructor during war, 9 mos.
2. General farm work, 6 mos.; law, 14 yrs.; real estate salesman, 3 mos.; building and contracting manager, 2 yrs.
3. Surveyor, 6 mos.; stenographer and bookkeeper, 5 mos.; cream tester in creamery, 2 mos.; in charge of army canteen, 6 mos.; soda fountain clerk, 9 mos.; carpenter, painter, entomological work, lumber camp, 6 wks.; cattle boat, 2 wks.; farm work, 5 yrs.
4. General farming, 15 yrs.; carpentry and painting, vacations.
5. General farming, 6 yrs.; building, 2 yrs.; painting, 6 summers; manufacturing lumber, owner and manager; bookkeeper, 2 summers.
6. Post office clerk, 1 yr.; editorial work, reporter and business management, 4 mos.; general farming, 1½ yrs.; real estate salesman, 4 mos.; factory timekeeper, payroll, 6 mos.
7. Farming, 8 yrs.
8. Army aviator in France, 2 yrs.; travelling salesman, electric motors, 1 yr.; aeronautical materials testing engineer, 4 yrs.; machine shop work and installing telephone switchboards, summers.
9. General farming until 21 yrs. old; salesman, books, aluminum, clothing, hardware; carpentry, 1 summer.
10. Farming, salesmanship in canvassing.

11. Asst. minister, 9 mos.; missionary, 16 yrs.; recruiting for church vocations and counseling, 7 yrs.

12. General farm work, several summers; plumbing, 1 yr.; meat packing, 3 wks.; clerical work, 1 summer; post office work sorting mail, vacations.

13. General farming, several yrs.; selling, 3 mos.; store manager, 4 mos.; mason, 3 mos.; book salesman, 3 mos.; public service, 6 yrs.; guardian, 2 yrs.; business manager of 2 farms, 5 yrs.; homemaker, 7 yrs.

14. General farming, 5 yrs.; construction work, 3 mos.; selling, 6 mos.; undertaker's assistant; baseball player, 3 summers; canvasser, 1 summer; bookkeeping machine salesman, 1 summer.

15. Newsboy, 3 yrs.; chore boy, farm, 5 yrs.; gardener, 3 yrs.; general farming, 3 summers; selling, 1 summer; deputy city clerk, 1 summer; bill collector, 1 summer; hotel janitor, 3 mos.; hotel night clerk, 5 mos.; truck driver, 3 mos.; delivery boy, 1 wk.; ice-cream factory hand, 3 summers; carpenter, 6 mos.; auto mechanic's helper, 6 mos.; electrician's helper, 1 wk.; painter, 4 mos.; paper hanger's helper, 2 wks.; business manager college annual, 9 mos.; soda fountain clerk, 2 mos.; unskilled laborer, 3 mos.

16. Sales manager, 1 yr.; account clerk, 3 mos.; grocery clerk, 6 mos.; manager grocery store, 2 yrs.; railroad passenger trainman, 3 mos.; construction, 1 yr.; stock clerk, 3 mos.; office and mailing boy, 3 mos.

VOCATIONAL COUNSELORS: WOMEN

1. Clerical work, insurance, 3 summers; library assistant, 4 summers; assistant in Red Cross office, several mos.; clerk in quartermaster corps, 1½ yrs.; director girls' camp, 1 summer.

2. Cashier in tea-room, evenings occasionally; pastry cook, 4 summers.

3. Director of city playground, 4 summers; secretarial work, 7 mos.; secretary in appointment bureau, 4 yrs.

4. Clerk, candy counter, 3 summers.

5. Homemaker, 17 yrs.; Camp Fire Girl Guardian, 2 yrs.

6. Director of Junior Red Cross, 2 yrs.; social work; homemaker, 7 yrs.; supervisor of large department in church, 8 yrs.

7. Homemaker, 22 yrs.

8. Dressmaker, 2 wks.; summer camp director, 1 mo.
9. Private secretary, 1½ yrs.; court reporter, 6 mos.; Y.W.C.A. secretary, 8 mos.; general office work, summers.
10. Homemaker, 14 yrs.; private secretary to an author, 1 summer.
11. Placement work, 3 summers; homemaking, 22 yrs.; quartermaster's department during war.
12. Retail selling, 5 wks.; factory work, assembling radios, 3 wks.
13. Retail clerk, 1 yr.; mail order clerk, 1 yr.; assistant manager tea-room, 2 summers; club waitress, 2 summers; library work, 1 yr.
14. Factory work, 1 mo.; general office work, 3 mos.; stenography and typing, 6 mos.; selling; practical nurse, 3 mos.; head of family, 10 yrs.; director of industrial department Y.W.C.A., 2½ yrs.
15. Bank clerk, 1 summer.
16. Bank teller, 2 yrs.; bank work, 3 yrs.; selling, department store, 2 mos.; employment service, 1 yr.
17. Bank clerk, 1 yr.; farming, 1½ summers; playground worker, 1 summer; executive secretary, 1½ yrs.; camp counselor, 1 mo.
18. Assistant in dentist's office, 1 mo.; milliner, 1 yr.; orange growing, 2 yrs.; homemaker, 2 yrs.; department store personnel work, 3 yrs.
19. Homemaking, 1 summer, irregular short periods.
20. Purchasing work, 1 yr.; economic research work, 1 yr.; research assistant, 2 yrs.; secretarial work.

Commenting on this showing Dr. Brewer writes:

If four major fields of occupational experience for men are designated agricultural, industrial, commercial, and the professions other than teaching, it will be found that five of the men responding to this questionnaire have had experience in all four, five in at least three, four in two, and only two of them were confined to one field. If for the women we consider the four fields homemaking, industry, commerce, and the professions other than teaching, two had experience in all four, three in three, 11 in two, and four in one. In addition to the experiences in these four groups of occupations there were two women who had had experience in farming and one man in homemaking.

The median length of experience was about eight years for the men and slightly less for the women. It should be noted that our tabulation includes all of those who responded to the questionnaire and the list presumably included all the active counselors in our classes.

It seems safe to conclude that counselors in American schools are not without occupational experience other than teaching, and that therefore they have in their equipment this desirable background for their work.[11]

It was in the hope of obtaining just the sort of information given above by Professor Brewer that Question 17 was included in our questionnaire: "Please enumerate all the different positions you have held since leaving school and indicate the length of time spent in each." Replies to this question were received from 101 counselors. The following table includes all the positions held by more than one person and the number of persons holding each position the specified number of years, as well as the number failing to state years of tenure.

POSITION	YEARS							
	1–5	6–10	11–15	16–20	21–25	OVER 25	YEARS NOT STATED	TOTAL
Teacher . . .	23	20	15	4	4	3	9	78
Principal . . .	14	1	..	..	..	..	3	18
Asst. principal	2	1	..	..	..	..	2	5
Univ. or college teacher . .	6	..	..	..	..	..	..	6
Counselor . .	6	2	1	..	..	..	4	13
Teacher of occupational studies . .	2	..	..	..	..	..	..	2
Toolmaker . .	..	..	3	..	..	..	..	3
Y.W.C.A. sec'y	1	1	..	..	..	..	1	3
Factory mgr. .	1	..	..	..	..	..	1	2
Soldier . . .	2	..	..	..	..	..	..	2
Office worker .	2	..	..	..	..	..	..	2
Contractor . .	1	..	..	..	..	..	1	2
Social worker .	3	..	..	..	..	..	..	3

The following includes positions mentioned by one person each, arranged according to duration of tenure:

[11] John M. Brewer, "The Vocational Experience of Counselors." *The Vocational Guidance Magazine*, Nov., 1928.

Less than one year: Y.W.C.A. secretary, director girls' camp, waitress, department-store worker, newspaper work, financial secretary church, assistant dean of women state university

One year: Athletic director, statistician, statistical clerk, director of research, industrial-welfare worker, personnel worker, salesman, supervisor, training and placement, federal board for vocational education, publicity, helper R.R. shops

One and one-half years: Girls' adviser, manager road graveling crew, farmer, veterans bureau

Two years: Dean of girls, librarian, stenographer, apprentice engineer

Three years: County superintendent of schools, director of industrial training

Four and one-half years: Executive secretary club

Five years: Director physical education

Eight years: Instructor manual training, bank clerk, "active in organized labor"

Nine years: Department-store worker and executive

Ten years: Instructor, machine shop

Fifteen years: Machinist

Years not stated: Y.W.C.A. physical director, draftsman, engineer

The total number of persons listed above and in the table as holding different positions is greater than the number of persons replying to the questionnaire because most replies mentioned several positions successively held by the same person.

The following gives a somewhat clearer picture of the number of years of experience in different positions prior to entering their present positions, reported by the 101 counselors replying to this question.

YEARS	COUNSELORS
Over 25	3
21–25	4
16–20	4
11–15	20
6–10	30
1– 5	85
Less than 1	7
Years not stated	24

It should be pointed out that this list, like those immediately preceding, contains many duplications. It is more accurately informing at the top than at the bottom. The three who had taught more than twenty-five years before entering vocational guidance had done nothing else. On the other hand, the seven who are listed here as having less than one year's experience, held other positions for greater or shorter periods of time. The figures, in the main, must be understood as representing number of positions rather than number of counselors.

A similar question was asked of all counselors interviewed in the field study. Complete information was thus obtained from thirty-nine counselors. The following table lists all positions held by more than one person together with number of years of tenure, in so far as the latter was obtained.

POSITION	YEARS					
	1–5	6–10	11–15	21–25	NOT STATED	TOTAL
Teacher	12	7	..	1	9	29
Principal and asst. principal	3	2	..	..	1	6
Superintendent of schools .	2	..	1	..	1	4
Vocational guidance . . .	3	..	..	..	..	3
Accountant	2	..	..	..	..	2
Social work	5	..	..	..	2	7
Children's bureau	2	..	..	..	..	2
Visiting teacher	3	..	..	..	..	3
Factory work	2	..	..	..	2	4
Army	2	..	..	..	1	3
Railroad	1	..	..	..	2	3
Salesman	..	..	..	..	2	2
Clerk	1	..	..	..	1	2
Y.M.C.A. secretary . . .	1	..	..	..	1	2
War work	1	..	..	..	1	2
Personnel work	2	..	..	..	..	2
Lumber jack	..	..	..	..	2	2

In addition, the following positions were held by one person each, arranged according to years of tenure.

One to five years: Employment certificating; employed in U. S. Veterans' Bureau; contractor; research worker; registrar (college).

Six to ten years: Preacher; factory manager.

Eleven to fifteen years: Manager printing office.

Years not stated: Playground director; newsboy; telephone operator; boat hand; farmer; insurance agent; director of Chautauqua; housekeeper; stenographer.

Both lists indicate that teaching far outranks all other fields as the background experience of present counselors. At the same time the array of other types of position tends to support Professor Brewer's contention as to the variety of experience possessed by persons in guidance work.

One further bit of information tending to throw some light on the qualifications of counselors is to be obtained from the questionnaire. It was believed that alert, professionally-minded counselors would be apt to become members of organizations concerned with education, guidance, or allied fields. Consequently this was included, "Please name any professional or semi-professional organizations in which you hold membership."

After eliminating certain organizations that seemed irrelevant, such as honor societies, fraternities, etc., the answers seemed to fall into three groups.

1. Educational organizations (National Education Association, State Educational Associations, teachers' associations, etc.).

NUMBER OF ORGANIZATIONS	NUMBER OF COUNSELORS BELONGING
1	14
2	22
3	32
4	12
5	3
"Several"	9
None	3
No answer	10
Total	105

Altogether ninety-two out of ninety-five counselors replying belonged to one or more educational organizations.

2. National (or local) Vocational Guidance Association: member, 48; no answer, 57.

It is probable that if the question had been "are you a member of the National (or local) Vocational Guidance Association?" there might have been more affirmative replies. At the same time it seems reasonable to suppose that most counselors would be apt to recall their membership in such an association without having their memories jogged. The question called for the name of any organization that seemed pertinent. Where there was no mention of any guidance association, the reply was checked under the heading "No answer."

3. Several other organizations mentioned that did not seem to belong with either of the two preceding groups are included here because of their interest or importance.

ASSOCIATION	NUMBER OF COUNSELORS
Mental Hygiene Society	3
American Association of Social Workers	2
State Conference of Social Work	2
Consumers' League	1
National Association of Visiting Teachers	1
National Committee on Mental Hygiene	1
Personnel Association	1
Southern Sociological Conference	1
Teachers Union	1

CHAPTER VIII

CONDITIONS OF WORK

A recent annual report of the director of the counseling program of one of the large cities of the country contained the following:

Need for quiet place for vocational conferences.—At present most of the vocational conferences are held on noisy and drafty stair landings. Quiet and seclusion are necessary if the pupil is to be at ease and feel free to discuss his problems. A small private office would make this possible, would save the counselors' time, and would also enable the counselors to build up small libraries on occupations which might be loaned to pupils, and make available space for important records. A quiet place where counselors may meet with individual pupils without being disturbed is recognized as essential to a vocational counseling program.

In our field investigation we were constantly impressed with what seemed to be inadequate office arrangements for the counselor. In some cases the only place available for a conference with a pupil is a stair landing or a corridor. In many schools otherwise well equipped the counselor shares office space with others—sometimes as many as four desks being placed side by side. The inevitable result in a small room is lack of privacy. When the room is large and the desks placed some distance apart, a reasonable degree of privacy is achieved. In some of the newer school buildings, built after counseling had become a recognized activity, we found thoroughly adequate provision in the way of office space for the counselor.

Eighty-one of the 105 counselors who replied to our questionnaire said that they had separate offices with privacy for interviews; twenty-three said that they did not have such facilities; and one replied "not entirely."

Clerical assistance for the counselor is important on account of the large amount of record-keeping, filing, etc., that must be done if the work is adequately performed, and because such assistance makes a heavier program possible.

The 105 counselors who turned in questionnaires answered the question, "Do you have clerical assistance?" in this wise:

Yes 34
"A little" 9
Student help 20
No 39
No answer 3

It appears from this showing that thirty-four had adequate assistance. Those who answered "a little" apparently did not have sufficient aid nor, probably, did those who depended on student help. However, altogether there were sixty-three who had some kind of assistance as against thirty-nine who had none.

The following information with respect to work requirements and remuneration is derived, except where otherwise indicated, from the returns from seventeen directors of centralized guidance systems who filled out the questionnaire intended for directors. The returns are from cities having a combined population of more than four and a quarter million persons, and are located in thirteen different states.

Working Hours

The following shows the number of cities in which the indicated time schedule obtains.

DAILY		SATURDAY		OVERTIME	
Six hours	4	None	9	None	5
Seven hours	4	3 hours	1	"Occasionally"	1
7½ hours	3	3½ hours	2	"If necessary"	1
Eight hours	1	4 hours	2	"Often"	2
"Same as teach-		"Paid extra"	1	"Much"	1
ers"	3	No answer	1	"Great deal"	1
No answer	1			No answer	5
	—	Total	16[a]		—
Total	16[a]			Total	16[a]

[a] One director wrote in answer to the question relating to hours, Saturday work and overtime "School day and as much besides as necessary to complete the job."

The length of the working day is important to counselors just as it is to iron molders or street-car conductors and for the same reason—because of its relation to rest and recreation and to the physical and nervous strain involved. To judge of the latter we need also to know something of the amount and character of the work done. We made an attempt therefore to discover the average pupil load carried by counselors. It developed, however, that little dependable or significant information could be secured.

As we have seen, counselors perform a great variety of tasks. Information as to number of pupils being counseled does not give us, therefore, a complete or accurate picture, nor would it do so even if the work consisted exclusively of counseling. The sum total of energy required is affected by the division of time between individual and group counseling; by the time of year, since one period differs from another with respect to the nature and intensity of the demand upon the counselor's time; and by the inevitable fact that pupils differ from one another with respect to the amount of time their particular problems require. Hence, with the same number of pupils in the counseling area the task of one counselor will differ markedly from that of another at the same time, and the work of the same counselor will differ from term to term as the school population changes in numbers and in variety of problems. It follows that no counselor can speak of "pupil load" with the same assurance that a case worker can speak of "case load." He can only tell approximately what it was last week or last month or how it was distributed last year.

The Committee on Vocational Guidance and Child Labor of the White House Conference made no attempt to measure pupil load. It did, however, obtain some useful information with respect to the ratio of number of counselors to the number of pupils of "counseling age" in the school systems of various cities. "Counseling age" was defined as referring to pupils in the seventh to twelfth grades, inclusive. Information on this point was summarized in the report for "largest," "medium sized," and "smallest" cities.

In the group of largest cities:

Baltimore has one full-time counselor for every 1,100 pupils of counseling age; Chicago, one for every 5,000 pupils of counseling age; Cincinnati, one full-time counselor for every 2,700 pupils of counseling age; New York City, one for every 35,000; Providence, one for every 700.

In the group of medium sized cities:

Allentown, Pennsylvania, has one full-time counselor for every 2,600 pupils of counseling age; Long Beach, California, one for every 5,000; and Niagara Falls, N. Y., one for every 600.

In the group of smallest cities:

Madison, Wisconsin, has one full-time counselor for every 1,100 pupils of counseling age; San Jose, California, one for every 1,200; and Superior, Wisconsin, one for every 2,200.

In general, the committee reported the ratio between full-time counselors and pupils of counseling age as one to 1,595 in the smallest cities, one to 1,503 in the medium sized cities and one to 3,340 in the largest cities. Commenting on these figures the committee said:

Some authorities in vocational guidance have estimated that at least one full-time counselor is necessary for every 500 pupils of counseling age. On this basis the smallest and the medium-sized cities studied are in need of three times as many counselors as they now have, and the largest cities should multiply their present number by seven.[1]

One inescapable fact that emerges from this report is that millions of pupils of "counseling age" are without

[1] White House Conference Report, pp. 46–47. These figures are useful as indicating the effort, or lack of it, in the various cities to meet counseling needs. They do not reveal the number of pupils interviewed by each counselor.

counselors. With it there is the justifiable inference that conscientious workers in the field of vocational guidance are over-taxing themselves in an attempt to carry the load.

Vacations

In response to our inquiry, "What is the policy as to vacations?" the seventeen directors answered as follows:

VACATION PERIOD	DIRECTORS REPLYING
2 weeks	1
1 month	4
10 weeks	1
12 weeks	1
3 months	2
"Same as teachers"	8[2]

This indicates that in twelve of the seventeen cities, counselors have the same vacation periods as teachers, a tendency which data secured in our field study tend to confirm.

Sick Leave

The answers to the question "What is the policy as to sick leave?" reveal great lack of uniformity in practice. Five of the sixteen directors replying to this question mentioned a period of leave but did not state the amount of pay allowed, if any, during this time. Presumably, however, full pay is allowed for the period indicated. One director reports a period of ten days. Two mention two weeks, one of whom states that this time is "cumulative for five years." One month is the period given in another questionnaire, and the fifth states that a "schedule of time is allowed in accordance with years of service."

Eight directors state that full pay is allowed for varying

[2] In one school system reporting that counselors have the same vacation as teachers, counselors also do placement work. The placement office is always open, consequently some members of the staff are always on duty at the central office. Those who are thus retained during a period when the schools are not in session are paid $8 a day in addition to their annual salaries.

periods of time.   In three cases the period is ten days, in one of which the time not used in one year can be added to the allowance of the next, apparently without limit.   In another case a ten-day period with full pay is followed by ten days on half pay.   One director reports five days on full pay followed by fifteen days of half pay.   Another director writes "five days on full pay and fifteen half days on full pay during the school year."   In another case the allowance is "salary up to six months, varying with number of years of service," and in another the director writes, "Fifteen days are allowed for illness for which the worker will be paid.   For any time lost after fifteen days, a doctor's certificate must accompany the application for pay.   The School Board has sometimes allowed teachers a full year's leave with pay for sickness."

Two directors report half pay for sickness.   One states that it is "for a certain number of days," the other does not indicate any time limit.   One replies "Same as teachers."

Pensions

In fourteen of these centralized guidance systems, counselors are eligible for pensions after a term of years.   In the other three, there is no such provision.   Few details are given.   In one case the annual pension is $400 after twenty-five years, in another it is $500 after thirty years of service.   In the main, the pension plans appear to be identical with those to which teachers are eligible.

Salaries

From the directors' questionnaire and from our field study we have information on salaries from nineteen cities. The variations are so great that it is impossible to make any general or comprehensive statement beyond the fact that size of city seems to have little relation to amount of salary. An attempt was made to secure beginning salary, rate of annual increase, maximum and present salary schedule. The lowest beginning rate was found in one of the small cities, and the highest beginning rate in one still smaller. The lowest, $1,000, was the beginning salary in a city of 60,000, and $2,600, the highest beginning rate, was paid in a city of 45,000.

The lowest maximum reported under any set of conditions was $2,200 in a city of more than 700,000. This, however, is for counselors in junior high schools whose maximum is based on "service" only. The "maximum with credits" for these counselors was $2,600. In this school system counselors in senior high schools have a maximum of $2,550 for "service" and $3,000 "with credits." The highest maximum provided for was $4,000 in a city with more than 500,000 population.

Annual increases up to the maximum, range from $50 to $200. The salaries being paid in 1928 and 1929 in the cities for which we secured information ranged from $1,695 to $3,750.

The following table, with cities ranged in order according to population, contains the salary data secured in 1929 and, for purposes of comparison, similar information for 1934. One city in the 300,000 to 500,000 group and one in the "over 500,000" group paid slightly higher average salaries in 1934 than in 1929. In all of the others giving information there were substantial reductions.

SALARIES OF VOCATIONAL COUNSELORS AND DIRECTORS OF VOCATIONAL GUIDANCE IN PUBLIC SCHOOLS

CITIES RANGED ACCORDING TO POPULATION	BEGINNING SALARY 1929	ANNUAL RATE OF INCREASE 1929	AVERAGE SALARY OR SALARY RANGE IN 1929	AVERAGE SALARY OR SALARY RANGE IN 1934	SALARIES OF DIRECTORS 1934
	.....	.....	$1,800–2,000	$1,500–1,580	.....
	$2,400	$150 to maximum of $3,500	.....	Positions abolished	.....
	$2,600	.....	$3,080–3,300	$2,040–2,975	$3,060
25,000 to 100,000	"Teachers Schedules+$100"	.....	$1,850–3,100	$2,500	$5,000
	$1,000–1,400	$100	.....	30 percent cut	.....
	$1,350	$50–100	$1,850–2,200	$1,800	$2,770 (cut from$3,500)
	.....	.....	$1,500–1,800	$1,600	$2,700
	.....	.....	$1,850–2,750	$1,625–2,325[a]	$3,700
200,000 to 300,000	$1,572	$150	$2,750–3,750	$2,000–3,000	$3,024
	$1,740	$120	$2,820	.....	.....
	$1,400	$100	.....	.....	.....
300,000 to 500,000	.....	$100	$2,422	$1,100–1,961	$2,500 (cut from$3,300)
	$1,500	.....	$1,695	$1,236–1,584	$2,340
	$1,600	$150 to maximum of $3,500 withM.A.degree	$1,725	$1,778	$3,025
	$1,450	.....	$1,800–3,000	$1,240–2,400	.....
	Men—$2,016 Women—$1,728	$144 to maximum of $3,888 $96 to $3,092	.....	.....	.....
Over 500,000	$1,500	$100 to maximum of $3,300	.....	.....	.....
	$1,800	$150 to maximum of $3,300	.....	Positions abolished	.....
	$2,100	$150 to maximum of $4,404	.....	$3,000	.....

[a] One counselor was receiving $2,850 in 1934.

Part Three

PLACEMENT

CHAPTER IX

PLACEMENT AS VOCATIONAL GUIDANCE[1]

Placement as an organized activity existed long before the term vocational guidance was known. We have already seen that the latter in the sense of counseling with young people about the choice of, and preparation for, an occupation came to be recognized as a socially necessary activity in 1908 in Boston. Agencies for the placement of persons seeking work, on the other hand, have probably existed since comparatively early in the development of the present industrial system. Dr. Mollie Carroll states that such an office was opened in Dresden as far back as 1840.[2] So far as we are aware, there is no record of the initial development of employment offices under private auspices in this country, though one competent observer says that they existed as early as 1820.[3] An employment bureau was opened in Chicago by a philanthropic agency in 1870,[4] and in New York one was organized by the United Hebrew Charities in 1885.[5] The first public employment offices in this country were set up under municipal auspices and began to be established in the late sixties.[6] Ohio was the first state to establish a public employment agency, the law to bring that about being enacted in 1890.[7] By 1910, two years after Professor Parsons had organized his Voca-

---

[1] The explanation, if any is needed, of the exclusion from this and following chapters of any discussion of private commercial employment agencies, lies in the fact that they are commercial. We are considering placement agencies as having a social purpose. Where the very reason for being is commercial, it follows that a social purpose cannot be uppermost.

[2] Mollie Ray Carroll, *Unemployment Insurance in Germany*, p. 10.

[3] Stewart, Annabel, and Bryce Stewart, *Statistical Procedure and Public Employment Offices*, p. 215.

[4] Bulletin 68, U.S. Bureau of Labor Statistics, p. 1.

[5] Harrison, *Public Employment Offices*, 1924, p. 80.

[6] Stewart, *Statistical Procedure of Public Employment Offices*, p. 22.

[7] Harrison, p. 116.

tional Bureau in Boston, there were fifty-five public employment offices in operation in twenty-one states.[8]

Whether placement is to be considered as an aspect of vocational guidance or whether it is a distinct though related activity is a matter about which there is some difference of opinion. One of the most frequently cited publications in the field of vocational guidance is a report by the U.S. Children's Bureau entitled "Vocational Guidance *and Junior Placement.*"[9] The number of school systems doing counseling seems to be considerably greater than those doing placement. Of the 150 school systems replying to the questionnaire sent out in connection with the White House Conference, ninety-nine, or 66 percent, had vocational counselors, but only fifty-nine, or 39 percent, had organized placement.

This seems to indicate that even if placement is considered a vocational guidance activity it is less generally recognized than counseling as an essential part of the field. Nevertheless, its acceptance as a logical part of a vocational guidance program is widespread. The report of the Children's Bureau, mentioned above, contains this statement:

When the school assumes the responsibility of guiding the child toward a vocation and preparing him for it, it becomes difficult to avoid taking the logical third step, that of placing him in it. The dependence of the junior, the interest of the teacher and vocational counselor, the pride of the school in its output, all urge in this direction.[10]

There are placement workers, who, like many counselors in the appraisal of their own field, are so far from doubting the importance of their work in a vocational guidance

[8] Harrison, *Op. cit.*, p. 624.
[9] On the other hand, Professor A. H. Edgerton, a former president of the National Vocational Guidance Association has written a book entitled "Vocational Guidance *and Counseling.*"
[10] Children's Bureau Publication No. 149, p. 68.

program, as to claim that placement alone is vocational guidance. On the other hand an experienced placement worker writes,

There is so much confusion about the term "vocational guidance" that before one discusses the placement office, it seems necessary to state that the writer is perfectly aware that vocational guidance is not placement work, that unless there has been a certain amount of vocational guidance previously in the schools the efforts of the placement counselor are often futile; in other words that placement is only one part of a thorough program for vocational guidance.[11]

The relation of placement to a well-rounded vocational guidance program is well summed up in a standard treatise on public employment offices.

Vocational guidance must, after studying each case, take other possibilities into account than immediate employment; it must consider, also, the question of further education and vocational training and methods of the applicants' advancement after work is secured. Indeed, there is danger here that the experienced placement worker will unduly magnify the importance of placement information which is "reliable, comprehensive, concrete, accurate and up-to-the-minute" to the exclusion of other necessary features, just as contrariwise, some who advocate the keeping of the vocational guidance movement within the schools may become lost in a maze of "counseling" and overlook the necessity for providing organized employment assistance. Both are important and one should not be emphasized to the exclusion of the other.[12]

Counseling in the Placement Office

One reason for the less general acceptance of placement as an aspect of vocational guidance is the fact that not all of it can be so classified. Adult placement that is truly adult has very little to do, as a rule, with vocational guid-

---

[11] Dorothea de Schweinitz, in *Practice in Vocational Guidance*, F. J. Allen, editor, p. 261.

[12] Frederick A. King, in Harrison, *Public Employment Offices*, 1924, p. 566.

ance in its ordinarily accepted sense. The adult has made his decision. He has received whatever training he is likely to get, and he is apt to be permanently settled in an occupational group, if not in a specific trade. As a rule he comes to a placement office not for advice about occupations, but for information about the state of that part of the labor market in which he is interested.[13] An English authority writes,

> The Juvenile Labour Bureau is faced with a problem differing greatly from that of the Adult Exchange due chiefly to the fact that the material in the two cases differs greatly. The applicants at the latter are a more or less finished product, whilst the Juvenile Exchange deals with the raw material. The adult is assumed to be a free agent to have some acquaintance with the Labour market and industrial conditions; the child is immature, inexperienced and almost totally ignorant of industrial affairs. The former is embarked upon his industrial career; the latter is about to embark upon it.[14]

In the overwhelming majority of cases, it is the youth, standing at the very beginning of his occupational career, who is in a position to make use of guidance in the placement office. It is in the junior field, therefore, that we should expect to find the type of placement in which guidance is a factor. But the work of counseling in the junior office is limited by two important facts. On the one hand, the time of the placement worker is taken up mainly with finding jobs and discovering applicants who may fill them. As a general rule there is insufficient time for the deliberation essential to satisfactory counseling. On the other hand, the young person coming to a placement office comes there for a job, not for advice or how to choose or get ready for one. He is in a hurry as a rule, and in no mood either for an

---

[13] This statement refers to "normal" adults under "normal" economic conditions. It is otherwise with the handicapped, and with the younger adults in a time of economic depression.

[14] Arthur Greenwood, *Juvenile Labour Exchanges and After Care*, 1911, p. 48.

extended conference or for a change in plans.[15] Says the White House Conference Report,

Persons who apply at employment bureaus are ready for jobs and are not deeply concerned with *right* jobs. This holds for adults as well as for children, and makes it necessary for the employment worker to surmount one more obstacle in the achievement of a successful employment adjustment. To the applicant real employment information, real vocational counsel, real consideration of all the threads which weave a complete picture, are merely red tape from which he must somehow disentangle himself to reach the thing he really wants—a job![16]

It is this attitude which makes vocational guidance exceedingly difficult in the placement office. But the necessity for guidance at this point is nevertheless clear. Even if the child has had able assistance from a school counselor, he stands in need of the kind of advice that a trained and experienced placement worker is prepared to give him.

Evidence of a clear recognition of the need among guidance technicians and leaders appears in the following excerpt from a recent publication:

The function of the placement office is to render assistance to the individual in entering upon the chosen occupation and making progress in it. This function may be satisfactorily performed

[15] After reading this paragraph the following comment was made by one whose long experience with both school counseling and placement gives exceptional authority to her opinions: "While the attitude of the applicant may be quite hurried and his main object in coming there is to get a job, there is something to be said on the other side, in that he is coming to the office in the 'buyer's attitude' and is a bit more ready to take suggestions from people who have jobs to offer than he is from the counselor in the school who is giving him advice about something that is a long way off and about which he feels his opinion is probably as good as the counselor's. I am referring to such practical matters as the fact that an employment worker can tell a girl that she won't get a job at Wanamaker's if she indulges heavily in make-up, whereas if she is told this by a counselor in the school she is inclined to regard it as a bit of 'moral guidance' and discount it accordingly."

[16] White House Conference Report, pp. 232, 234. See also *Proceedings 9th Annual Meeting International Association of Public Employment Office*, Bulletin 311, U. S. Bureau of Labour Statistics, pp. 35–36.

without actually finding a specific job for the individual. In general, however, the placement service is obliged to assist the applicant to secure a job, and for that reason it has come to be regarded by many as a job-finding or employment office. In some cases an over-emphasis has been placed on the finding of jobs, with the resulting over-shadowing of the guidance activities. Even in the most favorable situations it requires great caution and diligence to make the placement service known to pupils and employers without exaggerating its place in the whole scheme of guidance.[17]

Child Labor Laws

Despite the obstacles to counseling in the placement office the junior placement worker possesses certain strategic advantages. One advantage lies in the fact that the compulsory school laws and the child labor laws combine to limit the independent judgment of the child.

The legal restrictions placed about the employment of children constitute an invaluable aid to the placement worker in the task of protecting the child against the consequences of his own impulse and ignorance and it is one of the factors tending to make the work of junior placement essentially different from placement of adults.

Legal restrictions center about age, scholastic achievement, and physical health. In most states the minimum age for leaving school to go to work is fourteen, though it is sixteen in a few states, and the NRA codes temporarily, at least, have made that the general rule. In most states the child must have completed the first six grades of the public schools and in some states the requirement is eight grades.

These requirements raise difficulties in the case of subnormal children who, on arriving at the prescribed age for

[17] Richard D. Allen, *Organization and Supervision of Guidance in Public Education*, p. 291. This section was written in collaboration with Archibald Taylor, Counselor in the Department of Vocational Guidance, Boston, and Alice L. Weeks, Supervisor of Guidance and Placement, Providence. See also "Guidance in the Placement Office," by a committee consisting of Archibald Taylor, Alice Weeks, J. D. Stark, and Mary Stone, *Vocational Guidance Magazine*, February, 1930, p. 208.

going to work have not completed, and are seemingly unable to complete, the academic requirements. Obviously unfitted for continuing in an academically motivated school system, it has frequently been suggested that they ought to be permitted to go to work as soon as they reach the minimum age or even earlier. In some states the educational authorities are authorized to excuse a child from attending school when it becomes evident, after suitable tests, that he is unable to do so with profit.

There is another point of view, and it is probably held by most of those in vocational guidance work, which suggests that the remedy is not to be found in taking the child out of school so much as in adapting the school to his needs. The Children's Bureau report on vocational guidance, speaking of these mentally backward children, says,

The provision of suitable work for older children in this group has many difficulties and has not been thoroughly worked out or even tried out except in a few places, but it is becoming more and more generally recognized among experts in the education of mental defectives that instead of permitting them to leave school for work as soon as they cannot keep up with the work of the regular schools, some sort of supervised training up to at least 16 years of age is even more necessary than for the normal child.[18]

Another statement in the same report, dealing with keeping normal children in school is apropos here.

Incidentally, keeping dissatisfied children in school will hasten the day when the schools will provide instruction to suit the needs and abilities of all types of pupils, for it has been the presence of large numbers of children kept in school only by the compulsory education laws that has been largely responsible for such attempts at individual adjustment as have been made hitherto.[19]

[18] *Vocational Guidance and Junior Placement,* Children's Bureau Publication No. 149, pp. 42–43.
[19] *Ibid.,* pp. 44–45.

Having fixed the point at which children may leave school to go to work, the law generally sets standards that must be maintained for the employment of all children during the first year or two of their working lives, and in a limited area, regulations are frequently laid down for all minors. Children under sixteen are not permitted to work in certain dangerous occupations and in many states those under eighteen or even under twenty-one are excluded from occupations considered physically or morally dangerous. In practically all states hours of labor are limited by law during at least the first two years that children are permitted to work.

The administrative device that has generally been adopted for making as certain as possible that these restrictions shall be effective is the work certificate. By this device much of the burden of proof is placed on the child himself, but school and employer are put definitely on record also.

Where the placement bureau works in close coöperation with the school system or is a part of it, the child's school record, academic and otherwise, may be available. Often other aids to counseling are present, such as results of tests, opinion of teachers, child's previously expressed vocational preferences, etc. All of these are of great assistance in the placement office in helping to determine the type of job the particular child should or should not have. It is obvious that where there has been an adequate counseling system in the school which the child has been attending, the work of the placement office is simplified and the amount of additional counseling required of the placement office is lessened. At best, however, the problem of counseling in the junior placement office is so difficult that many believe it can be done effectively only after the first job has been secured and the child comes back, with imagination stimulated by experience and ready for advice.

Placement and the Social Agencies

In addition to public schools and the state departments of labor, social agencies are also interested in the matter of placement and their interest is both natural and logical. Unemployment stands first as a cause of economic distress, and though its intensity varies with the seasons and with changes in general business conditions, it is an ever-present economic phenomenon and thus remains a constant factor in the case load. Even if this were not the case, social agencies would be compelled to turn their attention to the matter of placement because of their concern for the handicapped. The mentally or physically limited are not only subject to the economic needs that are common to mankind, but often their ability to conquer their handicaps is directly dependent on getting and holding a job.

Consequently, social agencies for many years have been active, directly or indirectly, in promoting facilities for placement. A quarter century or more ago this activity manifested itself in the organization of employment bureaus. Bradley Buell states that "before the end of the nineteenth century all the large social work organizations dealing with families in New York had started something in the way of organized employment agencies as a part of their regular programs, and the same was true of similar organizations in Boston, Cleveland and a number of other large centers."[20]

These agencies, carried on as a part of the work of family societies, have now been abandoned for the most part.[21] It became evident before long that placement is as distinct a field of activity as case work and that the possession of training and experience in the latter field without other specialized training and experience did not provide the

[20] Harrison, *Public Employment Offices*, p. 80.
[21] *Ibid.*, p. 81.

necessary qualifications for effective placement work. Accordingly, the tendency now is for the social agencies to refer their clients to regularly established employment bureaus. To carry on the work for the handicapped, specialized placement bureaus are being organized, often by the social agencies themselves but under separate or independent leadership and with a technically qualified staff.

In this section of the report, the major emphasis will be on those aspects of placement in which vocational guidance is an actual or a potential factor. That means that attention will be given to junior placement and to agencies dealing with the handicapped.

CHAPTER X

ACTIVITIES AND PROBLEMS OF THE PLACEMENT OFFICE[1]

The work of placement is somewhat more definite and circumscribed than is that of counseling, but no one would suspect it from the titles in use. Persons who filled out the questionnaire intended for "directors" of employment offices designated themselves variously as follows:

Assistant, Department of Research and Guidance
Special Assistant in Charge of Employment
Coördinator
Director of Vocational Guidance
Director of Guidance and Employment
Director of Division of Junior Placement
Director of Employment
Director of Placement
Assistant Director in Charge of Guidance and Placement
Assistant Director of Vocational and Industrial Education
Employment Bureau Director
"In charge of Bureau"
Placement Officer
Superintendent of Junior Placement
Supervisor of Junior Employment
Supervisor of Guidance and Placement
Supervisor of Junior Employment Bureau
Special Agent Educational and Employment Work
Vocational Adviser
Vocational Counselor

Persons who interview applicants for work listed themselves as:

Counselor
Assistant Counselor
Assistant Junior Placement Counselor
Guidance Counselor
Guidance and Placement Counselor
Guidance and Employment Counselor
Employment Supervisor
Employment Secretary
Employment Worker
Interviewer
Junior Counselor

[1] For a detailed statement of the essentials of organization in a placement office, see Appendix J.

Junior Placement Assistant
Placement Clerk
Placement Counselor
Placement Secretary

Placement Worker
Vocational Adviser
Vocational Counselor

Despite this confusion of titles, the prevailing tendency is reasonably clear. Ordinarily the head of an employment office is a "director." A person who interviews and places applicants for work is more frequently called "placement clerk," "placement secretary," or "interviewer" than any of the other titles listed.

Duties of Placement Workers

The answers to the request for a list of duties did not bring forth so wide a variety of answers as did the same question addressed to school counselors. All placement workers have certain basic duties which, so far as a bare listing is concerned, do not vary much from one office to another. An irreducible minimum includes interviewing applicants, receiving or soliciting employers' orders, referring applicants to positions and verifying placements. The extent to which these bare bones are clothed with the flesh of individual service varies very greatly with the community, the nature or auspices of the agency, the type of worker placed and the imagination of the placement worker.

Here, for example, is a listing of duties by a placement worker whose office is a part of a state service and is located in a girls' continuation school.

1. Registration of applicants.
2. Consultation with clients who are working or who have left their employer.
3. Consultation with applicants about some special training they may take either to help them on their present job or better prepare them for a new one.
4. Follow-up work both from employers' and employees' point of view.

5. Field work at least two afternoons a week. This consists of visits to employers. Some are new firms, others are old employers with whom we are most anxious to keep in touch.
6. Contracts with social agencies such as Department of Public Welfare, Rehabilitation Bureau, Industrial Aid, Y.W.C.A., and Catholic Charities. All these have applicants whom they send to my desk for work and advice.
7. Interviews with teachers at the school as to the capability of certain applicants as far as can be judged from their school records.
8. Actual placement of people on the job, which means this:
    a) Call from employer.
    b) Interview and selection of applicant which may mean interviewing ten before a final selection.
    c) Calling employer to see if person applied.
    d) Calling next day to see if person is actually working on the job.
9. All of above notations must be kept on file so that they may be referred to at any time, so that there is any amount of clerical work connected with each and every person, firm or organization with whom a contact is made which all takes time, as each worker's records must be in such shape that a new worker can come into the office at any time and take up the work with very little difficulty.

The following is from a reply to the same question sent in by a placement worker attached to a vocational school. This reply included duties identical with some of those in the preceding list. Omitting these the following additional activities, peculiar to the area covered, are mentioned:

Verification of employment and authorization of diploma after girl has been employed at least three months in an *approved* establishment.
Firm visiting
    a) To solicit jobs
    b) To follow up placement
    c) With trade instructors to keep them familiar with any new workroom technique or practices.
Interviewing all applicants for vocational school who come from parochial, private, or out-of-town schools. Girls admitted on

probation are followed up at end of one month—those admitted regularly, after three months. This admission of applicants includes:

  a) Interview with child
  b) Interview with parent
  c) Physical examination
  d) Psychological examination
  e) Record from school

When these data have been accumulated, whole report with our recommendation is mailed to district superintendent of district in which girl resides, who in turn approves it and forwards it to superintendent of district in which vocational school is located. Then school is notified to admit the girl.

Graduates are interviewed, given physical (many have psychological) examinations, and age is established at least six months before graduation. In the meantime, arrangements are made for correction of any physical defects or any other difficulty involved.

Again leaving out of the reply the standard or basic duties, the following remain as the additional responsibilities of a placement worker attached to a public school system and dealing largely with the handicapped.

Prepare summaries re applicant for social agencies.
Collect and forward to State Bureau of Rehabilitation records concerning applicants referred for vocational training.
Visit schools.
Visit hospitals and other agencies primarily for handicapped.
Visit homes.
Arrange with schools for special services for individual handicapped pupils.
Attend conference and committee meetings.
Give talks to various groups.
Make recommendations re procedures in dealing with physically handicapped.

Types of Agencies

The agencies included in this study fall into five groups, when considered from the point of view of variation in activities.

First, agencies for junior placement under state or municipal auspices or operating independently and having no connection with any other enterprise or purpose. Such agencies vary in their activities one from another, but every activity is related to the major purpose of the agency.

Second, junior placement agencies which are a part of, or connected with, a school system. In such agencies the placement workers not only are more likely to emphasize the counseling aspect of their work and even to do school counseling having no immediate relation to placement, but they often have duties relating to the school system itself, such as teaching classes in occupations, advising with respect to curriculum, supervising scholarship funds, and even, on a part-time basis, teaching subjects having no direct relation to occupational interests. A counselor in the Department of Vocational Guidance in one of the larger cities, assigned part time to placement work, writes

Two members of the Department of Vocational Guidance are assigned to placement on a part-time basis. Each of these members is a counselor in a high school—one for three days a week, the other for two days a week; and on alternate days they are in the office of the Department of Vocational Guidance and handle the placement. However, their duties in the office include other things besides placement, one being also assigned to the testing department and the other acting as treasurer for the High School Scholarship Association in addition to handling various duties of office routine. Both are college graduates with additional courses in psychology, sociology and research.

Third, employment departments of local branches of the Y.M.C.A. and the Y.W.C.A. Here placement workers frequently have other duties not related to placement. Some of these duties mentioned in the questionnaires were "desk duty," "room registry," acting as membership secretary, promoting or conducting educational classes, "case work." Sometimes the work of placement itself is modified by the major purpose of the Association. A job analysis of the work of placement secretary in charge of office workers, compiled by a Y.W.C.A. employment department includes—"Being alert during entire interview as to other ways in which the Association may serve the girl."[2]

Fourth, social agencies (other than Y.M. and Y.W.C.A. and agencies for the handicapped). As indicated elsewhere only a few such social agencies doing placement work for juniors or the handicapped were discovered. Their activities are modified in some cases by handling only applicants referred to them by other social agencies, whose histories are available in the case records of the referring agency.

Fifth, agencies dealing with the handicapped. The workers in these agencies are concerned with physical or mental adjustment and often with placement as a means to that end. Placement workers in these agencies have direct and constant coöperative relations with other social agencies. Two agencies placing the hard-of-hearing reported the teaching of lip reading as an activity of a placement worker. One of the latter was herself a person with only 15 percent of normal hearing.

Major Activities of Placement Office

Some of these variations in activity will be discussed more extensively later and the duties of placement workers will be more clearly revealed as we consider in detail in Chapters XII–XV the major functions of employment work. It may be useful, however, to indicate here, briefly, the nature of these major activities as revealed by this study. They appear to be as follows:[3]

[2] See Appendix K for the full text of this job analysis.

[3] The following from a leading authority in the field presents the same set of duties more forcefully: "The principal functions of an employment office are to receive notifications of opportunities for employment from employers, to receive requests from persons seeking employment, and to bring into contact

1. Recruiting applicants and jobs.
   The extent to which this is done as well as the methods employed vary with the type of agency and the degree of business activity.
2. Receiving and registering applicants.
3. Taking employers' orders.
4. Obtaining information about
   (a) The applicant, through records, references and the interview.
   (b) The job, through investigation.
   In general (a) is much more thoroughly done than (b).
5. Counseling and guiding applicants.
6. Referring applicants to jobs.
7. Verifying referrals (that is, finding out whether applicant applied for and got the job).
8. Follow-up.
9. Recording information.

It is to be hoped that neither this bare list of minimum essentials nor what appears on the pages that follow will convey an idea of uniformity and monotony in employment work. The following statement of demands made in the office of the Junior Employment Service in New York will serve to indicate how mistaken such a notion would be:

Not only are the junior employment offices being crowded constantly with boys and girls seeking work, but they receive many other and diverse inquiries as well. For example, during June there were 2,515 calls made upon the junior offices by others than the boys and girls seeking jobs. Such applications come from teachers, counselors, parents, attendance officers, representatives of case work agencies, playground directors, a manager of a boys' club, a swimming instructor, and included also inquiries made by several members of local chambers of commerce. In other words, the junior officers are to a growing degree,

---

the opportunity and the persons seeking it. This is done by directing suitable applicants to prospective employers and ascertaining in each instance whether or not the person sent has been accepted, in order that the transaction may be considered closed and so recorded; or if the person sent has not been engaged that another may be sent if the employer so desires."—Stewart, *Statistical Procedure of Employment Offices*, p. 40.

a source of information for those who are interested in problems affecting working boys and girls.[4]

Employment Office Problems

In the operation of employment offices there are, as elsewhere, unsolved or moot questions. These are matters about which there are differences of opinion among placement workers or with respect to which they are experimenting in order to discover satisfactory methods. These problems fall into two classes. There are questions that are purely technical in character, and there are others that involve both practical and ethical considerations. The technical questions need not be discussed here in detail. Many of them will be brought out in considering the actual duties of placement workers. They include such questions as how long to keep an applicant's card in the active file; who should fill out the registration card, the applicant or the interviewer; what information should be secured from employer and applicant; what method of filing should be used; what forms should be chosen; what methods of clearance and record keeping should be used.

Besides these technical questions there is an area in which the placement worker must make decisions on the basis of social or ethical theories. One of the outstanding questions here arises out of the fact that the placement office has the responsibility of serving two sets of interests that are in part the same but which may at any time tend to come into conflict. These interests are those of the employer, who is seeking a particular type of employee, and the worker who is sometimes looking for a particular type of job and sometimes, with less discrimination, is merely looking for a job.

In meeting this problem it is clear that the placement

[4] N. Y. Industrial Bulletin, July 1932, p. 332. Report by Clare L. Lewis, director, Division of Junior Placement.

office must endeavor to meet the employer's requirements. There is no difference of opinion about that among competent placement workers. The employment office is offering service to the employer. If it does not render competent, dependable service there is no reason why the employer should continue to patronize it any more than he could be expected to continue to buy raw materials or equipment for his factory that failed to come up to specifications.

On the other hand, the applicant expects his interests to be served by being referred to a job. His desire is to get connected with a payroll. He may therefore be somewhat more willing to "try" a job that he is not quite certain about than the employer may be to "try" a worker who does not present the exact qualifications desired. This fact may create something of a dilemma for the employment worker. A student of the problem writes,

The chief business of an employment office is to select for referral to employers those candidates who fulfill two conditions: (1) Those likely to satisfy the requirements of the employer, and (2) those likely to be satisfied with the conditions of employment they will find. In this operation much the same kind of judgment is required of the interviewer as the employer himself uses in hiring workers. . . . The interviewer must act as his agent and thus finds himself between two interests that are not identical. . . . He must at the same time be the employer's agent and the applicant's agent. . . . In so far as there is an inherent difference of interest between the employer and the applicant in the employment process, amounting in some aspects to an antagonism of interests, just so far must the function of the interviewer become a judicial one rather than merely that of an agent or advocate of either party.[5]

As indicated here, the competent placement worker generally takes the position that the best way of meeting the problem is by acting as the employer's agent. No good

[5] Leslie Woodcock, in Harrison, *Public Employment Offices*, pp. 281–82, 370.

end is accomplished, he will tell you, either for the employer
or for the applicant by sending an applicant to a job he
cannot fill.   The employer will lose confidence in the
employment office and the worker will shortly lose his job.
It is believed that in the long run the applicant's interests
also will best be served by referring him only to those jobs
for which he is qualified.

Even those conducting specialized bureaus for the handicapped or for juniors accept the above as a correct principle.
When caught off guard, however, they sometimes give
evidence of a tendency to deviate somewhat from the
stated principle.   For example, the Children's Bureau
report on vocational guidance says that junior placement
"has for its objective the maximum development of the
individual child along the lines of his occupational possibilities into a happy and successful citizen."[6]   In the
report of the subcommittee on vocational guidance of the
White House Conference, we read: "Junior placement
offices should place the interest and welfare of the children
before all other interests,"[7] and a former director of the
junior employment service of a large city school system
writes, "The main function of the junior employment
office is to secure suitable jobs for John and Mary."[8]

None of the writers just quoted would take the position
that the deciding factor in referring an applicant should be
his need of a job.   It is evident, however, that they do not
conceive of the junior placement worker as in any sense
the "agent" of the employer.   This different point of view
is demonstrated also by the practices of both junior employment offices and those for the handicapped, which are
designed to afford protection to the worker.   These include
investigation of jobs and follow-up.

[6] *Vocational Guidance and Junior Placement*, Children's Bureau Publication
No. 149, p. 58.
[7] White House Conference Report, p. 253.
[8] Dorothea de Schweinitz, Junior Employment Work, an unpublished
manuscript.

Placement workers are confronted with another and more direct aspect of the divergent interests of employers and employees when the question arises of filling vacancies due to a strike. If the placement worker is the agent of the employer, he might reasonably be called upon to supply strike breakers when desired. Such an act would, of course, brand the office as an enemy of the labor movement and it could no longer attract and serve all classes of applicants. This problem, which at one time caused a considerable amount of concern and debate, has pretty generally been solved in the adult office by the practice of accepting the employer's order, but informing applicants of the existence of the strike. The employment office thus becomes merely an agency for the dissemination of information. It makes no recommendation, but does not leave the applicant in ignorance of the opportunities for employment. In junior placement offices the question is not so likely to arise.

The solution of these and other problems are often facilitated by the organization of advisory committees with representatives of employers and organized labor in its personnel.

CHAPTER XI

JUNIOR PLACEMENT—AUSPICES

Junior placement is carried on under three general auspices: boards of education; state or city public employment offices; and social agencies.

Placement Organization in Public Schools

The questionnaires filled out by school counselors in our study indicated that a considerable proportion of them do some placement work.[1] Our field investigations also have made it clear that some form of placement work, organized or unorganized, is carried on in public schools very generally. The most nearly complete information available on the amount of placement work done by public school systems is that compiled by the Committee on Vocational Guidance and Child Labor of the White House Conference on Child Health and Protection of 1930. As previously noted, questionnaires sent out by the Committee were returned from 150 school systems. Of these, forty-six reported an organized employment service, headed by a director, eighty stated that they had no such service, and twenty-four either failed to reply or gave "scattered information."

It should be noted that the question referred to an "organized, uniform employment service." All available information, supported by our own observations, would indicate that when there is no centrally organized system, individual high schools quite generally carry on some form of placement activity. Sometimes this is done even where there is a central employment office. In Cleveland, for example, where junior employment offices are maintained both by the Board of Education and by the state, coun-

[1] See Chapter III.

selors in nine high schools in the year 1927–28 reported that they had made 380 full-time placements, 486 part-time, and 783 temporary placements. The Board of Education placement office in the same year reported 1,470 full-time placements and 696 placements in part-time jobs.

The degree of activity of the forty-six centrally organized placement services reporting to the White House Conference is indicated in part by the number of workers on the staff, exclusive of clerks. To quote the tabulation of the Committee:[2]

PLACEMENT SERVICES	NUMBER OF MEMBERS ON STAFF
24	1
9	2
2	3
5	4
1	5
2	6
1	7
1	10
1	not indicated

Of the ten small cities having an organized service, six had only one worker. The same was true of twelve of the fourteen medium-sized cities, while sixteen of the twenty-two large cities had more than one worker.

Twenty of the forty-six school systems reported that their service was located in a "central" office, presumably not in a school. Five were in high-school buildings, six in continuation schools and the other fifteen were scattered, most of them having offices in more than one type of school. Twenty-four cities reported placement activities as independently organized in certain schools.[3]

[2] These figures are not printed in the White House Conference Report but are quoted from the original tabulation, a copy of which was made available through the kindness of Miss M. Edith Campbell, chairman of the Subcommittee on Vocational Guidance.

[3] "Eleven of these 24 also have a central organization; the remaining 13 have no central organization, but a decentralized organization."

The White House Conference Report[4] states that

School systems are by no means agreed that junior placement should be a public education function, though most of the larger systems have some kind of organized plan for including it. It is interesting to see that the percentages having placement within the systems increase as the city population increases, i.e., only 21 per cent of the 25,000–49,000 population cities which reported had placement service; 41 per cent of the cities of 50,000–99,000; and 75 per cent of the cities of 100,000 and over. Smaller cities tend to care for junior placement in more personal ways. The more intimate group of families, friends and teachers, make individual, personal contacts more possible and through these channels children often secure jobs.[5] . . . Disregarding certain exceptions, it would be safe to say that about a third of the school systems furnish and feel responsible for furnishing such aid (i.e., placement service) to the school population.

Junior Placement under City or State Auspices

New York is the only state in which there is a division of junior placement within the public employment service. This division has fourteen offices, seven in New York City and vicinity and seven up-state. In other states there are separate divisions for junior placement within the general placement office or, occasionally, an individual office separately organized. Cincinnati has a junior employment service organized under city auspices. Cleveland has two junior services, one under the Board of Education and the other in the State-City Employment Service. In Chicago there were until recently two junior services, one under

[4] Pp. 218–20.

[5] In connection with this statement it is interesting to refer to a study of placements of school children in Milwaukee a few years ago. More than 6,000 pupils of the Milwaukee Vocational School (Continuation School) who had jobs were covered, 3,700 of whom were boys and 2,600 girls. Eighty percent of the boys and 82 percent of the girls got their jobs either by applying directly for them or through the aid of friends or relatives. Only 13 percent of the boys and 9 percent of the girls got their jobs through employment offices of any kind. Newspaper ads and window signs accounted for the remainder.— Jean Bernard, *The Placement Problem in the Part Time Vocational School*, Vocational Education Monograph No. 12, Milwaukee Vocational School, 1927.

the Board of Education, the other under the State Free Employment Service.

The Committee on Vocational Guidance of the White House Conference received completed questionnaires from eighty-four junior placement offices connected with state employment bureaus. These offices reported the average number of persons under eighteen years of age applying each year as ranging from less than 100 to over 1,000, the median group receiving from 300 to 399. The number of placements as reported by these same offices ranged from under 50 to 500 and over. The median group placed from 150 to 199.

Junior Placement by Social Agencies

In an attempt to find out to what extent social agencies are doing placement work, a letter was sent early in 1933 to executives of community chests and councils of social agencies in all cities of 100,000 or over having such organizations, asking for the names of social agencies rendering that service. Such letters were sent to ninety-three cities and seventy-nine replies were received. Thirty-one of the replies stated that none of the social agencies of the community did employment work in an organized way. The forty-eight letters giving the name of one or more agencies doing placement work were not very productive since a great many organizations were included which obviously were not concerned with placement or which were not social agencies. As a result, questionnaires were sent to twenty-nine agencies, resulting in very meager returns.

Questionnaires were sent also to lists secured from the national headquarters of the Y.M. and the Y.W.C.A. Some very valuable data were thus obtained. The number of offices, however, which kept separate records for junior placement was limited.

The Committee on Vocational Guidance of the White

House Conference also secured from the community chests in various cities a list of social agencies doing vocational guidance or placement work. Using these lists, they sent out questionnaires similar to those sent to school systems and state agencies and received replies from 107 agencies.[6] In answer to the question "About how many individuals (under 18 years of age) do you place in a year?" replies were received as follows:

NUMBER OF INDIVIDUALS	NUMBER OF AGENCIES
Number negligible	5
Under 50	33
50–99	15
100–149	8
150–199	6
200–249	3
250 and over	10
Number not given	27
Total	107

An attempt was made without much success to find out through the White House questionnaire whether the social agencies considered junior placement a permanent feature of their work. The question dealing with this matter elicited an affirmative reply from fifty-nine agencies and a negative from twenty-six, the other twenty-two agencies either refraining from answering or giving uncertain replies. Another question asked whether placement was being carried on as an experiment or a demonstration. Twenty agencies said "yes," thirty-three said "no," and fifty-four omitted an answer or gave a vague or uncertain reply.

Following these two questions was one asking what agency seems the logical one to do junior placement if the

[6] There is no way of checking to determine whether the agencies covered were truly social agencies. For example, The Child Welfare Board in New York was included. There is a possibility also that adult placement activities were included in view of the fact that 94 agencies reported that they also did adult placement.

social agency does not do it. Ninety of the agencies failed
to answer this question, leaving seventeen which replied.
Of these, thirteen said the schools should be responsible;
the other four mentioned, respectively, the state, the city,
U. S. and State as joint sponsors, and "the employers
association"!

The committee asked a similar question of the state
agencies. Fifty-one replied that junior workers should go
to the state service and twenty-two said they should not.
Twenty-five said the school system should not be responsible and forty-one said it should be. About a third of the
latter group said the state and the school system should
work together.

The White House report comments as follows on the
facts emerging from this part of the questionnaire:

State employment bureaus believe, in an encouragingly large
number, that a plan of close coördination with school systems
would be valuable for this junior program. Some think that
boards of education should do all junior placement; others that
only the lower age levels, fourteen to sixteen years, should be
cared for by school systems. The fact that so many of the public
offices have urged coöperation hints of better standards, and a
better understanding of what the school guidance and placement
offices are trying to accomplish. One state office said that such
coöperation would free the school bureaus for more complete
attention to "vocational work," and two state departments in
cities having no separate junior placement service—Youngs-
town, Ohio and Springfield, Massachusetts—acknowledging
the work with juniors as a unit needing its own separate method,
reported that public employment bureaus should have special
junior departments. Some state departments feel that schools
should undertake junior placement because it is an extra burden
to the state, and some school departments would be glad to be
free of the burden on themselves; but that there is such general
sense of the value of responsibility and coöperation on both sides
is most hopeful.

Another position held by some state offices is that the state,
with its factory inspection department, is in a much better posi-

tion to do the entire job of junior placement, but this theory is in
the decided minority. Some of the factors in its support have no
substantial value and are often due to purely local conditions tied
up with local prejudices and attitudes. The position which some
of the schools take, that they know the children better, and that
they should therefore do the work of placement, has just as strong
foundation. The truth of the matter is that both kinds of information are necessary. Individuals must be known and followed
up, jobs must be known and investigated, in order that placement
may have value to the individual and to society and mean more
than a temporary, and all too often an unsatisfactory, hitching
up of work and worker.

Many privately endowed social agencies favor board of education control for junior placement as a whole, but regard special
problems of placement to be the function of agencies especially
equipped to solve them. Some agencies carry on a junior placement program as an experiment, and say quite frankly that it is
a temporary venture, its responsibilities to be diverted to other
channels when these are sufficiently developed to take care of
them. In some instances, the experiment is initiated as a means
of making this particular part of the vocational guidance program available to a community, and often as an answer to a
particular need. In others, it has been initiated with a long look
ahead; to the possibility of organizing a rounded program of
guidance in which its several activities are delegated to the community groups best able to handle them, both as individual units
and as parts of a complete program in which the general philosophy and method of development are the same. Some agencies
of the group studied specified particular activities, such as scholarships or special work with handicapped, which they hoped to
develop after another agency—often school or state—took over
placement. Organization of this second kind calls for very close
coöperation of the agencies represented, for an intimate understanding of the various phases of guidance, and for a deep deter-
mination to give individuals a balanced service rather than a
concentrated portion of one phase which is often valueless without the others.[7]

[7] White House Report, pp. 220–21.

CHAPTER XII

JUNIOR PLACEMENT—REGISTERING AND INTERVIEWING

The young person planning to leave school to go to work usually learns of the existence of a placement office through other young people already at work, from school counselors, from teachers, and from the clerk in the employment certificating office. Not much recruiting of applicants by the placement office itself is necessary. Most of the offices visited in our field study did no recruiting. Of the thirty-eight offices placing juniors who replied to our questionnaire, twenty-five were doing no recruiting in 1933, seven were doing some recruiting, and three were recruiting in "special cases" only. Three did not answer the question. In "good" times, fourteen do some recruiting, seventeen do none, two do very little, and five did not answer the question. Such recruiting as is done is mostly through the schools. Principals and teachers are circularized in some cases. Sometimes a representative discusses placement before the members of the class that is about to graduate. Other methods occasionally employed include the use of posters, ads, newspaper publicity, and contacts with social agencies. As a rule, however, even in prosperous times the agency placing juniors depends upon the applicants to come of their own accord.

Receiving the Applicant

When they do come, whom do they see, and how are they greeted? In eighteen of our thirty-eight junior agencies they are met by a special reception clerk who is stationed near the entrance and who finds out their needs and assigns them to an interviewer. In seventeen cases they are greeted first by the interviewer. In two offices the head of the department makes the first contact and in one case the answer was not clear.

At the 28th Street Office of the Junior Employment Service in New York City the receptionist obtains certain essential information: whether the applicant is "new" or "old," whether a new applicant has "evidence of age" and if not sends him to get it, whether applicant has working papers; name and address and, if the applicant lives outside the district covered sends him to the office in his own district.   She calls the applicants and assigns them to interviewers in the order of their arrival.   The receptionist, in this New York office is one of the interviewers, who are assigned in rotation to this work.   In most other offices having a receptionist, the work is combined with clerical service or with switchboard operation.

In the Junior Employment Service in Philadelphia the reception clerk has in addition the following duties:

1. Gets out registration cards of applicants previously registered and puts confidential "action cards" on counselor's desk.
2. Types name, address, and other identification, data regarding applicant on new registration card preliminary to interview with counselor.
3. Types name, date, and purpose of visit on "action card."
4. Gives information regarding ways of proving age for employment certificates.
5. Tabulates daily data from (1) counselor's record of action taken and (2) registration card.
6. Makes out "visible index" cards for registrants.
7. Keeps chronological file for follow-up of registrants and sends follow-up cards at dates indicated.

Registering the Applicant

After an applicant has been received, and either before meeting the interviewer or during the interview an application blank giving some essential information must be filled out.   Whether this is to be done by the interviewer who may jot down the applicant's answers to questions as the interview progresses or in advance by the applicant himself, is a question about which there is some disagreement.

Mary La Dame discusses this question and gives some of the arguments commonly advanced in favor of one practice or the other.[1] Our field study and the questionnaire indicate that the prevailing practice in junior offices is for the applicant to fill out the blank. This was true in twenty-two of the thirty-eight offices answering the questionnaire, while in twelve the blank is filled out by the interviewer. In the remaining four cases the work is said to be done by both applicant and interviewer. In some cases, also, a clerk assists the applicant in filling out the blank. Where the blank is said to be filled out by "both," the practice is to ask the applicant to fill out a part of the blank and bring it back to the interviewer for completion. In such a case the part to be filled out by the applicant contains simple personal information, such as name, age, address, education, etc., while the part filled in by the interviewer during the interview may call for an expression of judgment as to personal characteristics. The director of an office where this is the practice, which handles commercial and personal service jobs, writes:

Blank is given (to applicant) after a preliminary interview, to ascertain bare outline of education and experience and make sure that person comes within occupational classification we cover. If she belongs to another group, interviewer writes the whole history in concise form on a special card, tells the applicant that the bureau does not cover her particular field and refers her to an office that does. In this way the applicant is not given the hope which filling an application arouses. If in proper field for placement here, applicant fills blanks in part, interviewer supplements it later with personal data after a more intensive interview.

In offices affiliated with school systems, the card may be filled out in part from the records sent to the placement office by the school counselors, or as in some cases, the school counselors may fill out a complete personal record

[1] See Appendix J.

card for each graduate, and send it to the placement office to be used instead of an application blank. A member of the staff of the Department of Vocational Guidance of a large city school system explains their practice as follows:

The majority of our applicants are graduates of the public high schools, which are of two types—academic and commercial. All commercial high school graduates fill out their application blanks in school before graduation, the school record and teachers estimate are added by the school and the (placement) counselor visits the school and holds an individual interview with each applicant before the blanks are brought down to the office of the Department of Vocational Guidance to be placed on file. Academic high school graduates and students who leave school before graduation are usually referred by the principal of the school which they have been attending. They fill in application blanks at the office and then the school record is secured by the counselor.

Name, age, address and telephone number, scholastic training, and date of registration are items appearing on all of the blanks used in junior offices that were examined for this study. Other information generally called for includes work record, type of work sought, nationality, race, and religion; information concerning applicant's family such as nationality and occupation of parents, age and occupation of brothers and sisters, etc. Items frequently recorded include special interests, courses most enjoyed or most disliked in school, extra-curricular activities, plans for further training.

Some application blanks include space for scholastic record, record of tests, teacher's estimate and opinion of interviewer on personality. Some space is usually provided on the reverse side of the card for record of placements and on many of them the entire space is devoted to that purpose. Occasionally both sides of the blank are used for personal information and a record of placements is made on a separate card. Y.M. and Y.W.C.A. agencies are apt to add an inquiry about church memberships and some of them a few questions about personal habits. One of these agencies uses a blank including the following questions:

Do you smoke cigarettes?........Drink?........Gamble? ....Are you a church member?........Are you a member of the Y.M.C.A.?........If not, why not?........

These application blanks are generally filed by occupational groups and alphabetically within the group. Two files are usually kept, one active and the other inactive. In general, applications are kept in the active file as long as the applicant is in need of a job and keeps in touch with the office by returning from time to time to make inquiries. Thirty-four of our thirty-eight junior offices answered the question covering this point, with the following result:

LENGTH OF TIME APPLICATION BLANK
IS KEPT IN ACTIVE FILE

TIME	NUMBER OF OFFICES
Until applicant is placed	5
Six weeks to two months	1
One to three months	6
Two months	2
Three months	3
Six months	3
One year	4
Two years	3
Indefinite period or permanently	5
Until age limit handled by office is reached . .	2

The Interview

No matter who fills out the application blank it is followed or accompanied by the interview. In the overwhelming majority of cases this is conducted in private. In only one of the questionnaires was "no" written in answer to the question covering this point. One answered "usually" and one did not answer. The field investigation bears out the impression thus received. In answer to the question "about how long is the first interview," the lowest figure was two minutes and the highest, mentioned by ten agencies, was thirty minutes. The average appears to be between fifteen and twenty minutes.

The interview is the most important of several methods of obtaining information about the applicant. This information must be of sufficiently complete and precise a character to enable the interviewer to judge of the applicant's occupational fitness and thus to become equipped to perform the placement function with skill and effectiveness. The more information there is available to the interviewer in advance in the form of records and reports the better will he be able to make the interview itself an effective instrument. The child begins to lay the basis for some helpful records the moment he starts his school career. In the schools that are best organized and administered a cumulative record follows him through the school system. Teachers form opinions of him as he passes before them and frequently record their estimates of his ability and character. Intelligence tests increasingly make possible a record of the psychologist's attempt to measure intellectual capacity. The extent to which these records are available to the interviewer depends in part upon the degree to which the schools coöperate even with their own placement agencies and in part, of course, upon how closely the agency is connected with the school system. Nineteen of the twenty-two agencies closely affiliated with school systems, which reported to us, were provided with the school record, and the same number had the teachers' estimates. Only thirteen of them, however, had the results of intelligence tests.

Altogether, of the thirty-eight agencies reporting, thirty had access to the school record, and two 'did not. One had it "frequently," one in "special cases," and four did not answer. Twenty-seven had the teachers' estimate, two definitely did not have it, three had it "occasionally" or in "special cases" and six did not reply. Seventeen were provided with the applicant's intelligence quotient, and, again, two were not. Nine had it "occasionally" or in "special cases," two "rarely," and eight did not answer. Other records mentioned by one or more agencies as available in some cases, stated in order of frequency, included "work experience" where there had been any, employer's rating, reports from social agencies, health record, character rating, record of extra-curricular activities, "police record," and "juvenile court record."

If the records are lacking or incomplete, it is possible for tests to be made at the time of application. The questions on this point did not elicit altogether definite replies. It is clear, however, that while interviewers sometimes give tests, it is not the usual practice. When it is felt that tests are needed they are given either by a psychologist who is sometimes, but not often, attached to the placement staff, or the applicant is sent to a psychologist provided by the board of education or some other agency. The test most frequently given in this way includes intelligence, aptitude, trade ability (this is often given by the interviewer), interest and achievement tests.

Attitude of Interviewer toward Leaving School

Most workers in junior placement offices feel some responsibility for discovering not merely the most suitable job, but whether the best thing for the applicant is any job, however suitable. Discussion of this point with placement workers during our field study created the impression that there is a very general tendency to assume that all young persons should be in school and that the practice is to attempt first to dissuade them from their desire for employment and to induce them to return to school. To check on this impression a question inserted in the questionnaire was as follows:

Does interviewer advise applicant to return to school?
                    Always...........
                    Sometimes........

Every one of the thirty-eight agencies answered this question. The nearest approach to an unqualified "yes" was the answer of a large agency which reported affirmatively with respect to all applicants fourteen or fifteen years of age. Thirty-four checked the word "sometimes," two wrote "no" after the word "always," leaving open the possibility that they do recommend a return to school in certain cases. One answered, somewhat cryptically "every placement interview is an educational prescription." It is evident then, that very nearly all, if not all, these agencies, do advise a return to school under certain circumstances. In explaining what these circumstances are it was evident that the largest number would advise a return to school for every child capable of profiting from it if economic circumstances would permit. Some agencies take great pains to make sure that their recommendations are sound. One director wrote that the recommendation is made "after careful consultation with school, study of school record, psychological test and the total picture of the individual, educational, social, economic, etc." And another said "always talk with teachers, often parents and others before taking a definite stand."

In the section on counseling it was shown that school counselors interviewing prospective "drop-outs" urge the promising ones to stay in school and often try to help solve the financial problems that make continuance in school seem impossible. One method is the securing of a scholarship. Replies to our questionnaire revealed the fact that many placement agencies, also, concern themselves with this problem. Twenty-six of the agencies reported that where it seems probable that the applicant would profit from further school attendance and his reason for leaving school is economic, they refer him to a scholarship fund. Three said they did so in "rare cases." One said that this was done by the school counselor, three stated positively that they do not follow this practice, one replied, "no scholarship fund available," and four did not answer the question.

Thirty of the agencies refer applicants to social agencies where circumstances seem to warrant it, and three of those answering do not. Five failed to indicate their policy. All but three of the thirty-eight agencies clear through the social service exchange. Five clear all cases and thirty clear "special" cases or when "necessary."

Purpose of the Interview

Because we wanted to know as specifically as possible what service the placement office tries to render the applicant, we asked in the questionnaire whether the interviewers "advise the applicant about further training opportunities" and about his "vocational choice." We asked these particular questions because we hoped to find out whether interviewers think of themselves as counselors with the duty of helping the applicant to the best possible decision or merely as channels through which the applicant finds his way to any sort of job. Following these was another question addressed even more directly to the point:

What is the primary purpose of the interview?
  a) Placement?...
  b) Vocational guidance?................................

The answers to these questions were interesting. In the first place, the two questions asking "Does the interviewer advise" about training and vocational choice brought a secondary response that had not been anticipated. One director put a question mark over the word "advise" and substituted for it the words "give information." Another wrote in an additional word, making the phrase read "advise with." A third, checking "yes" in answer to both questions, wrote after them, respectively, "interviewer always points out that final decision rests with the individual," and "applicant must make his own choice after information has been furnished." Another replied "not always advise, but discuss opportunities." It was obvious that the word "advise" suggested to these placement workers the idea of direction, or the writing of a prescription. It was not so intended, but their obvious opposition to such a concept does more than the mere answering of questions to indicate their belief that an interviewer, like a school counselor, should avoid substituting his judgment for the voluntary decision of the applicant. The director of an independently organized placement agency for girls, on the other hand, wrote "the job for which the girl is best fitted is determined upon in conference of case worker, psychologist, and placement secretary."

Thirty-seven of the thirty-eight agencies replied to the two questions about advising. With the limitations quoted, every one of the thirty-seven said that they do advise about further training opportunities. Thirty-five said that they advise about vocational choice. Of the other two agencies, one does so "sometimes" and one to a "limited degree."

The third question in this group was the one asking for the "primary purpose" of the interview. Every one of the thirty-eight agencies replied. Twenty-two indicated that placement stands first; only six put vocational guidance first; but ten either wrote "both" or indicated that it was impossible to state which is more important. A typical comment reads "vocational guidance is such an integral part of placement that it is difficult to say which is really primary."

No other question elicited so much additional comment as this one. Because they throw light both on the interviewer's point of view and on the problems met in a placement office, some of these comments may well be reproduced. A few indicated that present policy is influenced by the depression. For example, one who said that placement is the primary purpose of the interview added, as in explanation, "just now the financial need is great." Another emphasizing placement wrote "For the past few years it has been impossible always to find the job that is most suitable for applicants" and consequently the office has been "helping her to adjust herself to a work situation"; a director in a large eastern city said that while placement would be the primary purpose "under ordinary business conditions" vocational guidance "assumes more than usual importance now"; and one in a western city wrote: "Both. The emphasis depends upon the case. In these days much emphasis is put upon advising further education and the utilization of leisure time."

Two directors of agencies which function as part of a school system indicated that because there were counselors in the schools, the placement office could concentrate on job finding. Just the opposite position was taken by another, who said that vocational guidance is "often necessary to continue and strengthen the information given by the counselors in the school."

Others in public school placement offices put vocational guidance as the primary purpose of the interview. One said, "We regard placement as a part of the guidance program of the school system, instead of merely an employment referral service," and another, "I am convinced that a real thorough job of placement cannot be done without vocational guidance." Some emphasized the strategic opportunity for vocational guidance that the placement office affords:

The immediate purpose of the interview varies, but desire for placement gives an excellent opportunity for the giving of educational and vocational information preliminary to and in addition to placement.

First approach is to gain good will by meeting immediate interests or needs.   Guidance follows upon better acquaintance.

Two other comments indicate that applicant and interviewer may look at the matter differently.   One said: "The applicant's purpose is placement.   The worker often finds other needs and has vocational guidance in mind"; and the other: "Many of our girls come from the country and from small towns and have had no guidance.   Placement to them is the major problem.   We find vocational and occupational information the major need."

CHAPTER XIII

JUNIOR PLACEMENT—REFERRAL AND FOLLOW-UP

There is widespread objection among junior placement workers to sending more than one applicant to an employer at a time. Most of them would avoid it if they could. Yet only two of the thirty-eight agencies reporting said that they did not do it. Fifteen said that they send more than one "sometimes" or at "employer's request," and most of the twenty-one who checked the affirmative answer to the question said that they did so because the employers required it. One wrote "This is not our policy unless as now happens occasionally an employer insists. If it is done applicants are told of the fact before they go out. We resist this policy as much as possible, however."

Investigation of Places of Employment

There also appears to be a general feeling that jobs to which juniors are to be sent should be investigated in advance. Both in the field study and in the questionnaire an effort was made to discover whether this is the prevailing practice. From neither source is it possible to piece together a consistent and integrated picture. No uniform practice was discoverable in the field study, though there was generally a defensive attitude on the part of those who did not investigate all jobs before referral. The answers to the questionnaire were so frequently qualified that a clear-cut statement concerning them is impossible. About half of the agencies replying said that they investigate all places of employment not previously encountered, either before referral or immediately after. Others investigated "suspicious" cases, or places of "doubtful" location, or when conditions were "unusual" One said that investigations are made in "special cases where things look fishy," or "when we challenge the attitude of the employer on account of reticence, queer requirements, unsavory reports, etc." Two said that investigations are unnecessary because the employers are already known.

The inferences to be drawn from these statements would seem to be these: placement workers as a rule feel that for the protection of young persons the nature and environment of a job and the character of the employer should be known in advance. They obtain this information whenever time and resources permit, but do not generally sacrifice volume of placement activity to accomplish it.[1]

Verifying Referrals

Every placement office attempts to "verify referrals," that is, to find out whether an applicant referred to a position is hired. When sending an applicant to an employer who has placed an order with the agency it is customary to provide him with a card of introduction to the person at the place of employment who interviews applicants. This card is usually intended to serve also as a means of notifying the employment office whether the applicant has been hired. There is usually space at the bottom of the card where the employer may indicate action taken. Some of them ask also for a statement of reasons, if the applicant was not hired, and some provide space for indicating whether other applicants should be sent. The reverse of the card carries the address of the office together with a stamp or government frank, in order that the card may be put into the mail as soon as the employer has checked his action.

[1] A director of an adult placement office who read this section said: "It is extremely difficult to ascertain moral conditions through visits to the employer. These are matters that are easily covered up and become known to the agency, as a rule, only when the worker reports back. Investigation of places of employment is, however, essential to good placement as this is the means by which the placement worker may become familiar with the job, the type of shop and the type of worker desired."

Some agencies depend chiefly upon the return of the card
for information about hiring, but telephone the employer
if the card does not come back promptly. Others do not
wait for the card, but telephone as soon as the applicant
has had time to reach the place of employment and obtain
an interview. This is done in order that the agency may
know both whether the applicant has been placed and thus
is no longer looking for a job, and whether the position is
no longer open for the consideration of other applicants.
A few agencies depend for information, on the applicant
telephoning or calling at the agency. The great majority,
however, depend on communicating with the employer
by telephone.

If no opening for which a particular applicant is fitted
is known, twenty of the thirty-eight agencies endeavor,
over the telephone or otherwise, to find a job for him.
Eight do so occasionally. One of these writes "can't do it
except for outstanding cases—load too heavy." One
"seldom" follows this practice. Nine refrain altogether,
though three of these have done this in "ordinary times"
but are not now doing so.

If the agency gets word of an opening for which an
applicant who is not present is fitted, thirty-six of the
agencies reporting will send for him. Two will not because,
respectively, there are "too many applicants on file" and
there is "no time."

In view of the great number who were looking for work
at the time of the sending out of the questionnaire, many
agencies were trying to discourage applicants from coming
frequently or remaining for any length of time in the
waiting rooms. They were told that they would be sent for
if a job should present itself. In order to find out whether
this tended to work a hardship, the following question was
asked: "If applicant previously registered who is absent,
and new applicant who is present are equally qualified for

a job that has just come in which is sent?" Thirty-five agencies answered this question. Seven said they would send the first applicant. Seven would do so "ordinarily" or "if possible" or if he were "available." Nine would send the one present (one director adding "I'm afraid"). Four would send both, and five the one most urgently in need of a job. One would let the employer's urgency decide it, one would send the "better known," and one stated simply "it seldom happens." One, who would send both wrote "No two people are 'equally' qualified for a job." One who would send the applicant who was present, explained "Quick action is the order of the day," and another "Employer wants vacancy filled as soon as possible."

A statement by a director of guidance and placement in a large vocational school describes the methods employed by the interviewer in selecting an applicant to be referred to a specific opening. It is included here for the light it throws on procedure as well as on guiding principles.

The detailed specifications for each job are written on a separate card known as the Employer's Order. In receiving an order, much skill and tact is used in directing the conversation so that a maximum of information is secured with a minimum of direct questioning. Long experience in placement will enable the guidance counselor to know specifically the information which is necessary to achieve satisfaction to the applicant and the employer. Particular attention is paid to special requirements such as a tall boy, six feet tall, or, a girl who can meet people.

A selective device (Findex) almost instantly discloses every student who will answer the detailed requirements of the job. This is an improvement on the occupational cross-file in that, in addition to cross-reference by occupation, any other characteristic desired, such as education, experience, age, or residence, can be found. It assures the placement office that every person qualified will be considered, and it enables a selection in one minute which formerly took hours.

The employment application cards of the students who meet the requirements are secured and checked to ascertain (1) if the attendance record is clear, (2) if the physical examination indicates fitness for this job, (3) if the "Teachers' estimate" is up-to-date, and (4) if the past job history as shown by "previous employment" and "follow-up" reveals suitability for this opening. Next, the shop or home room teacher who is responsible for these pupils is consulted for more detailed information and for a re-rating of the card.

The selection has now been narrowed to one or two individuals. The final interview with the student in the guidance office occupies considerable time and is the most important part of the placement procedure. The interviewer obtains any further information about the student which has not previously been brought to light. He carefully notes appearance, bearing, manners, and attitudes in their relation to this particular job.

The final decision is made by matching all of the factors making up the pattern of the job with detailed information about the pattern of the student. Finally, the placement worker will always ask himself this question, "If I were the employer, would I hire this person myself?"

The final interview is a tense occasion for the student and can be utilized as a strategic time for effective counsel to the individual. The guidance worker learns through bitter experience that placements based on sympathetic reasons instead of personal qualifications and a meritorious work record invariably end in failure and dismissal, and consequently hurt the individual more than help him.[2]

Follow-up

Speaking before the National Vocational Guidance Association in 1924, the Director of the Junior Division of the U. S. Employment Service said:

We take it that merely getting a job for a junior which is probably no better than that junior would be able ultimately to get for himself, and then forgetting all about him until in the course of events he shows up for another job of the same sort is in no sense professional or educational work, and that the responsibility of the state and society toward the junior is in no way fulfilled by such a service. On the other hand, we think that the

[2] *Applications of Vocational Guidance.* Syllabus of course of lectures given to faculty of Milwaukee Vocational School by Wm. F. Patterson, Director of Employment and Guidance. (Mimeographed.)

placement office coöperating with the school authorities should establish a supervision over the working junior, whether he be in part-time school or released for full-time work in industry.[3]

A good general statement of the value, purpose, and method of follow-up is given in the report of the White House Conference as follows:

After the work of actual placement comes a third kind of interview, and a most important one if any of the others are to have their full value—the follow-up interview, in which there is a chance for discussion of the job and the child's growth on the job, his education along the way, what the later opportunities are, and how he can make ready to meet them. Many departments, even many school departments, do their follow-up work through the employer only, by personal visit after a placement has been effected, by letter, or by telephone call. When a visit is made it is sometimes possible to see the child on the job and to have a short interview with him there. A more satisfactory follow-up of the child is possible if he can return to the employment department, away from restraint and free from criticism because of seeming interference which such an interview on the job might create. These interviews are held generally in evening office hours, arranged for this particular purpose, or in time reserved for the child by special appointment. Some employers are willing to give children time from work to have this consultation, particularly if the child is very much in need of counsel at which the employer himself has been unsuccessful. Tardiness, overtime, illness, and countless other matters sometimes can be adjusted successfully in the placement department after conference between the child and the employer have proved fruitless. A continuation school child can generally call at the employment office on his day in school. If an office interview can be combined with a visit to the employer, the worker is able to get the clearest picture of how the child is progressing. The most important thing which the follow-up can hold is often not the particular adjustment, but the method of adjustment which the child and the employment worker devise together; so that the child may have a working basis on which to operate when a similar situation next arises.[4]

[3] Mary Stewart, *The Vocational Guidance Magazine*, March, 1924, p. 161.
White House Conference Report, pp. 239–40.

The purpose of follow-up in a junior placement office appears, from the answers to our questionnaires, to be threefold—service to the worker, service to the employer, and the securing of valuable information for the placement office itself. All of the thirty-eight offices gave some information on this matter. The service rendered the worker that was mentioned more frequently than any other was "adjustment." This appears to mean assistance and advice to the worker in meeting problems that arise in employment. The junior office, in the nature of the case, is placing applicants who have had very little prior work experience or none at all. They are frequently unprepared for the conditions confronting them in the place of employment and do not understand them. Conference with the placement worker at this point is very important. One placement secretary attached to a large vocational school never places a graduate in the first job without inducing him to agree that he will not quit of his own accord without first consulting her. Thus, when the action is impulsive or based on misunderstanding she may be able to straighten the matter out and save the youth from establishing at the very outset a habit of instability.

"Adjustment," however, means something more than trying to keep a worker in a particular job. It includes a study of both job and worker to see whether the position is a good one for him. It is not adjustment to a particular job that the placement worker is concerned about but adjustment to work opportunity and work environment. Consequently replacement may prove to be as important as placement, and advice about further training opportunities as important as either.

The placement worker has a further responsibility to the junior applicant, and follow-up helps him to discharge it. That is to protect him to a certain degree against exploitation and physical and moral hazard. Consequently follow-

up should include a check on the place of employment
to ascertain labor-law violations, low wages, and other
forms of exploitation.

Service to the employer involves discovering whether he
is satisfied with the worker sent him as well as studying
his requirements so that future orders may be filled satisfactorily. This is service to the employer but it is also
service to the placement office since the success of the latter
must depend on knowledge of the employer's requirements
and ability to meet them. It is difficult to distinguish
therefore between service to the employer and the gathering
of information that is of value to the placement office. In
Chapter XV reference will be made to visits to places of
employment for other purposes. It is obvious, however,
that visits for the purpose of follow-up of workers make
possible the gathering of information about the job itself
and its requirements.

In addition to these purposes of follow-up some of the
agencies connected with school systems reported that visits
to the work place frequently made possible recommendation to the school regarding training, and curriculum
revision designed to keep the school abreast of business and
industrial practice.

The telephone seems to be the instrument most frequently
resorted to in follow-up. Twenty-eight of the thirty-
eight agencies reporting said that they made use of it for
this purpose. Only three depended on it exclusively,
however. The others used it in connection with other
devices such as writing letters or the maintenance of office
hours. Eighteen maintained contact by means of letter
writing—again only three depending on this means alone.
Thirteen made use of office interviews, two of these by
special appointment and the others by the maintenance
of office hours, usually in the evening or one day in the
week, to which all workers recently placed are invited.

Twenty-five of the replies included other means of follow-up. Six of these mentioned visits to the place of employment and six merely used the word "visits," but these were also, presumably, to the place of employment. Other methods included calling in the continuation school pupil on his day in school, attendance at meeting of a workers' club, "supervision of case worker," and other methods not clearly specified.

A few excerpts from the replies will throw additional light on the methods and purpose of follow-up:

From the Department of Research and Guidance of the Providence, R. I., public schools we learn that the purpose of follow-up is:[5]

(1) For the child—to find out any difficulties he may be having; (2) for placement office, to measure success of service and provide information about jobs and employers; (3) For counselor, to measure her guidance; (4) For administration, to provide curriculum suggestions which will keep schools abreast with the current business practices.

As contrasted with the purposes thus set forth, the following statement of purpose by another agency seems rather limited:

To ascertain whether or not employee is satisfactory and also whether the place might be available in case she was not satisfactory.

Another method of follow-up is:

"Entirely by telephone, for lack of time."

Another agency faced by the same difficulty writes:

With a limited force we follow-up when and where we can. In many cases we must omit follow-up because we cannot spread ourselves thin enough to cover all.

The placement division of the Department of Vocational Guidance of New Orleans proceeds as follows:

[5] See Chapter VI and Appendix L.

When applicants are referred to jobs they are asked to notify counselor how they get along on the job. Frequently, they do this voluntarily either by telephone or personal calls. If they do not, counselor telephones the home and either gets information from parent or arranges for applicant to telephone or call at some convenient time.

From the Director of Placement of the Minneapolis Public Schools we learn that:

Every third year, a complete follow-up study is made of all high school graduates of one year. This includes those going on to school as well as those working. This study shows the percentage of pupils from each school who go on to school, the percentage going on to business, college, etc.—those taking jobs, those unemployed and the types of jobs secured by the pupils who go to work.

In the Baltimore public school placement service (discontinued in March, 1933) the practice was to send a

Letter in form of questionnaire to applicants and employer— 1 mo. after placement; 3 mos.; 1 yr.; 2 yrs.; 3 yrs., and 4 and 5 yrs. were contemplated. We did not get that far in our work.

In the Junior Employment Service in Philadelphia:

a) There is a regular follow-up of young people who have secured positions through Junior Employment Service.

b) Applicants who are suffering with malnutrition or other physical defects.

c) Applicants for placement for whom Junior Employment Service has been unable to secure positions (in general, an applicant, for placement is not "closed" without an attempt to find out if a position has been obtained or if the applicant still wishes Junior Employment to keep on trying to get a job for him).

d) Applicants for whom there is an educational opportunity in which interest has been expressed.
A card indicating the date for follow-up and the type of follow-up desired is filed in a chronological file. Each day cards filed under that date are removed and a personal letter or form post card sent to the applicant. In the follow-up or

placements, each interview serves a special purpose. The first contact is made as soon as possible after the position has been secured to talk over first adjustments on the job. In the second conference, about a month later, the emphasis, in general, is on the duties of the job and the possibilities of advancement. The third is held usually just prior to the time of registration for evening schools. Subsequent follow-ups occur according to the needs of each case with a minimum of one a year until the applicant becomes twenty-one years of age.

An interesting statement regarding the purpose, methods, and value of follow-up in the Milwaukee Vocational School is contained in a syllabus of a course of lectures on "Applications of Vocational Guidance" given to the faculty of the school by Wm. F. Patterson, Director of Employment and Guidance in the school:

Pupil follow-up is accomplished by automatically calling in the student for a conference on his school day six weeks after he has been placed on a job. Subsequent interviews are held at the expiration of each three months period. After the young worker has discontinued day school attendance, the follow-up is made at three-month intervals through a questionnaire.

Employer follow-up is made by the guidance counselor or instructor during field contacts made about every three months at the place of employment. Work processes are observed and conferences are held with foremen, inspectors, managers, and other supervisors to learn how the student is progressing, what is the next higher job, and what is needed to secure it.

The Value of Follow-up
  A. To the Placement Service
     1. Initial placement is not a complete and final solution.
     2. Placement technique is improved through knowing mistakes.
     3. Intimate knowledge of the job and conditions in the place of business become an addition to the working capital of the placement office.
     4. Desirable and undesirable employment conditions are revealed.

B. In Disseminating Occupational Information
   1. Shows what fields are overcrowded or undersupplied.
   2. Promotional opportunities for different types of junior workers are made known.
   3. Information obtained through follow-up can enrich occupational studies because it is representative and it is founded on hundreds of contacts.

C. To the School
   1. Discloses personality traits which need to be developed.
   2. Suggests changes in teaching methods and in the curriculum.
   3. Is a method of demonstrating the sincerity of interest in the welfare of a student.
   4. Aids in advising on new machinery and equipment needed.
   5. Provides a check or inspection on our guidance.
   6. Links the interest of the school and the community more closely.

D. To Employers
   1. Enables a better matching of the applicant and the job.
   2. Causes him to focus his attention on the performance of adolescent workers.
   3. Greatly improves a replacement and re-guidance.
   4. Often prevents a separation from employment.

E. To the Young Man or Young Woman
   1. Is spurred to greater effort when a kindly interest is manifested in his problems.
   2. Violations of child labor laws on prohibited employments, minimum wage, and hours of labor regulations are prevented.
   3. His job is frequently saved through intervention.
   4. Suggestions made relative to educational preparation and personal efficiency result in rapid progress and satisfaction on the job.
   5. The training value and future of his occupation is interpreted to him and happiness in his work ensues.

CHAPTER XIV

JUNIOR PLACEMENT—THE EMPLOYER AND THE JOB

Finding the Job

How does the interviewer know where there is a job to which the applicant may be sent? Job seekers may come of their own accord but jobs ordinarily require some solicitation, despite the obvious truth of the reply of one director of an office who said "as good service as we can give has been our best publicity." An hour of observation spent in an employment office in reasonably good times will probably leave the visitor with the impression that employers telephone in their job requirements without any effort on the part of the office. As we shall see, a relatively high proportion of jobs do come to the attention of the office in that way; but it is obviously true that before employers begin to telephone their orders they must somehow have become aware of the existence of the office and their confidence in its ability to render service must somehow have been aroused.

A director of vocational guidance and placement in a large vocational school gives the following list of the common sources of "help wanted" orders:[1]

1. Through field coördination (i.e., visits to employers, schools, social agencies, student homes, etc.)
2. As a result of former placements
3. Through students, former students, and their relatives
4. Faculty members and their acquaintances
5. Telephone calls to place special cases
6. Employers organizations and labor unions
7. As a result of apprentice committee activities
8. Following visits to the school by outside organizations
9. Careful study of all "Help Wanted" advertisements in the newspapers

[1] Wm. F. Patterson, *Syllabus of Lectures on Applications of Vocational Guidance.*

10. Through coöperating agencies, such as the Public Employment Office, Industrial Commission, and fraternal employment bureaus

All of the thirty-eight agencies answered the question "what methods are used in recruiting jobs?" The greatest dependence, it appeared from the replies, is on visits to employers. Thirty-five checked that method, though one resorts to it in "special cases" only. Twenty-nine rely also on the telephone, though four do so only "occasionally" or "sometimes." Twenty-seven use both telephone and visits, and all but two use one or the other. Only thirteen make regular use of advertising. Twenty-five mentioned other types of publicity or recruiting. These included, in order of frequency, circular letters sent to employers, speeches to clubs or over the radio, the publication of periodical bulletins or occasional leaflets, newspaper publicity.

The foregoing is a statement about recruiting and has no reference to results. When orders are actually received from the employer, how do they reach the office? A question directed to this point revealed that far the largest proportion of orders are received over the telephone, the employer calling. Every one of the thirty-eight offices mentioned incoming phone calls and in general it would appear that in these offices about 80 percent of employers' orders are received in this way. The replies that did not mention a definite percentage generally used some such expression as "majority," "bulk," "nearly all," etc.

Twenty-nine of the offices obtain orders through "personal contact" mostly when calling at places of employment, the replies indicating that the proportion of orders received in this way ranges from "a few" to 50 percent of all orders with a possible average of 10 percent. Twenty-four of the offices obtain some orders by calling the employer on the telephone. In general not more than 5 to 10 percent of the orders are thus obtained. Only thirteen offices indicated that orders are received by mail and the proportion so received was very low.

A question of some importance, discussed by Mary La Dame, who is quoted in Appendix J, is, Who shall receive the employers order over the telephone? Several possibilities are suggested, including the employment of a special "order clerk." Through the questionnaire an attempt was made to find out whether any of the agencies have assigned this duty exclusively to a clerk, or whether the interviewer or someone else regularly receives the call. It is clear, as a result, that the prevailing custom among the thirty-eight agencies replying is for the interviewer to receive the employer's call. Thirty-one agencies so reported, definitely. One reported that the telephone operator takes some of the calls but that most of them are taken by the interviewer. One Y.M.C.A. agency checked impartially "telephone operator," "interviewer," and "membership secretary." Only two agencies checked "special order clerk." One of them did so after crossing off the word "order," and on this questionnaire the word "interviewer" was checked also. In the questionnaire from the other agency the words "mostly refers cases to interviewer" were written in the margin. It seems unlikely that either of these agencies employed a special order clerk in the sense intended by Miss La Dame. However, the practice does exist among some junior offices, the Boston Vocational Guidance Bureau being a notable example. In three agencies the office secretary regularly takes employers' orders over the telephone, and thus might be considered special "order clerks" though they are not so designated.

In junior offices the items almost always found on the employer's order form include the name of firm, address and telephone number, nature of business, name of person to whom application is to be made, kind of work, wages offered, and hours of work. Other items frequently included are age or sex desired, race or nationality, educational or other qualifications. Still others occasionally appearing on the forms submitted in this study are promotional possibilities, physical requirements, whether plant has been investigated, and physical condition of plant.

Order forms are filed according to occupation and usually a cross reference file of employers arranged alphabetically is maintained. The interviewer usually has either on his desk or immediately accessible the active file of employers' orders for the occupations handled. When an applicant appears he can turn at once to all of the positions available to him for which the applicant is fitted.

Twenty-nine junior offices reporting stated that employers' orders were retained in the active file varying periods.

NUMBER OF OFFICES	LENGTH OF TIME RETAINED
1	Two days
4	One month
1	Three months
2	One year
1	"Variable" periods
2	"Indefinitely" or "permanently"
1	"Until we hear from the employer"
16	Until filled
1	Uncertain reply

In explaining this practice Stewart says:

The offices try to fill orders as quickly as possible, and openings reported are usually considered valid until filled or cancelled. Cancellation may be made by the employer if he has found the desired workers elsewhere or if his requirements have changed, or automatically by the office when the order, as given, expired if not filled by a certain date. In practice the efficient placement official keeps in close touch with the employer so that an unfilled order is not likely to remain in the files without recent information as to its status. As orders are filled or for other reason become inactive they are transferred from the active to an inactive file.[2]

[2] Stewart, *op. cit.*, p. 48.

When an applicant has been sent to an employer, his application card is generally clipped to the employer's order card and the two placed in a temporary file until word has been received as to the result of the interview. If the applicant has been hired the fact may be indicated on the back of both cards and both may then be placed in their respective inactive files.   If the applicant is not hired both are returned to the active file.   As previously noted most of the placement offices studied do not wait for the introduction card to come back but telephone the employer the same day, if possible, in order that steps may be taken at once, if the interview did not result in a placement, both to fill the opening and to find another job for the applicant.

Clearance

Twenty-six of the agencies in the junior group clear all unfilled orders at the end of each day with a central clearance bureau.   Eight reported that they do not clear.   One replied "Have no unfilled orders"!   Three did not report on this point.

Clearance as it is practiced in Philadelphia is thus described in an unpublished report on file in the U. S. Children's Bureau and made available to the writer:

The clearance system on employer's requests for workers which is used in junior employment offices contributes greatly to the success of decentralized placement.   By agreement, every local junior employment service office that receives an employer's "request for workers" that it can not fill immediately, telephones it to the supervisor in charge of clearance, who, in turn, notifies other offices of the opening.   By the same agreement employment supervisors do not solicit jobs from employers outside the school districts served by their respective offices without first calling the clearance supervisor to learn whether there has already been solicitation and, if so, what were the results.   This method saves duplication of effort and prevents the annoyance to employers of having several employment supervisors call during a day to inquire about jobs for juniors.

Every hour during the morning, and once or twice during the afternoon, the clearance supervisor checks on the information received in local offices through job soliciting and also on the filling of jobs referred from one office to another. Orders coming to the central office from employers in the territory of a local office are referred at once to that office. As a result of this system of clearance, employers have the advantage of a selection of applicants from all school districts, and young people have a choice of jobs in all parts of the city.

Visiting Places of Employment

We have already seen that interviewers sometimes visit places of employment in connection with recruiting and follow-up. Three specific questions were inserted in the questionnaire in order to ascertain the practice with respect to field visits. Thirty-four of the agencies reported that interviewers do, as a regular practice, visit places of employment, and four that they do not. Two of the latter, however, emphasized the fact that they do not do so "now" (one on account of lack of personnel), but that normally, interviewers give fifty percent of their time to such visits. Thirty-two of the thirty-four agencies reporting regular visits to places of employment answered the question asking for the proportion of time devoted to such visits. Twenty-two agencies reported that five to forty-five percent of the interviewer's time was used that way with an average of about twenty-three percent. Seven indicated in one way or another that very little time was devoted to this purpose,[3] two said that there was no "allotted time,"[4] and one had "never noticed" how much time it took.

[3] One said that it varies with the circumstances. When the agency was first established 40 percent of the interviewer's time was given to visits to places of employment. Later it dropped to 20 percent and recently it has been "very little."

[4] One of these said "Just when she can get to it."

Of the thirty-four agencies whose interviewers visit places of employment, twenty-five indicated that their purposes included recruiting, investigation, and follow-up. Twelve of the twenty-five gave other reasons in addition. Five agencies have as their purpose investigation and recruiting, but not follow-up, and two of these listed additional reasons. Two are concerned with investigation and follow-up only, one with recruiting and follow-up, and one with recruiting alone.

To put it another way, recruiting and investigation each are mentioned by thirty-two agencies. Follow-up is mentioned by twenty-eight agencies, and "other" purposes are listed by fourteen. The purposes listed under the last heading include "adjustment"; the establishment of "friendly relations"; acquainting the interviewer with shop practice, employment conditions and trends, job specifications and possibilities of promotion; the collection of information for occupational studies; securing the co-operation of employers, checking the legality of employment, "impressing the employer with activity."

The unpublished report of the Children's Bureau referred to above describes the practice in Philadelphia.

A study of time reports shows that each employment supervisor spends on the average about 16 hours a month in "firm visiting." At least once every two years the supervisors in each local office visit and revisit all the firms located in their respective districts. This procedure involves continuous visiting, for some districts include a very large number of establishments. In addition, supervisors also make occasional studies of a particular occupation or industry. For this purpose, they visit not only the firms in the local district, but also, by arrangement with central clearance office, survey similar firms in the other districts, so that a complete report for the city may be written. All information gained through visits to business and industrial establishments is recorded in duplicate. One copy is filed in the local office, and one is sent to the central office for the use of the clearance supervisor, and other out-of-district supervisors whose applicants may obtain positions with the firm.

About 2,000 employers are visited each year, and whenever working conditions are suitable for the placement of young people under twenty-one years of age, the employers are urged to call the junior employment service when they need additional junior workers. As a reminder of the service available, the supervisor leaves her business card, which contains the address and telephone number of the local office, with the employment manager. In addition to personal visits, special letters advertising the junior employment service, printed leaflets of information, and double post-cards soliciting special types of jobs are sent to employers at regular intervals. An industrial calendar for junior workers in Philadelphia has also been made, and the information contained in it is used each month in soliciting jobs by letter, telephone, and personal visit in the industries which are "in season."

Applicants for positions are usually referred to jobs at once if any suitable openings are available. It is a rule of the office, however, that they are not referred to firms which have not been previously visited by an employment supervisor. When occasional exceptions to this rule are made, a supervisor visits the firm within 24 hours.

The Agency and Conditions of Employment

Visiting the place of employment for the purpose of "investigation," "checking the legality of employment," or "acquainting the interviewer with employment conditions" indicate the widespread belief that the agency should assume some responsibility for protecting the junior worker. The feeling is evident also in the attitude of most junior placement agencies with respect to investigating work places before sending young workers to them. The belief that this should be done is general even where the rule is more honored in the breach than in the observance.

Some questions intended to throw light on the manner in which agencies attempt to discharge this responsibility were included in the questionnaire. For example, do the agencies accept orders from all employers, without discrimination, and attempt to fill them? In answer to the question "Do you list all jobs offered?" eighteen agencies said "yes," one qualifying the answer with the word "usually";[5] eighteen said "no"; and two did not answer.

In order to discover as definitely as possible what specific conditions might lead to refusal to accept an order and therefore to fill a job the following enumeration of undesirable situations was presented, with the question,

Would any of the following conditions lead you to refuse to list a job?

a) Absence of educational content
b) Absence of promotional possibilities
c) Illegal conditions
d) Long hours
e) Low wages
f) Accident hazard
g) Health hazard
h) Moral hazard
i) Labor trouble
j) Other (specify)

The answers to this question, which come from thirty-seven of the thirty-eight agencies, indicate much difference of opinion and some confusion of thought on the part of the directors of agencies. As indicated above, eighteen answered "yes," to the question "Do you list all jobs offered?" yet everyone of the eighteen checked some of the items enumerated above as representing conditions under which they would not list jobs. The number of such conditions checked by the eighteen ranged from three to eight.

Only one agency checked all ten items in the list, and one checked nine. Eight items were checked by four agencies, seven, by eight agencies; six were checked by nine; five, by four; four items, by five; three, by four; and one agency checked only two items.

[5] One director wrote "Yes, but not try to fill them. We list the bad ones and try to get volunteer workers to go to find out about them."

Only one in the suggested list "illegal conditions," was checked by every agency replying. The other conditions, listed in order of number checking ran as follows:

Moral hazard	34
Health hazard	33
Accident hazard	29
Low wages	25
Long hours	23
Labor trouble	22
"Other"	8
Absence of educational content	3
Absence of promotional possibilities	3

It may be of interest to record here that the three agencies which did not check "moral hazard" included two public school placement bureaus, one of which recorded, comfortably, "covered by the child labor law," and a Y.W.C.A., the employment director of which wrote on the line indicated "Thank heaven everyone isn't weak!" Another agency sponsored by a community chest, which did check this item, qualified it by adding "in a good many cases."

Every item except "(c) illegal conditions" called forth comment from one agency or more. Since the comments throw significant light on the attitude of the agencies reporting, they are reproduced herewith:

a) and b) *"Absence of educational content" and of "promotional possibilities"*

"Perhaps" (would refuse to list); "seldom now due to lack of jobs"; "not these days."

d) *Long hours*

"Usually"; "If longer than the law allows"; "If illegal"; "If excessive"; "If exceedingly long"; "Not these days."

e) *Low wages*

"Usually"; "Sometimes"; "If very low"; "If excessive"; "Depending on capacity and need of girl and offsetting cultural advantages in employer's home" (from an agency placing house workers); "If much lower than the law allows; wages are shifting so rapidly that it is necessary to readjust our standards in regard to what are 'low wages' "; "Employers are informed that applicants will not accept such low wages. As a result the wage offer may be increased or job withdrawn"; "Something would be said to the employer"! One agency wrote, after both (*d*) and (*e*) "NRA"!

f) *Accident hazard*

"In some cases"; "For some people"; "Covered by Child Labor Law"; "Might tell applicant about job but would make hazard clear and would not urge placement."

g) *Health hazard*

All of the comments on accident hazard presented above were repeated with respect to health, and this in addition, would "put it up to the applicant."

h) *Moral hazard*

Comments quoted above.

i) *Labor trouble*

"Unless conditions favorable."

j) *Other (specify)*

Three said they would not place an applicant at "selling on a commission basis." Other conditions that would prevent listing were as follows:

"Unreasonable demands."
"Previous unsatisfactory experience, but not always, as conditions may have been corrected."
"If employer has made a practice of telling us one wage and then repeatedly offering applicant much less."
"Meanness of employer."

Further comments relating to the list as a whole were these:

Would list all jobs "if they are legitimate for the age child we have."
"Any one of above conditions might prevent our sending a particular candidate."
"We use blind alley jobs primarily as temporary measure until more suitable employment can be secured."

"There can be exceptions to all of these (by an agency which checked every one of the ten conditions).

"Attitude toward these topics is different with juniors than with adults. Would guard the junior but let the adult, if capable of a judgment herself make up her own mind. In all these cases except (*a*) ('absence of educational content')—and sometimes even then—we should discuss situation frankly with worker and employer. Illegal conditions we should list in order to report them"(by an agency which places adults as well as juniors).

CHAPTER XV

PLACING THE HANDICAPPED

For the purposes of this chapter a handicapped person is assumed to be one who on account of some physical or mental difficulty is confined to a narrower area of job activity than others, or finds it difficult to get a job because of a belief that he is so restricted, whether the belief is well founded or not. Included in this category are those with obvious physical handicaps, such as amputations or blindness, and those making use of conspicuous appliances, as well as those whose handicaps are not immediately obvious, such as cardiacs, the tuberculous, the hard-of-hearing, and those with mental difficulties or limitations.

This chapter is based upon the information derived from observation of the work of a half dozen agencies for placing different types of handicapped people, from conferences with placement workers in this field, from documents and reports and from eleven questionnaires returned from agencies placing the handicapped. As stated elsewhere, forty-four questionnaires were sent to agencies for the handicapped. Thirteen were returned, of which eleven could be used.[1]

Methods of Placing the Handicapped

All of the essentials of placement work that have been discussed in preceding chapters and that are set forth in Appendix B apply with equal force to the placing of the handicapped. There are, however, some additional essentials to successful achievement in the latter field. The first of these may be described as the necessity of discovering not only whether the applicant is fit for a particular job, but whether he is ready to do work of any sort. In a

[1] See Appendix I.

general sense, this is the same problem that confronts any placement worker, since he must in every case have some evidence of the fitness of an applicant for a job before referring him to it; but while the normal worker starts at scratch, the handicapped person starts somewhere further back, and the work of placement cannot even begin until he has somehow found his way to the starting point. To put it another way, when a normal person comes to an employment office there is reasonable ground for assuming that he is ready for some sort of job: when a handicapped person registers for work, that assumption is not justified and the facts must be ascertained.

In the ordinary employment office if evidence of fitness for work is not available, that is the end of the matter; the agency simply does not refer such an applicant for employment. In an agency for the handicapped, that may be the beginning of the matter, instead. If the trouble is that the applicant has not fully recovered from an injury or an illness, he may be referred to a clinic or otherwise helped to secure the necessary treatment. If the applicant lacks some necessary appliance, such as an artificial limb, or a hearing aid, the agency may assist him to secure it; some agencies have a loan fund for this purpose.

Sometimes the chief necessity is building up self-confidence in the applicant—a belief in his own ability to carry on. In an agency for the hard-of-hearing which we visited, the ability of the staff to do this is greatly enhanced by the fact that they, too, are hard-of-hearing. Having themselves overcome this difficulty, they are able to discuss the matter convincingly with others. Confidence is sometimes restored by a period of work in a sheltered workshop, such as that maintained by the Institute for the Crippled and Disabled in New York, or that of the American Rehabilitation Clinic.

A second characteristic of the agency in this field that

marks it off from others is the greater amount of counseling done. The paragraphs immediately preceding indicate that the placement interview in an office for the handicapped necessarily covers a wider range than is customary. In addition to the topics mentioned, there is much more of vocational counseling than in the general placement agency. The interviewer is deeply concerned about the occupational background of the applicant for it is likely to afford a clue to the plan that should be made for the future. The applicant suffering from a handicap which has developed since beginning his occupational career is apt to come to the agency believing that he must turn to some other occupational field. The interviewer may be able to discover means by which he may remain in the occupation for which his training and experience fit him. If a change must be made the previous occupation may have provided essential training for a new one. In either case the interviewer tries to build upon the previous work experience.

In the case of juniors who have not yet entered an occupation a specialized sort of vocational guidance is necessary. The interviewer's acquaintance with the areas within which persons having the handicaps under consideration have made satisfactory vocational adjustments, makes him an especially valuable counselor.

From the foregoing, it is evident that the office placing the handicapped is much more than a placement office. It is a case-working agency also, and its work is as much that of rehabilitation[2] as it is of placement. Not only is

---

[2] "In her daily work the placement secretary often meets other needs than placement. One applicant is in serious need of medical treatment or convalescent care; another has a family in distress; another is homeless, as his friends can no longer lodge him; another cannot even apply for a job until he gets shoes or a clean shirt; another needs help to get a reduction in alimony he pays his wife as even the prevailing wage in his line does not cover it; another is found to be eligible for the old age pension; another wants information on art schools where he can study at night. Such are a few of the many problems that the applicants present to the placement secretaries in their daily work of attempting to find jobs." *Annual Report Employment Center for the Handicapped, 1930–31,* New York.

this true with respect to counseling, it is equally marked with respect to the technique of placement. Much of the placement work of the agencies for the handicapped is a case by case matter. The agency must find a job that will fit not merely a man with a particular technique, it must find one for a handicapped man having that technique. The agency placing the nonhandicapped does not need to look for a job involving a minimum of stair climbing, but the agency placing cardiacs must.

The agencies for the handicapped must campaign among employers to break down the general prejudice that exists against all handicapped persons as employees. Consequently, very much more active solicitation of jobs is required than is the case in other agencies.

People often ask: How do you find any jobs for the handicapped? The answer is: By getting personally acquainted with employers, by constant telephone solicitation, answering advertisements, by letter or telephone in behalf of individual applicants, by circular letters about specially qualified ones to employers. Much direct solicitation of employers is necessary if any results are to be obtained. . . . Visiting of places of employment is an important phase of the work to interest employers to consider the handicapped and to learn the requirements of jobs and places.[3]

The following excerpt from a magazine article by two experts, one of whom is the director of the Employment Center for the Handicapped in New York City, emphasizes certain points of difference from the work of other agencies:

When the handicapped are ready to go to work, many, like their nonhandicapped friends, manage to secure jobs through friends or relatives. But the majority must rely upon other means—answering advertisements, direct application, or the general employment office. In such cases they are handicapped in their competition with the nonhandicapped. To get employment, the handicapped child needs special placement assistance—

[3] From annual report 1932–33, New York State Employment Service, Section for the Handicapped.

the visibly handicapped because of their appearance, and the others because of the special supervision they need in choice of work and work-place.

Whether such placement service is provided by the regular vocational counselor or junior placement worker or through special workers, there is need of special information and procedure.

The procedure followed in the Employment Center for the Handicapped in serving the younger group who apply there for employment may serve as an illustration. Each year, between 300 to 400 new applicants under 21 years of age register for help in securing work.

A careful first interview is given each applicant, who is questioned about his education, training, social history, experience at work, and handicap. A physician's statement with diagnosis, prognosis and work limitations is secured. In some cases school reports are obtained, and if there has been any work experience, references are secured from previous employers. The majority of the applicants under 21 are given a psychological examination, including general intelligence and mechanical aptitude tests. Those with commercial training are usually given a typing test.

Few of these young applicants have had any vocational training, and many of them have little conception of the kind of work they want or are able to do. Taking into account all the available information, the placement secretary tries to help the young person decide upon the general lines of work that may be most suitable. In most cases there are several possibilities to be tried. Realizing the limited training possibilities in industry for many of this group, the secretary makes every effort to stimulate the applicant's interest in vocational training and to direct him to available sources. The Bureau of Rehabilitation in the New York State Department of Education can provide further education and training for those over 16 years of age. Others are referred to the Institute for the Crippled and Disabled, which provides training in printing, welding, jewelry making, commercial art, leather crafts, and optical mechanics. Others are referred to the general educational institutions in the city. Such training is of vital importance to the handicapped, who must aim to be even better prepared than others in order to meet the severe scrutiny and close competition in industry.

It is occasionally necessary to refer applicants to the proper agencies for appliances, such as an artificial leg or brace, which will often help to overcome the physical limitation and give them a better chance of employment. If, as often happens, the applicant feels that he is unable to spend time in formal training, or if he has no interest in it but, first and foremost, wants a job, an attempt is made to place him in a job where he may have some opportunity to learn. Because of their eagerness to get a job when they have once left school, in spite of limited opportunities open to them, it is all the more important that training be obtained before they sever their school connections.

When a young person is considered ready and able to work, the placement secretary tries to secure suitable openings by visiting, telephoning and writing employers. Considerable time is given to visiting employers, to interest them in the employment of the handicapped and to explain how the latter may fit into various occupations. But most of the soliciting must be done on an individual basis for each particular applicant. The work qualifications of the applicant are emphasized with the employer, and the point made, for example, that even though he is lame, this does not interfere with ability to do the particular job. It has been found by experience better to talk in terms of a particular disability rather than generally of the handicapped, as this term apparently often suggests only the more severely handicapped persons, such as those who must use two crutches. An employer is never asked to take a handicapped person out of pity or charity but only because he is qualified to do a certain job as well as anyone else.[4]

Types of Agencies

There are three types of placement agencies dealing with the handicapped. First, there are specialized agencies handling specific types of handicap. Some of these are departments of social agencies that are concerned with the problem in a broader way, such as leagues for the hard-of-hearing, associations for the blind, etc. These agencies are so definitely allied with the organizations of which they are a part that placement does not assume an importance all its own but becomes a step in a process the objective

[4] Seville Mellar and Louise C. Odencrantz, "Vocations for the Handicapped." *Occupations—the Vocational Guidance Magazine*, October, 1933.

of which is rehabilitation.   Thus, we find a placement secretary in a league for the hard-of-hearing, devoting a part of her time to organizing classes in lip reading.   In such an organization the executive of the agency is often the director of placement and sometimes the only placement worker.   Such an executive, in an organization for the blind, writes:

Placement of blind people necessarily follows a different course than placement of juniors or others without a handicap. We do not have any regulations regarding recruiting jobs, employees and possible employers, but use common sense, case work, and personal knowledge of the individual, to do as good a job at placement as possible.

Specialized agencies exist also which are independent of other organizations, such as the Vocational Adjustment Bureau in New York which is concerned with girls manifesting nervous and mental difficulties.

A second type of organization in this field is the independent agency concerned with placing the handicapped in jobs, regardless of the nature of the handicap.   Not being a part of an organization for general rehabilitation, and not being concerned about any one type of handicap, these agencies are freer to devote themselves to placement in its strict sense, and thus they are more apt to take on the characteristics of general placement agencies.   Here, too, however, there is concern about the total well-being of the applicant, and the procedure and method of placement are influenced by that fact.   Typical of these agencies are handicapped divisions—where they exist—of public employment agencies or of school placement offices and agencies under private auspices such as the Placement Service for Handicapped People of Minneapolis.

The third type is found in the rehabilitation departments of the various states, working under the direction of the Vocational Rehabilitation Division of the Federal Board for Vocational Education. These departments are definitely concerned with placement only as a phase of rehabilitation. Most of them are organized as case-working, rather than as placement, agencies. Each worker carries a definite case load in which, at any given time, all stages of rehabilitation may be represented. The steps through which each client is taken are authoritatively described as involving six fundamental elements:

a) A survey of the case to serve as a basis for rehabilitation service; to establish the need for and to show what is to be accomplished through rehabilitation service in the case under consideration.
b) Guidance and assistance in the selection of a job objective.
c) Preparation for the job objective by physical restoration through surgery or artificial appliance, by training, or by counsel and advisement for adjustment in employment, or by combinations of these services.
d) Supervision and guidance through the entire process of rehabilitation.
e) Placement in employment upon completion of preparation.
f) Follow-up and guidance for a reasonable period after placement in order to insure the rehabilitation plan has been effective.[5]

The first four of these, it will be noted, involve the technique of vocational and educational counseling, the last two the technique of placement.

The eleven agencies placing the handicapped which answered our questionnaire included the first two types referred to above. No questionnaires were sent to rehabilitation bureaus on the ground that as primarily case-working agencies, their form of organization and methods would not be as significant in an analysis of the work of placement agencies as would those of organizations in which placement is the major objective. Their objective is seldom

[5] *Vocational Guidance*, in Rehabilitation Service Bulletin 148, "Vocational Rehabilitation Series," No. 20, Federal Board for Vocational Education, June, 1930, p. 24.

placement as such, but rehabilitation through intensive case work carried on over a considerable period of time, in which obtaining employment is one of many important elements and is not always accomplished by the bureau itself. Many workers in this field encourage the handicapped person to find his own job on the theory that such action on his part has a definite morale-building value.

Our eleven questionnaires were returned by five specialized, and six general, agencies. The specialized agencies included one handling mental and nervous cases, one handling the tuberculous and the cardiac, one dealing with the blind, and two with the deaf. The first two mentioned were independently organized agencies, the last three were departments of social agencies specializing in the field indicated. Of the six which were concerned with placing the handicapped generally, one operated under the auspices of a board of education, one was a division of a state employment service, two were divisions of social agencies, and two were independently organized.

These eleven agencies employed thirty-four full-time and three half-time workers, interviewed 9,925 applicants in the last fiscal year and made 3,038 placements. The following pages present information derived from the eleven questionnaires. Since all of the questions were stated and discussed in Chapters XII to XIV they are not, for the most part, repeated here. In most cases, also, the replies are stated briefly and without comment, their significance having been made evident in the preceding chapters.

Duties of Placement Workers

The replies to the question relative to duties brought out clearly the activities referred to above which are different from and additional to those common to all placement agencies. Nineteen individuals gave information on this point.   All mentioned the usual essential placement activities.   In addition, the following activities were mentioned by the number of persons indicated:

Coöperation with social agencies 10
Various health activities (including medical follow-up,
    "Securing medical data," referring for medical treatment, and "assisting doctor in otological clinic") . . 5
Case work 4
Home visits 4
Teaching lip reading 2
Planning special training courses 1
Verifying work records 1
Vocational counseling in schools for crippled 1

Excerpts from some of the replies to the question about duties in the questionnaire will serve to indicate how the placement of the handicapped both resembles and differs from the work of offices dealing with normal individuals.

The first is the statement of the executive of an agency with a small staff which places all types of handicapped.

The duties of the director, who is not only the executive officer in this bureau but is also the only field worker, are too numerous to report in detail.   However, the main duties grouped under three headings are as follows:

1. An average of about 15 percent of the time is devoted to directing the office work and to interviewing applicants who report at the office for conference.   The main object of these interviews is the evaluation of the applicant's native capacity, acquired ability, and personality for the purpose of classifying for proper placement.   Each candidate is listed for the jobs which it is believed he can perform efficiently and in which he can be employed satisfactorily.

2. About 5 percent of the time is devoted to visiting applicants in their own homes.   The purpose of these visits is to become better acquainted with the applicant to insure higher efficiency in his proper placement.   The home life of a worker frequently pictures his personality much more definitely than the office interview.   Some of this time is also devoted to checking-up the applicant through his friends or references.

3. Approximately 80 percent of the time is spent out in factories, offices, and shops of various kinds where some of the director-field-worker's duties are as follows:

a) To interpret the service to the employer, to acquaint him with our philosophy of proper placement, to inform him concerning the service we are prepared to render to him in his own business.

b) To observe workers in their performance of various jobs with a view to determining the motion and sense demands of the various jobs upon the worker.

c) To become acquainted with the working environment in various plants so as to render better service in the selecting of workers with suitable personality for maximum service in various positions.

d) To render follow-up service by visiting both workers and employers or foremen to secure definite first-hand information concerning the success of the worker as well as the suitability of the job to which the worker has been assigned.

The director of an independently organized agency for placing the handicapped reports her duties as follows:

Administrative—about 15 percent of time

Planning and organizing the work of the office—intake, methods of procedure, division of work, planning duties of each member of staff.

Financial; plan budget, approve expenditures, etc.

With Board, work out general policies of the center and branch offices; act as secretary to Board, prepare agenda, make recommendations as to policies of procedure, personnel policies.

Oversight of office—space, equipment, supplies.

Prepare monthly annual reports, and special reports.

Supervision of staff—about 55 percent

Selection of staff; training.

Supervision through frequent consultation on individual cases, reading records, staff meetings.

Recommend meetings and lectures to be attended; recommend reading material.

At staff meetings, work out policies, special difficulties, etc.

Supervision of clerical staff.

Publicity—about 10 percent
Prepare written material about the agency and general subject
of employment for the handicapped.
Make speeches.

Contact with other agencies—about 10 percent
Serving on various committees of the Welfare Council for the
Employment Section, Section for Crippled, Sheltered Work-
shops, Coördinating Committees, etc.
Working out methods of coöperation with other organizations
dealing with same applicants.

Miscellaneous activities—about 10 percent

A placement worker in the placement section for the
handicapped of a social agency reports that his day is
divided as follows:

8:30–12:15   Field work
1. Making new contacts with employers and renew-
ing old contacts to strengthen job possibilities.
2. Visit applicants' home: visits made with younger
group where training is being considered or
vocational guidance needed.
3. Follow-up on placements: visit employers within
a few days after placement and again one
month later before closing applicant's case.
4. Verifying work records with former employers
and visits for further references on character,
etc.
5. Conferences with relief, medical, and char-
acter-building agencies.

1:15– 2:30   Dictation—narrative-style case records

2:30– 5:00   Interviews
1. First interview.
2. Seeing old applicants: encouragement.
a. Vocational guidance.
b. Referral to financial, educational, recreational,
medical and job resources.
Clear with Social Service Exchange with possible
conferences with medical, relief and character-
building agencies.

Send applicant to job: telephone, telegraph, home visit.

The following is a statement of her principal duties by a placement worker in a League for the Hard-of-Hearing:

Taking employment applications.

Job solicitation by letter, phone and in person (not much of last named at present time).

Welfare work.

Vocational guidance of adults.

Vocational and educational guidance of juniors.

Lecture on vocational guidance of the hard-of-hearing, aural hygiene, etc.

Assist doctor in otological clinic.

Make group hearing tests in schools and individual tests on league premises.

Give hearing aid consultations.

Give information on all subjects relating to the handicapped.

Registering the Applicant

Most of the agencies for the handicapped do little or no recruiting of applicants; the problem is rather that of finding jobs. Any sort of publicity designed to interest employers is apt to bring in new applicants. Occasionally efforts are made to acquaint the handicapped with the facilities of the bureau and these take the form of letters to school counselors or other contacts with the schools, some use of radio and newspaper publicity. Applicants coming to the Employment Center for the Handicapped in New York are referred, in the majority of instances, by hospitals. Other sources from which applicants come are, in the order named, social agencies, schools, and employers.

When the applicant comes to the bureau he is greeted by a receptionist in only three of our eleven bureaus. In six of them he is received by the interviewer, in one by a psychologist and in one by the secretary to the executive. The application blank in agencies for the handicapped calls for information similar to that required in other agencies and in addition information relating to the disability. When and how did it occur, what sort of treatment, what appliances, etc.? What sort of work did applicant do before disability, and what after; what work is suitable, etc.? Some application blanks reserve space for a medical report, and some for a list of "agencies interested." The blank is filled out by the interviewer in five of the eleven agencies, by the applicant in three, by a clerk in two, and in one by the "social worker referring the applicant."

The interview is conducted in private in ten of the eleven agencies and takes about thirty minutes in a majority of the cases. The information available to the interviewer through other sources than the interview includes—for the younger applicants—the school record and teacher's estimate in eight agencies. The results of intelligence tests are available to six agencies, and two make their own tests. Four have the social history from the referring agency, four have a medical report.

There is no uniform practice among these agencies with regard to tests. The most common practice is to secure a medical report either from a physician on the staff of the agency or by referring the applicant to a clinic or a co-operating physician. Next to the medical report, an intelligence test is most frequently insisted upon though occasionally arrangements are made for trade tests, test of mechanical ability, aptitude, etc.

Nine of the agencies advise the applicant to return to school in cases where the circumstances seem to warrant it; one agency does not do so; and one did not answer. Since agencies placing the handicapped include adults of all ages, this question had less pertinence than in the case of the junior offices. A return to school doubtless means, to most of them, enrollment in training courses designed to aid a person made ineligible for his old job by illness or accident, to prepare for a new one.   Seven of the agencies when advising a return to school refer the applicant either to a social agency or to a scholarship fund—four of them checking both.   One does so "sometimes," one refers only to the state rehabilitation bureau though two others do so in addition to other referrals.   Two agencies did not reply to this question.

Eight agencies clear all cases with the Social Service Exchange, two clear "special cases" only.   One clears no cases.

All eleven agencies, as might be expected, advise applicants about training, and about vocational choices.   As in the case of the junior agencies (see Chapter XII) the word "advise" in this question caused some misgivings.   The director of one agency wrote "We guide rather than advise."

In answering the question about the primary purpose of the interview, four checked impartially both "vocational guidance" and "placement," four "placement" alone, and one "vocational guidance" alone.   Two stated that in the case of older persons placement was the primary objective and with the younger applicants it was guidance.

Referrals

Five agencies never refer more than one person to a job at the same time; three refer more than one; and the remaining three do so only if the employer wishes it.

The agencies placing all types of handicapped and two of the specialized agencies, one for the deaf and one for the cardiac and tuberculous, require references.   They are not required by the other three specialized agencies.

For verifying referrals three agencies depend upon the telephone alone, usually calling the employer the same day or within 24 hours.   One of them phones the applicant also. Two depend upon personal visits only.   Three use telephone and depend also on return of card. One relies on telephone, card and letter and one on card, telephone and letter in the order named. One uses the phone and writes letters to applicant.

Jobs are always investigated before referral by two agencies, "usually" by two, "sometimes" by one, and by one "if there is any question." Four investigate either before or immediately after. Only one agency makes no investigation, the director writing in answer to this question, "The personnel manager's word is enough."

All but one of the agencies solicit jobs for a particular applicant if none for which he is fitted is known at the time of his application. All send out for an applicant previously registered if a suitable job is discovered when he is absent from the office. Most of the agencies use the phone, send a telegram or a special delivery letter or even a messenger for this purpose. A messenger is usually sent by an agency for the hard-of-hearing since their clients cannot use the phone.

When an opening is reported for which two persons "equally qualified" have registered, six of the agencies will send out for the one registering first even though the second registrant is in the office at the time. Only one would send the applicant who happened to be present, as a matter of course. Two would send the one having the "greater need." Two did not answer this question.

Follow-up

If follow-up is desirable in the case of juniors in order to further "adjustment," it is doubly so in the case of the handicapped. In addition to the question of personal suitability to the particular job or work environment, there is the problem of the effect of the work upon the physical well-being of the worker. Necessarily, therefore, the follow-up work of agencies placing the handicapped is in part medical in character, as the following explanations of method show.

The first two statements are from agencies placing all types of handicapped; the third is from one dealing with cardiacs and the tuberculous.

1. Applicant is sent a letter with a post card enclosed, a month after he is placed, to find out how he is getting along, and inviting him to come in for an evening hour. We follow up also through clinics, especially for tuberculosis. Thereafter, applicants are followed up at longer intervals for vocational help and medical oversight.
2. Frequently follow-up is made by telephoning employers. Where there is any doubt of jobs being suitable to handicap (especially with cardiacs and arrested pulmonary tuberculosis patients) follow-up medical examinations are required.
3. Letters are sent to placed applicants to determine if job is suitable from a health point of view as well as other angles. If necessary, the employer is visited to make adjustment, if work proves unsuitable. A close contact is kept with clinic referring applicant to learn whether or not health declines or improves on job.

The special need of follow-up of the handicapped is indicated further in the statements of purpose given by the directors of these agencies. The usual objectives are mentioned such as desire to promote the economic progress and vocational adjustment of the individual, improve his relation with the employer, etc. Most of them stress also the need to discover the effect of the handicap and whether the job is appropriate in view of the worker's physical condition. Other purposes mentioned include discovery of whether the employer is satisfied, cultivation of his good will and finding new openings.

Finding the Job

As in the case of the junior offices, the most fruitful source of new jobs is found in visits to employers. All eleven agencies use that method. Nine use the telephone also, and eight use want ads. One office depends solely on visits, one on visits and ads, two on visits and telephone and seven use all three methods. Other methods used by a few of the agencies include letters to employers, publicity leaflets, newspaper articles, and contacts with organizations.

When orders are received from employers, most of them in the junior offices come over the telephone. In the handicapped offices most of them are secured personally through direct contact with the employer. The other sources, ranged in descending order, are telephone, employer calling; telephone, office calling employer; and incoming mail. Telephone orders are received by the interviewer in nine of the offices. In one the director of the office receives them and one office gave no information.

Visiting Places of Employment

Every one of the eleven agencies reporting stated that interviewers visit places of employment, though one replied in answer to the request for the proportion of time given to this purpose, "practically none at present." The replies from the others indicated a range from 15 to 80 percent of the interviewers time given to such visits. The general offices seemed to give more time to visits than the others, though an agency for the tuberculous and cardiac reported two-thirds of the interviewers' time and one placing the blind wrote "as much time as it requires."

The chief reason for visiting places of employment is job solicitation, every one of the eleven agencies mentioning that purpose. Ten mention follow-up as a purpose of the visit. Nine speak of "investigation" or "job analysis." Other purposes specifically mentioned were to "strengthen the position of the handicapped," "adjustment of differences," "adjustment, at the request of the employer," and "to go with the applicant, who is deaf and timid."

The Agency and Conditions of Employment

Ten of the eleven agencies answered the question "Do you list all jobs offered?" Six answered affirmatively and four in the negative. As in the case of the junior agencies, however, all who stated that they do list all jobs indicated in answer to the next question certain conditions that would cause them to refuse to do so. This question was, as a reference to Appendix A or Chapter XIV will reveal:

Would any of the following conditions lead you to refuse to list a job?
a) Absence of educational content
b) Absence of promotional possibilities
c) Illegal condition
d) Long hours
e) Low wages
f) Accident hazard
g) Health hazard
h) Moral hazard
i) Labor trouble
j) Other (specify)

This question was answered by ten agencies. The one not replying had answered "no" to the preceding question. "Do you list all jobs offered?"

None of the ten checked either (*a*) or (*b*), and only one checked (*j*) "Other," indicating that he would not list a job for a "dishonest employer." This left seven items which received the greater amount of attention. Two of these items "Illegal conditions" and "Moral hazard" were checked by every one of the ten. Two items "Accident hazard" and "Health hazard" were checked nine times. Five checked "Labor trouble." "Long hours" and "Low wages" were each checked three times.

In addition, certain items were checked with qualifications. One executive indicated that he would not list a job with long hours "for certain types." Another checked "Long hours" with the qualification that he would refuse to list such a job only for cardiacs and arrested tuberculosis cases. "Others allowed to choose for themselves."

One checked "Low wages" but added "Would let applicant decide if health not involved." After "Labor trouble" another wrote "Would state case and let applicant decide." One director who checked only "Illegal conditions" and "Moral hazard" added the following: "We only place in factories where conditions are good. But there are almost always long hours and low wages; sometimes 'illegal conditions' as far as hours go." This is the executive referred to above who does not investigate jobs since "the personnel manager's word is good enough."

CHAPTER XVI

QUALIFICATIONS AND CONDITIONS OF WORK

Placement workers, when writing of their problems, have not been quite as articulate about qualifications as the vocational counselors have been. When they have expressed themselves, however, they have placed the requirements on a high level. This is illustrated by excerpts from two addresses given at the 17th annual meeting of the International Association of Employment Offices, September, 1929. Sidney W. Wilcox, then of the Department of Labor of Illinois, now of the U. S. Department of Labor, said:

The placement officer should have an effective knowledge of machines and processes, occupations and industries, job specifications and the kaleidoscopic changes that are taking place in them; he should know which are blind-alley occupations and which will lead to the portals of the future; he should be able to understand and even to forecast fundamental economic conditions, not merely in the aggregate, but industry by industry and even firm by firm; he must know the firms, likewise, according to their personal policies, whether they are enlightened or benighted; he should know and have the confidence of their personnel officers or employment managers; he must be wise to all the devices, good and bad, of the employment game. . . . The placement clerk must know languages and racial characteristics.[1]

Another speaker offered the following as essential qualifications.

Employment men should be personnel men. Personnel men should be among the highest types of men to be found—well-met, personable, keen, thoroughly trained, psychologists. . . . (The employment man) must be a psychologist and know something of mental hygiene. He must be able to measure the intelligence and aptitudes of those seeking employment. This implies that he must be familiar with the field of psychology,

[1] U. S. Bureau of Labor Statistics, Bulletin 538, p. 95.

both general and applied, and must be familiar with the field of tests, both of intelligence and aptitudes. . . .

The employment worker must also know the occupations in which men engage; he should have special training in studying occupations and should have read much about them. Moreover, he should have had experience that has brought him in intimate personal contact with industry. He should have had experience in surveying industries, in order that he may have a real knowledge of what should be looked for in studying a vocation. He must know the advantages and disadvantages, the income, the opportunities for advancement, the special qualifications needed, and the training desirable. . . . He must be acquainted with methods of occupational research. . . .

As to educational background and training the speaker suggested that the placement worker should have:

The equivalent of graduation from a recognized college, with emphasis on the following fields:
He must have adequate training in English; broad training in the social sciences, especially in sociology, economics, psychology, both general and applied, and mental hygiene; the field of testing. He should have at least one general information course in the vocational guidance or the personnel movement, followed by work in vocational information and courses in vocational counseling.[2]

Required Qualifications

Our questionnaire sent to directors of offices asked what experience is required of new staff members. Two said they do not have new staff members any more! Five reported that no definite requirements had been formulated, one answer was not clear, and fifteen did not answer, leaving twenty-six which gave some information.[3] The answers are so lacking in uniformity that it is hard to give their substance. However, the types of experience mentioned as desirable, listed in order of frequency were:

[2] F. G. Davis, *Ibid.*, pp. 107, 108–9.
[3] In this chapter all types of agencies studied are considered together. Consequently the total number of agencies replying to the questionnaire is 49.

Social work, or specifically, case work 9
Industrial experience, including personnel work 5
Business or office experience 4
Training in same organization 4
Teaching 4
Placement or counseling experience 3

Other replies were so individual that nothing but direct quotation would serve to indicate their character. A few of the more significant replies follow:

This from a Y.W.C.A. placement department:

Exceptionally well-trained workers have been accepted with no experience. We give it to them here under supervision. Have had training seminars, discussions of office technique, of books on subjects covered in the bureau, placement, psychological testing, case work, etc. Education and training requirements for the job? College graduate or equivalent, with sociology, economics, psychology, case work or business experience (if progressive business) taken as additional asset.

In this case, in addition to these requirements there is a "very careful interview for the job, and careful consideration of credentials. Performance reviewed each year, growth or lack of it, noted."

The director of a public school placement agency mentions as requirements for new staff members, "Several years in meeting and dealing with people: (a) teaching, (b) counseling, or (c) office management in a department within a large organization, or combination of all three."

In an agency supported by a community chest new staff members "must have had psychology and sociology and be interested in people. Must have a great deal of personality and college training."

On the other hand, in an office conducted under the direction of a state department of labor "civil service regulations vary with the title. Assistant supervisors (the beginning job) can start with no placement experience whatever. Junior placement counselors are all people of considerable placement or industrial experience."

In most of the agencies attached to public school systems, placement workers are expected to meet the requirements for teaching positions, including the holding of teachers' certificates. The only exceptions specifically noted are Chicago, where the placement workers in the Vocational Guidance Department were required to meet the same requirements as school counselors and Philadelphia where the employment supervisors in the Junior Employment Service are subject to civil service examinations.

In general, civil service requirements for school placement workers are more rigorous than for workers in public employment offices under state auspices. In Chicago, as stated, the requirements for a school placement worker included college background with special designated courses together with related experience definitely outlined. In the Illinois state service the requirements for a placement clerk are "education equivalent to two years high school work, preferably with experience in placement work." For the higher positions no educational requirements whatever are laid down and the experience requirements are vaguely stated. The superintendent of an office and a department superintendent are expected to have "experience in soliciting for employment agencies, or selecting applicants for positions; administrative ability." The general superintendent besides having administrative ability must have had "experience with employees and employers" and "familiarity with labor conditions," and the chief of division is required to have "familiarity with laws and regulations administered by the Department of Labor; special experience in free employment work and management of a large office."

Civil service requirements in Ohio for the position of superintendent and assistant superintendent of a public employment office are somewhat more definite than in Illinois as to experience but contain no provision as to educational training. The superintendent must have "at least four years of experience in employment work, or such equivalent experience as would indicate ability to perform the duties of the position." The requirements for assistant superintendent include two years experience rather than four, but otherwise are the same. In a report on a study of employment agencies in Cincinnati made a few years ago, the following comment on these requirements is made:

The alternative to four or two years of employment-office experience is a very general one, possible of a broad interpretation. Contrasted with the City Civil Service Commission's requirements for work of a somewhat similar nature, the standard set by the State Commission seems rather indefinite.

For instance, the minimum qualifications demanded by the City Civil Service Commission for the position of Supervisor of Social Service, in connection with the Department of Public Welfare, are:

Education equivalent to that represented by graduation from a university of recognized standing, with specialization in social sciences; four years of responsible experience in social service, case and office work; good knowledge of modern social service practice; supervisory ability; sympathetic understanding of human nature; tact; good judgment; and good address. . . .

The minimum qualifications necessary to take the city examination for Senior Social Investigator, another somewhat comparable position, are:

Education equivalent to that represented by graduation from a university of recognized standing, with specialization in social science, or from an accredited school of civics and philanthropy; two years of successful experience in social service case work; sympathetic understanding of human nature; firmness; tact; initiative; good judgment; and good address.[4]

In New York State, workers in the Division of Junior Placement must be high school graduates.[5] In the Voca-

[4] Frances R. Whitney, Employment Agencies in Cincinnati, 1928. Published by the Consumers' League of Cincinnati.

[5] Though many of them are college graduates with professional training.

tional Service for Juniors of New York City, the most prominent service in that field under private auspices, placement workers must have a college degree or the equivalent.

Education and Experience

The qualifications actually possessed by the placement workers covered in our study, were, in the main, much beyond civil service requirements. The forty-nine agencies replying to our questionnaire reported on the educational status of 124 staff members. Of these, ninety-one were graduates of colleges; seven had had two or more years in college, but were not graduates; one was a graduate of a normal school; twenty-four were graduates of high schools but did not go to college; and in one case educational experience was not clearly stated.

An inquiry covering this point in the questionnaire answered by individuals brought replies from eighty-five indicating that sixty were graduates of colleges; twelve had had two or more years in college but were not graduates; six had attended college—years not stated; three were high school graduates and had attended normal schools; one was a high school graduate and had gone to business college one year; and three were high school graduates only. In addition, one of the above had the degree of doctor of education, twenty-one had master's degrees; four were graduates of a school of social work; twelve had attended schools of social work; twenty-five had taken other graduate courses; two had law degrees; and one had attended law school.

Ninety-eight placement workers gave a list of the positions held since leaving school and most of them gave the number of years in each position. The following table includes all the positions held by more than one person, and the number of persons holding each position the speci-

fied number of years. Each job is recorded as many times
as it was mentioned, and since most of the persons replying
had held more than one job the number of jobs recorded is
greater than the number of persons replying.

POSITION	YEARS					
	1–5	6–10	11–15	16–20	YEARS NOT STATED	TOTAL
Teaching in public schools						
a) Academic	21	13	7	3	1	45
b) Shop or vocational	3	3	1	..	..	7
Personnel work	10	2	..	..	1	13
Placement work	7	3	1	..	..	11
Case work	7	..	1	..	..	8
Y.W.C.A.	5	1	..	1	..	7
Research	6	..	..	..	..	6
Business	2	3	..	..	..	5
Office work	4	..	1	..	..	5
Salesman	5	..	..	..	..	5
Attendance office . . .	4	..	..	..	..	4
Principal	3	1	..	..	..	4
Stenographer	4	1	..	..	..	5
Red Cross	4	..	..	..	..	4
U. S. Children's Bur. .	4	..	..	..	..	4
Clerk	3	..	..	..	..	3
Editorial work	2	..	1	..	..	3
Farming	3	..	..	..	..	3
Instructor—college . .	3	..	..	..	..	3
Secretarial work	2	..	1	..	..	3
Bookkeeper	2	..	..	..	..	2
Industrial work	1	..	..	1	..	2
Psychologist	1	1	..	..	..	2
Supervisor industrial arts	1	..	..	1	..	2
Telephone operator . .	1	1	..	..	..	2
Vocational counselor . .	1	1	..	..	..	2
Social investigator . . .	2	..	..	..	..	2

The following includes positions mentioned by only one person each, arranged according to duration of time.

ONE YEAR

Agent, Division of Minor Wards, State of Massachusetts
Assistant to manager
"Bell hop"
Footman and horse trainer
"Industrial work"
Inspector under the British Unemployment Insurance Act
Law clerk
Pageant director
R.R. caller
Visiting teacher

ONE AND ONE-HALF YEARS

Adjustor, surety company
Manager, apartment house
Marine corps

TWO YEARS

Assistant, field-work department, school of social work
Credit manager
Manufacturing
Office manager
Supervisor of apprentices
Swimming instructor
Veteran's Bureau

TWO AND ONE-HALF YEARS

Aviator
Delivery boy
Engineering work
Supervisor, substitute teachers

THREE YEARS

Chauffeur
Promoting school bank
Superintendent of schools
Secretary women's industrial club

FOUR YEARS

Personnel director, public school
Practicing law
Staff, State Board of Public Welfare
Rehabilitation work
Lecturer and public-relations supervisor, Telephone Co.

FIVE YEARS

Counselor
Coachman
Secretary, Consumers' League
U. S. Women's Bureau

SIX YEARS

Certification office
Claim agent
Free lance writing
Secretary life insurance company
Statistician

SEVEN YEARS

Settlement work
Clerk, Income Tax Bureau

EIGHT YEARS

Efficiency manager, department store

NINE YEARS	FIFTEEN YEARS
Principal, automotive engineering school	Machinist

	YEARS NOT STATED
TEN YEARS	Carpenter
Laboratory technician	Construction foreman

Eighty persons gave also the number of years they have occupied their present positions in placement work. They ranged as follows:

NUMBER OF YEARS	NUMBER OF PERSONS
1	3
2	9
3	10
4	10
5	14
6	8
7	7
8	4
9	2
10	2
11	4
12	3
14	2
15	2

Working Hours

Eighty-three placement workers gave their daily hours of work, exclusive of lunch. They ran as follows:

NUMBER OF HOURS	NUMBER OF PERSONS REPORTING
6	14
6–7	1
7	35
7–8	22
8	6
8–9	4
12	1

The above represent the first five days of the working week. Seventy-eight workers reported their Saturday hours as follows:

NUMBER OF HOURS	NUMBER OF PERSONS REPORTING
None	4
3	32
3–4	18
4	20
4½–7	3
"Every 3d Saturday evening"	1

Of eighty-two workers in placement offices reporting on the length of the lunch hour, seventy-two had one hour, six had from 1¼ to 1½ hours, three had a half hour, and one reported no time.

One hears much talk about overtime among placement workers. Two questions were asked on this point. One asked for the amount of overtime in the week preceding the day on which the question was answered, the other asked for the average amount of overtime required. Fifty-four replied to the first question, and sixty-nine to the second. The two following tables summarize the replies:

OVERTIME IN PRECEDING WEEK

NUMBER OF HOURS	NUMBER OF PERSONS REPORTING
None	8
1–2	7
2–3	17
3–4	13
4–5	2
5–6	3
9	1
11	1
16	1
3 evenings	1

AVERAGE OVERTIME

HOURS PER WEEK	NUMBER OF PERSONS REPORTING
None	6
1 or less	2
1– 2	12
2– 4	21
3– 6	1
4– 6	5
6– 8	2
8–10	2

One reported "three evenings" a week; four "very little" or "occasionally"; eight indicated varying schedules of overtime without stating the amount; two said they had "much" overtime, one had kept no record and two replied "cannot estimate."

One in charge of a placement agency for the hard-of-hearing, who reported a regular twelve-hour day said, with respect to overtime—"I spend practically all my time at this work, but am not overworked. I work Sunday also, frequently."

Seventy-five out of eighty replying had vacations with pay as follows:

VACATION PERIOD	NUMBER OF PERSONS REPORTING
2 weeks	9
3 weeks	9
4 weeks	7
5 weeks	4
6 weeks	1
7 weeks	1
8 weeks	14
11 weeks	1
12 weeks	1
1 month	24
1½ months	1
2 months	3

Of five who had vacations without pay, one had eighteen working days, one had twelve weeks and three had one month.

Three of those who said they had two weeks' vacation reported that until 1930 the vacation period was one month. Those who now have vacations without pay had substantial vacations with pay before 1931.

Nineteen directors of employment offices reported their present salaries as follows:

SALARY	NUMBER RECEIVING
$1,200	1
1,800	1
2,000–2,499	5
2,500–2,999	2
3,000–3,499	4
3,500–3,999	2
4,000–4,499	2
4,500–4,999	1
5,000	1

One director wrote in April, 1933, "Haven't had any salary since January, 1933."

Several indicated that present salaries are below the level of 1929 or 1930. One receiving $2,100 before the depression is now getting $1,800. Other reductions mentioned were from $2,280 to $2,107; from $3,000 to $2,565; and from $5,100 to $4,531. Doubtless other reductions took place but were not mentioned. One stated that his salary of $3,068 was to be in effect "until a new and lower schedule is adopted."

Only eleven of the twenty directors indicated the maximum salary for their positions. These were as follows: $2,100; $2,500; $2,640; $3,000 (which was the maximum in three cases); $3,600; $4,000 (which was the maximum in two cases); $5,000; and $5,400.

Only two of those reporting were actually receiving the maximum—one of whom received $4,000, the other $5,000.

Fifty-nine placement secretaries gave information about their pay. Salaries received at present were as follows:

SALARY	NUMBER OF PERSONS
Under $900 (876)	1
900–999	2
1,000–1,499	9
1,500–1,999	15
2,000–2,499	8
2,500–2,999	16
3,000–3,499	8

Sixteen of these stated that their salaries had been reduced since the depression:

PRE-DEPRESSION SALARY	REDUCED SALARY
$1,600	$1,172
1,800	1,378
2,100	1,700
2,100	1,995
2,200	1,500
2,250	2,025
2,300	2,231
2,400	2,100
2,650	2,400
2,800	2,520
3,000 (two)	2,700
3,000	2,800
3,300	2,805
3,600	2,736
3,800	2,888

The maximum rate possible was reported on in thirty-six cases. These maximum rates ranged from $1,500 to $3,300. In detail they were as follows:

MAXIMUM RATE	NUMBER OF CASES
$1,500	1
1,740	1
1,800	6
2,000	2
2,100	3
2,640	2
2,650	1
2,700	2
2,800	1
3,000	2
3,200	12
3,250	1
3,300	2

In only nine cases was the present salary equal to the maximum. This was true of one case where the maximum salary was $1,800; in two cases where the salary was $2,640; in one case when it was $2,700; and in five cases where it was $3,200.

APPENDICES

Part One: Counseling

APPENDIX A

METHOD USED IN COUNSELING STUDY

As stated in the Foreword, this study of counseling included about six months devoted to interviews with school executives, directors of guidance organizations and counselors in the schools, coupled with direct observation of the work. This was followed by the sending out of questionnaires in the following manner.

A list of cities was made up from the census of population which included: (a) all cities of 150,000 population or over; (b) all cities having 25,000 to 100,000; (c) the largest city in each state having no city with as many as 25,0c0 inhabitants.

The following letter was then sent to the Superintendent of Schools in each city, excepting those covered in the field study:

Dear Sir:

The American Association of Social Workers, a professional organization covering the entire country, is making a series of job analyses in different fields of social work and in allied fields. I have been asked to make such an analysis of positions in the field of vocational guidance. I am writing you therefore to ask if you will be kind enough to give me the following information:—

A. The name and address of the person in charge of guidance activities in your school system—
   or, (if there be no centralized organization)
B. The names and addresses of all persons in your schools giving 25% or more of their time to vocational guidance activities.

If you will be kind enough to give me these names it will enable me to send them a brief questionnaire concerning their activities.

I shall greatly appreciate your coöperation in this study.

Yours very truly,

(Signed) John A. Fitch.

Letters were sent to 154 superintendents and replies were received from 83. A few, of course, stated that no vocational guidance activities were being conducted in their schools, but most of them gave the names of persons doing counseling. Additional names were secured by writing letters to secretaries of regional vocational guidance associations as listed in the *Vocational Guidance Magazine*. As a result letters were sent to sixty-seven persons said to be directors of guidance activities, enclosing a questionnaire (see page 200), intended for directors. Replies were received from twenty-eight, seventeen of which were used for tabulation.

The directors were asked to give additional names of counselors, and altogether 256 names were secured either from superintendents or directors of guidance. To these, the counselor's questionnaire (see page 201) was sent with the following letter:

Dear........................:

The American Association of Social Workers, a professional organization, covering the entire country, is making a series of job analyses in different fields of social work and in allied fields. As a member of the teaching staff of the New York School of Social Work, I have been asked to make such an analysis of positions in the field of vocational guidance. I am visiting as many cities as it is possible for me to cover and obtain the information in person. I cannot, however, cover a very wide territory in that way. I am trying therefore to make the study more representative by sending out questionnaires to cities I cannot visit.

I should appreciate it very much if you would be willing to fill out the enclosed questionnaire and return to me as soon as it is convenient.

Yours very truly,
(Signed) JOHN A. FITCH.

Replies were received from 126 counselors, 105 of which were found to be usable.

Altogether, then, questionnaires were sent out to 323 individuals, counting both counselors and directors. Total replies numbered 154, about 48 percent of the total number. Of these, 122, or 79 percent of all questionnaires received, could be used.

Replies were received from one or more localities in forty-five states. The questionnaires that are used in this study were returned from twenty-two states and represented forty-six cities, as follows:

Alabama	*Connecticut*	*Indiana*
Montgomery	New Haven	East Chicago
Pine Level		Richmond
	Georgia	South Bend
California	Atlanta	
Berkeley		*Kansas*
Long Beach	*Illinois*	Topeka
Los Angeles	Joliet	
Oakland		*Kentucky*
Pasadena		Louisville

Louisiana	*New Jersey*	*Ohio*
New Orleans	Bayonne	Cleveland[a]
	Newark	Dayton
Maryland	New Brunswick	Toledo
Baltimore		
	North Carolina	*Pennsylvania*
Massachusetts	Charlotte	Johnstown
Boston[a]	Durham	Wilkes-Barre
	Winston-Salem	
Minnesota		*Washington*
Minneapolis	*New York*	Seattle
	Jamestown	
Michigan	Kingston	*Wisconsin*
Kalamazoo	New Rochelle	Appleton
	Schenectady	Cudahy
Missouri	Rochester[a]	La Crosse
St. Louis		Madison
		Milwaukee[a]
Nebraska		Sheboygan
Lincoln		West Allis

When the cities visited in the field study and the states in which they are located are taken into account, it is evident that the information on which this report is based has been gathered from fifty-one cities scattered through twenty-two states. The distribution by sections is as follows:

South	*Mid-West*
Alabama	Illinois
Georgia	Indiana
Kentucky	Michigan
Louisiana	Ohio
Maryland	Wisconsin
North Carolina	*West*
	Kansas
East	Minnesota
	Missouri
Connecticut	Nebraska
Massachusetts	
New Jersey	*Far West*
New York	California
Pennsylvania	Washington

[a] A small number of questionnaires were received from these cities which were also visited.

Questionnaire Sent to Directors of Centralized Systems of Vocational Guidance

STUDY OF VOCATIONAL GUIDANCE UNDER AUSPICES OF
AMERICAN ASSOCIATION OF SOCIAL WORKERS
AND
NEW YORK SCHOOL OF SOCIAL WORK

(Information asked for on this sheet is desired from director of vocational guidance or Board of Education)

Date...

1. Name and position of person answering these questions....................
....
2. City..
3. Is there a central organization for vocational guidance?.......................
4. What are its principal functions. (Include organization chart if possible)..
....
....
....
....
....

5. Please fill in information called for in following table.

	NUMBER OF SCHOOLS	NUMBER OF SCHOOLS IN WHICH COUNSELING IS DONE	NUMBER OF COUNSELORS		
			Giving Full Time	Giving Half Time	Giving Quarter Time
High Schools					
Jr. High Schools					
Elementary Schools					
Continuation Schools					
Trade Schools					

6. Do Counselors make occupational studies?
7. If there is a staff for making occupational studies, how many persons
   a) Are giving full time to the work?..
   b) Are giving part time to the work?...
8. Is there a placement office conducted under auspices of school system?..
   How many on staff?..
9. Qualifications required for counselors
   Education..
   Experience...
   Other...
10. Are qualifications for placement and occupational research workers different?..
    If so, please indicate...
11. Total Working hours required (exclusive of lunch):
    Daily..
    Saturday (if different)..
    Overtime (if any)...
12. What is the policy as to vacations?...
13. What is the policy as to sick leave?..
14. Are there provisions for a retirement pension?.....................................
15. To whom are counselors administratively responsible?.......................
16. What is the beginning salary for each grade of work?.......................
17. What provision is there for salary increases?....................................
18. Present salary of each member of staff..

Questionnaire Sent to Individual Counselors

STUDY OF VOCATIONAL GUIDANCE UNDER AUSPICES OF AMERICAN ASSOCIATION OF SOCIAL WORKERS
AND
NEW YORK SCHOOL OF SOCIAL WORK

(Information asked for on this sheet is desired from individual counselors, placement secretaries, research workers, et cetera.)

Date..

1. Name...
2. City...
3. Position...
4. What are your principal duties?..
....
....
....
....
....
....

5. Do you teach classes in occupations?...

6. Do you interview parents?..
    If so, where?...
    What proportion of all parents do you interview?..........................

7. To what extent do you have contact with social agencies?...............

8. Do you make plant visits or occupational surveys?..........................

9. Do you administer
    a) Aptitude tests...
    b) Psychological tests..

10. What proportion of your working time is given to—
    a) Group counseling...
    b) Individual counseling...
    c) Placement...
    d) Obtaining occupational information...
    e) Other (specify)..

11. Do you have a separate office with privacy for interviewing?..............

12. Do you have clerical assistance?...

13. To whom in the school system are you responsible?...........................

14. What schools (high school, college, normal school, university) have you attended? (Please indicate year of graduation and degrees)
....
....

15. Name any specific courses that have contributed to your understanding of the requirements of your present position...........................
....
....

16. In which of the following fields have you had courses?
    Economics..
    Sociology..
    Psychology...
    Labor Problems...
    Vocational Guidance...

17. Please enumerate all the different positions you have held since leaving school and indicate the length of time spent in each..................
....
....

18. Please name any professional or semi-professional organizations in which you hold membership...
....
....

APPENDIX B

DUTIES OF COUNSELORS

In Chapter III the duties of counselors were set forth as they were revealed by the questionnaire and the field study. Here are presented somewhat formal statements of purpose and practice drawn up by vocational guidance practitioners.

I. Below is a descriptive statement drawn up by the vocational advisers[1] in the junior high schools of Chicago, and used by them as a guide until their work was ended in 1933. This statement, mentioning duties in order of sequence, together with some description of method, gives meaning and significance to the classified list of activities in Chapter IV. It is typical of the work done in the better organized guidance systems.

DUTIES OF VOCATIONAL ADVISERS IN JUNIOR HIGH SCHOOLS

1. Contacts with entering pupils

Forming contacts with students at the time of entrance constitutes one of the duties of the Vocational Adviser in some of the schools. At the close of the semester classification tests are given at the contributing elementary schools to 6A pupils who expect to enter Junior High School. Four of the advisers assist in this function. The process includes (1) giving and grading of tests, and (2) recording scores on office test cards.

When the new semester opens there are always other pupils to be tested who were not present when the tests were given at the elementary schools as well as many pupils in all grades entering by transfer from various schools. These are all interviewed and tested by the adviser and if the child is above 7th grade, advice is given as to his choice of course. Children entering during the semester are likewise tested and counselled. For irregular pupils special programs must be arranged and these are recommended by the adviser. Personnel cards are filled out—usually by the adviser—at the time of entrance and problems uncovered through the interviews are followed up.

2. 7A Counselling

In the Junior High School choice of course is made in the 7A grade for the ensuing years. All but two of the advisers supervise this work. In these two schools usually a class period is devoted to explaining the courses in each 7A room. A few advisers talk to the whole grade in assembly, although the smaller group method seems more satisfactory

[1] Counselors in the Chicago schools were known as vocational advisers.

because chart materials can be used and more time is available for individual questions.

Letters of explanation are then sent to the parents and a reply required for each child, indicating the course chosen, the amount and type of education the parents expect to give their children, and the vocation in which the child is interested—if any interest has been shown.

Personnel records are filled out for each child. Five advisers have the records filled out wholly or partly by the child. The rest of the advisers fill out the records themselves. The cards contain the family history, out of school history, school history, including grades received and results of various classification tests, school activities, vocational interests, course chosen, and educational plans.

The children are then interviewed individually. Three advisers make a practice of interviewing every 7A child, while others see only those that seem to need further advice, such as:

(1) All pupils expecting to leave at the end of Junior High School.
(2) All pupils contemplating 2 year High School courses and whose scholarship record and economic status would warrant a 4 year course.
(3) All children with low I.Q.'s and poor scholarship records who should take practical training.
(4) All other cases where there is a discrepancy between the child's occupational interests, special abilities, and the course chosen.

Parents are urged to come to the school, and at times visits are made to the home before the course is finally decided upon.

The results are tabulated and reports are sent to each division room teacher, showing the course each child is to take and a summary is sent to the Assistant Principal to be used as a basis for the school program for the following year.

3. *Change of Courses*

The problem of change of courses occurs in all Junior High Schools. The Vocational Adviser is called in on the cases and is given partial, and in some schools, complete authority in allowing or refusing the request. Changes are made only after thorough investigation.

4. *9A Counselling*

The routine of counselling makes it probable that each child will be interviewed twice during his stay in Junior High School. He was counselled when his selection of Junior High School course was made in 7A, and his second certain contact is made when he is interviewed in 9A concerning his selection of course for Senior High School. If the course was properly chosen in 7A and there have been no changes, there should be little difficulty in articulating in 9A.

The interviewing of 9A pupils concerning High School courses is a universal function for all Junior High School advisers. In half of the schools, personnel cards are filled out by the advisers. In the rest, they are filled out by the pupils and the scholarship and test materials added by the adviser. Filling out of personnel records by the pupils is sometimes done in English classes as a lesson in the correct method of answering questionnaires.

The personnel card is filled out by the pupils early in the semester and the pupils interviewed individually before the applications are required for High School. About the 14th week, a Vocational Guidance Week is planned in some of the schools. Speakers are engaged to stimulate interest in going on to school and representatives from the Senior High Schools are brought to the Junior High Schools to explain their activities. High school courses are explained either in the classrooms or in class assembly—usually in classrooms—by the adviser. At this time materials are sent home to the parents including: (1) a booklet explaining High School courses, (2) application blanks to be filled out indicating the course chosen, (3) a letter from the Superintendent of Schools explaining what is expected of the children in Senior High School, (4) and some advisers include a personal letter from the school inviting the parents to consult with the adviser before making the selection. In two schools electives are chosen and children are programmed in advance. In one school children try out for musical organizations and are assigned to rooms and seats in advance. One adviser gives tests which are required by the Senior High School.

Children who are not going to High School are followed up and certificated for work or helped to secure employment.

5. *Occupational information*

Although the method of presenting occupational information varies in the different schools, each adviser is conducting a program which reaches the students individually or in groups. In this work, coöperation with the classroom teacher has been secured. In most cases the adviser works with the social studies classes, particularly during that part of the term in which the course requires a study of occupations.

Group Work
1. Talks on specific occupations by advisers to classes.
2. Information on reference sources given to classes.
3. Trips to industrial establishments taken or arranged for.
4. Occupational themes assigned in English classes.
5. Posters made in art classes.
6. Since the work comes at a specific time in the social studies program, some advisers organize a "Vocational Guidance Week," and give special emphasis to furnishing groups with occupational information at this time by displaying poster work, securing outside speakers or vocational films for junior and senior assembly, arranging for articles in the school paper by

pupils or by the adviser, and for trips for the occupations classes. Those who do not have a "Vocational Guidance Week," as well as those who do, conduct a program of this sort running through the term.

7. In two schools, the advisers sponsor Occupations Clubs which meet once a week during the "club" period of a half hour to consider vocational matters.

8. Practically all of the advisers confer with the school librarian in selecting books for the library and in most cases supply bibliographies for the librarian. In some schools a special shelf is reserved for vocational books and reference material.

Individual Work

The adviser maintains her own supply of pamphlet, book, and magazine material, occupational studies and leaflets published by the Vocational Guidance Bureau and those collected from other cities which she gives or loans to individual pupils.

In four schools the adviser consults with individual pupils about choosing the subjects for their career books, planning them, and about methods of securing material and first-hand information about the occupation they have chosen to study.

6. *Subject failures*

All of the Junior High School advisers do some case work with pupils who are failing. The groups dealt with vary from school to school. For example:

1. The Seven B's, because they have just come to the school and maladjustments are to be guarded against.

2. The Eight B's, because they have just begun a new course and may run into difficulties.

3. Pupils failing in two or three subjects are sometimes considered sufficiently grave problems to need special attention.

4. The Nine A pupils, because they are getting ready to go to Senior High School.

5. Special cases referred to the adviser by teachers, deans, and other administrative officials.

The procedure varies; though the end to be attained, a better adjustment of the child to the school environment, is the same.

1. The adviser secures information from teachers about the child, his abilities, and disabilities, his attitudes, and details concerning his out of school activities and home environment. In some cases this is reported on a form devised for the purpose.

2. By an interview with the child this information is supplemented, and his own reaction to the school and the school work secured.

3. She may give tests to determine the focus of difficulty.

4. She may call upon social agencies for special case work or treatment.
5. She makes contact with the parents either by letter, phone call, or office visit, or home call.
6. Recommendations are made to parents and teachers and an attempt to help the child understand his difficulties is made.
7. His work is watched and follow-up work is done at subsequent periods.

7. *Other problem cases*

Besides the failure group, other problem cases are handled by the advisers. They include behavior cases, poverty cases, special cases of backward and irregular pupils. They are referred by teachers, deans, and other administrative officers. The procedure is the same as in the case of failing pupils. In this work also, it is frequently necessary to call upon the social agencies.

8. *Clubs*

The club activities of the junior high schools afford a means, frequently, of bringing occupational information before these groups. In two of the junior high schools, advisers sponsor Occupations Clubs. Even where they do not sponsor these clubs they utilize their activities to present vocational information.

9. *Placement*

Full Time

Although in general, pupils dropping out of school are referred to the Central Office for placement, in five cases some placements are made from the schools. Two of the schools place graduates as well; some schools make part of the placements and utilize the Central Office for others. Personnel cards containing school history accompany children sent to the Central Office for placement.

The placement of children is handled entirely by the Vocational Adviser at the Wendell Phillips High School.

Part Time

In five schools part-time jobs are solicited; in one other, received but not solicited. Because of the local character of most of this work, no pupils are directed to the Central Office for part-time placement.

10. *Transfers*

In approximately half of the junior high schools, the Vocational Adviser has some responsibility in connection with the issuing of outgoing transfers and the accompanying records of credit. The adviser seems to be the logical person to see that the credit records and transfers for the graduating class are sent to the receiving schools, since she had charge of enrolling this group for their high school courses. In addition the handling of the other transfers and credits is often undertaken because of the advantage of having this work taken care of by one person. This work is sometimes assumed by the adviser to make certain that she has a complete record of all drop-outs or pupils leaving the school. The names of pupils who have failed to enter the receiving school are in many cases referred to the attendance officer.

11. *Drop-outs and certificating*

The issuing of employment certificates to graduates or undergraduates for after school vacation, or full-time work is taken care of by the Vocational Adviser in the school. In this way it is possible to be certain that children remain in school until all papers are complete and it has been determined that they are eligible for employment. It is also more convenient for both child and parents because of the location near the home. Parents are interviewed at school, at home, and at their work. Some appointments are made by phone, and some by letter, and because of this facility of communication with the home, the adviser may be certain that the parent is in accord with the plan from the start.

This work involves the establishment of a proof of age, securing a statement regarding hours, type, and conditions of work from the prospective employer, and issuing of school records.

An effort is made to see that every child between the ages of 14 and 16 who drops out of school secures employment and is properly certificated for this work; that pupils between 16 and 17 years of age establish their age and are enrolled in continuation school. Information about night high schools and trade schools is given to pupils over 16 years of age.

It is difficult to be certain that the adviser secures the names of all pupils dropping out of school. In one school the principal has ruled that the permanent records of all pupils be sent to the office of the adviser by the room teacher for examination before the name may be dropped from her roll. In another case, the adviser has charge of checking the return of books, locker fees, etc. The names of pupils under age who do not respond to notices or phone calls are turned over to the attendance officer.

II. The following list of duties was compiled by the counselor of the Roosevelt High School in Minneapolis:

DUTIES OF THE COUNSELOR

1. To interview:
    a) New pupils for purposes of making adjustments and to give them educational and vocational information.
    b) Withdrawing pupils for purposes of explaining opportunities at Vocational, Dunwoody, and Evening Schools.
    c) Pupils who wish program planning, including all 9A pupils.

d) Pupils who desire employment.

e) Pupils referred to her as dull or superior pupils, therefore requiring special programs.

f) All seniors to (1) check credits for university entrance; (2) interpret for each student the significance of his rating in the College Aptitude Tests; (3) help in securing placement.

2. To do other educational and vocational counseling:

a) Collect and record data necessary for counseling the individual child.

b) Explain the high school program of studies and educational opportunities of city to groups entering from other schools, parents, and teachers.

c) Collect occupational information and make it available and useful to pupils, parents, and teachers.

d) Arrange vocational conferences for groups of seniors definitely interested in special occupations.

e) Arrange for individual conferences between students and business men.

f) Handle placement by (1) preparing card file of seniors for Placement Bureau; (2) arranging for part-time work; (3) assisting girls to find homes in which to work for room and board.

g) To keep records of cases handled.

3. To collect information about occupations and educational opportunities by:

a) Directing an investigation of an occupation as part of a program of occupational research planned by the Central Office.

b) Assisting in other occupational studies by visiting places of business and interviewing business men.

c) Collecting and filing information about educational institutions.

4. To counsel failing students by:

a) Acting as chairman of Scholarship Committee of the senior high school.

b) Interviewing students, teachers, and parents regarding causes of failure and plans for eliminating failures.

c) Organizing plans for recognition and encouragement of honor pupils.[2]

III. The following list of duties comes from Edison Junior High School in Berkeley, Calif., a school where there is very little emphasis on the vocational aspects of guidance.

[2] *Vocational Guidance Bulletin,* Minneapolis Public Schools, April, 1929.

1. *Educational guidance*
    a) Talks to groups of pupils.
    b) Interviews with individual pupils for purpose of making out programs.
    c) Interviews with individual pupils for purpose of adjusting or changing programs.
    d) Interviews with pupils whose work is unsatisfactory.
    e) Checking records and progress of every child under her supervision.

2. *Contact with parents*
    a) Personal interviews.
    b) Telephone conversations.
    c) Contact with parents through P.T.A.
    d) Contact with home through visiting teacher.

3. *Tests*
    a) Giving group test.
    b) Giving individual tests.
    c) Scoring tests and recording results.

4. *Conferences with principal*

5. *Conferences with teachers*

6. *Assist principal in making term program for school*

7. *Handle some discipline cases*

8. *Clerical duties, e.g., checking credits of H9 and H8 classes*

9. *Coördinator*
    a) Between elementary school and junior high.
    b) Between junior high and senior high.

10. *Direct teachers*
    a) Regarding report cards.
    b) Regarding yellow record cards.
    c) Regarding bi-weekly reports (i.e., reports of pupils doing unsatisfactory work).
    d) Regarding pupil load.

11. *Director of*
    a) Problem children.
    b) Special class adjuster.

12. *Miscellaneous*
    a) Supervision of student teachers.
    b) Chairman of Honor Society Committee.
    c) Coaching.
    d) Visits to elementary schools.

APPENDIX C

A SAMPLE WEEK IN COUNSELING

DAILY HAPPENINGS TO THE VOCATIONAL COUNSELOR, JUNIOR HIGH SCHOOL[1]

Monday, Feb. 25

8:30 A.M.

Checked in at main office and stopped to see if any messages. Three boys waiting in my office.

Walter T. (old applicant for after-school job) asked if any openings today. Counselor explained about other things he had to do—for example, get birth certificate, and took family history on record which had not been done before.

Helen S. (old case) reports mother wants her to leave school. She herself wants to stay and wants me to tell mother she can not leave. Father not turning over all money to mother at present time. Counselor talked after-school job and explained about getting birth certificate and taking physical examination. She further asked Helen to invite mother over to talk over plans. (Helen said mother had wanted to come but she did not want her to.)

Frank S. (old case) wants after-school job. Counselor explained about getting birth certificate (mother thought baptismal certificate was sufficient).

Counselor sent messenger for Joseph T. who wants full-time job. Report came back that boy was absent.

While in office, counselor consulted with principal and dean of boys concerning Tony B. who is in trouble again. Father in office at request of school—he states that Tony really does not want either to go to work or to go to school. Tony had sold pass into Western Electric where he was to apply, to another boy, for 50 cents. Tony and father turned over to counselor, who ex-

---

[1] As children were interviewed, rough notes were taken on slips of paper and attached to the personnel card; the cards were arranged in order of the interviews. During the day at intervals the running record was made in rough; at the end of the week the typed copy was made. It will be seen that the pressure of work this week allowed no time for writing up entries on the personnel cards themselves. This will have to be done later from the notes on slips of paper, still attached. A similar record of happenings made in April or May would show much more educational guidance being done, for it is at this time 9A pupils who are about to graduate are interviewed. As the larger percent go on to high school, the interview is concerned largely with a discussion of courses of study and electives.

plained that Tony could go to Camp for malnourished boys, full time parental school (24 hours per day) or he could get a job. Tony said he would try to get the job. Father will apply with boy today at two places and he will try to go with him every day when he himself is not looking for work. (Explanation: B. of Ed. Placement Dept. at the present time does not try to place boy enrolled in full-time school. Boy already out of school given preference.)

9:20 A.M.

George O. reports he got his certificate for after-school job and started to work Saturday. He has to get his glasses changed within a month or lose the certificate. Counselor told George to bring in dispensary card tomorrow with note to be excused.

Homeroom teacher of Joseph T. stopped to ask if counselor had seen boy this morning. Counselor explained that she had tried to find boy in building and had concluded that he was applying for job.

Melvin F., graduate Feb., came in and reported he had been laid off—had been twice to Continuation School since leaving Farragut. Counselor got record from office and wrote summary of record to Placement Dept. at central office, and told boy to continue coming into school until placed.

9:35 A.M.

Joseph H. (old after-school applicant) who did not pass physical examination reported that he had started to get glasses. Wanted to know about how he could gain in weight. Counselor called Medical Dept. at central office and found that boy was to go to Nutrition Clinic—had not been given card. Medical Dept. will mail card to me. Joseph asked about working this summer— usually went to grandfather on farm but plans to be in city this summer.

9:40 A.M.

Genevieve S. (old applicant—full-time job) showed me baptismal certificate—had previously brought in statement from city hall. Counselor explained about bringing note to be excused for physical examination. G. reports that job in bank which father thought he could get her has been filled.

9:47 A.M.

Rose K. and mother in. Rose has job in candy factory—wants help in getting papers. Counselor explained about proof of age and employer's statement—Rose to return.

10:07 A.M.

Counselor sent for Miles D. on list for full-time job. Boy absent.

10:10 A.M.

Opened mail—contents as follows:
Dispensary card from central office.
Notice from employer that he was mailing complimentary book.
Folder on occupations from Minneapolis.
Report from Child Clinic—Spinal T.B. case.
Notification of registration at senior high school of Feb. grad.
Notice from dancing school.
Report from central office on six cases.
Notice from central office about sending in time sheet.

10:15 A.M.

Called central office to get instruction about filling in form requesting leave for going to Convention.

Josephine B. (old applicant for after-school work) stepped in to see
if I had job. Told her to get Elizabeth P. to see if she had got
job I had sent her to.

Casimir K. (old applicant for after-school job) in to talk over getting physical defects corrected. Counselor called central office to
find out about place where boy should get corrective feet exer-
cises and special shoe. Boy to return to same clinic. Casimir
has started work on teeth—did not go to clinic Saturday because
father did not have the $5 for X-ray pictures. Casimir wanted
me to call dispensary and make new appointment. Date set for
Thursday after father will have been paid.

10:30 A.M.

Josephine B. back with Elizabeth P. Elizabeth got job at doctor's
home to work from 3 P.M. until after supper and all day Saturday and Sunday—to get $4.25 or $4.50 and carfare. Counselor
explained to Elizabeth about importance of getting telephone
calls for doctor correct—told her how she should check back each
telephone call after she had written it down. Counselor wrote
note to assistant principal explaining need for Elizabeth's being
excused at 2 P.M. and asking that arrangements be made with
sewing teacher for work to be made up. Counselor talked to
Elizabeth about mother and explained that nurse at McCormick's
had said her mother was to get half of her pay while she was sick.
Counselor asked Elizabeth to talk over following things with
mother and to report tomorrow—Elizabeth wrote down following
points so she would not forget.
Mother should take up matter of sick pay with company.
Mother should list clothing Elizabeth needs so that counselor
can order through School Children's Aid.
Mother should let me know whether she wants her case reported to the county agent for food and coal.

Mother should let me know whether she wants card of introduction to office of Mother's Pension.

Elizabeth to report back if she had been excused by assistant principal. (Later did so.)

10:50 A.M.

Josephine B. interviewed about after-school work. Counselor called two employers to see if they wanted girl to help take care of children. One employer will call back this P.M., other will call Wednesday.

John S. stopped to tell me that he cannot work on Saturday mornings as he has an art lesson then—can work Saturday afternoons and after school.

10:55 A.M.

Truant officer brought in new girl whom she was enrolling. Left girl to wait for counselor.

Gerald L., graduate Feb., had registered at Harrison but is dropping out as he has job as printer's apprentice. Counselor told Gerald he would have to take release up with senior high school. Counselor telephoned senior high school—senior high school counselor away for weeks because of sickness in family—principal handling drop-out cases in her absence—out of office—will call back. Telephone from principal of High School—boy to be sent over. Counselor wrote note to principal, saying she would make out necessary papers if records could not be found at Harrison but requested a written O.K. if he sent boy back.

Max K. and father in. (Max previously was sent to Dispensary and was diagnosed as having acute rheumatic fever with myocarditis). They had just returned from another visit to Dispensary—Max to have X-ray pictures next Saturday, charge $4. Father wondered if this charge could be reduced. Counselor called Social Service at the Dispensary, was referred to social service worker in General Medicine. Counselor explained family situation. Social worker thought fee could be reduced or canceled. Max to return to clinic next Saturday with or without money. Counselor told social worker that if doctor advised special care and thought Arden Shore Camp advisable, she knew there were vacancies and could get the boy in.

Interviewed new girl brought in by truant officer. Girl wants to be released from school. Principal previously told her she was to stay. Counselor explained that we would help with after-school job—and about birth certificate and physical examination. Took girl to Dean to get test and be enrolled.

11:45 A.M.

Saw librarian on way to Dean. She reported to me about V. family to whom she had given some money through me. Talked also about Paul R. to whom she writes. Boy at present at Camp because of malnutrition.

While in office Mary L. stopped me and reported that she had had her tonsils out.

Consultation with truant officer on a number of cases:

Christine C.—June graduate, under 16, who has gone on the stage as dancer.

Mildred F.—drop-out who has not got certificate.

Frank D.—problem case—who was returned to school.

Godfrey S.—failure in February class.

Joseph B.—court case for truancy.

George K.—drop-out who has not got working cert.

And about a dozen graduates who are being followed up.

12:20 P.M.

Helen S., graduate June. Is going to Continuation School and Placement Dept. wanted her to go every day. She has places she wants to go to directly, e.g., Ill. Bell. Advised her to go to Out of Job teacher at Continuation School and talk matter over with her.

William V., graduate Feb., in office. Placed this A.M. by Central Office at counselor's request. William reported to me that he had been assigned to Continuation School. Showed me book of rules of new employer—asked me about punching clock. Talked over a number of problems he would meet and advised him to ask his mother to let him wear good suit every day as this employer wants boys looking nice.

12:30 P.M.

James V. in to ask about mother coming over to talk to me about summer job.

12:40 P.M.

Gerald L. back from Harrison. Thinks things are getting fixed up—school record to be mailed in and he is to go down when birth certificate arrives from Wisconsin.

Teacher spoke to me about three of her homeroom pupils, girls who want to leave school (9B and lowest mental group).

Helen S. came to be excused to go to dental clinic.

12:45–1:05 P. M.

Lunch.

While at lunch teacher spoke to me about Victor Z. (old case) who is absent a great deal. Asked her to send boy to me.

Another teacher said she would pay for the glasses of Edward F., February graduate, who used to be in her homeroom.

Sister of Feb. graduate stopped to report to me that Theresa likes the job very much where I placed her.

George K. stopped to ask me if I would call up Dispensary to see if they would give him earlier date for tonsilectomy. Is to return.

Mary P. who wants after-school job, came to ask about going to B. of Ed. for physical examination.

Mother of Anna M. came to talk over release of daughter from school. Explained girl has to stay in school until she gets job. Girl will be excused to apply at specific places for work. Explained about physical examination, urged necessity for further education.

1:25–1:45 P.M.

Fire drill.

Conferred with Assistant Principal about credit slip for Edward M. who entered technical high school but who has transferred to Military Academy. Counselor to call counselor at Crane and get credit slip back. Tried to get counselor, phone busy.

1:45 P.M.

Frances K., graduate Feb., brought in birth cert. Made out cards and gave instruction about getting average card. Frances wants job at Ill. Bell. Told where and how to apply.

1:55 P.M.

Gerald L. back—last mail brought birth cert. from Wisconsin. Gave instruction about where to go to B. of Ed. and wrote note to interviewer explaining some things were irregular because of absence of counselor at Harrison.

2:00 P.M.

Tony B. returned—thinks he got job. At least was told to return Wednesday. Wants to be excused tomorrow as he heard of job through other boy. Gave me information about this boy who was former drop-out. Told Tony to have Charles come to see me as he is out of work.

2:30 P.M.

George T. wants after-school job, boy over 16. Is now delivering papers. Told him I wanted to consult with father before I considered him for job at 7 P.M., such as usher.

Homeroom teacher stopped to talk to me about case of George T.

Counselor went to office to turn over material on cases of two girls who had failed to enter this semester. Information obtained by counselor from visiting teacher at elementary school.

Later homeroom teacher returned in absence of George T. and told me he was suspected of stealing. Wanted me to know this so that I could do the best for the boy when placing him. Did not want me to put boy where there was temptation. This teacher reported to me also on case of Gloria R. who models for clothing houses. Dean of girls on case and suggested I get in touch with her.

3:00 P.M.

Joseph J., graduate Feb., stopped in from senior high school. Did not get shop he elected. Wrote note which he should give counselor at Harrison when she returns.

Howard T. (old applicant for after-school job). Counselor called employer to see if he needed boy—no openings but asked that boy put in application.

Girl from Feb. class stopped in to say she had changed course. Did not have time to talk further with her.

Wrote up roughly some of notes.

3:45 P.M.

Teacher came in to talk over cases of two boys.

Tuesday, Feb. 26

8:30 A.M.

Checked in at main office.

Interviewed Joseph T. (applicant for full-time job). Was hunting for job yesterday. Has place at 19th and California where he wants to apply. Suggested two other places. Had boy excused to apply—loaned 15c. carfare.

Tony B. thinks he will not apply today but will return at 2 P.M. to be excused Wednesday A.M. so he can go directly from home to apply for job at plant where he was Monday.

George O. brought note to be excused to go to eye clinic. Had boy excused to go.

Edward M. (applicant for full-time job) came to be excused to get teeth taken care of at clinic. Had boy excused.

Homeroom teacher of Victor Z. sent attendance record to show number of absences. Victor absent today.

Conference with truant officer on following cases:

George K.—drop-out.
Edward K.—graduate.
Chester L.—graduate.
Theresa S.—graduate.
Eleanor P.—June graduate.

Truant officer reported child whose mother is becoming mental case—child needs special watching at school.

Dean brought boy to me, Walter S. (old case). Wanted information about family situation and about after-school job where I placed boy. Conduct problem. Boy suspended until parent comes.

John S. in with note to be excused to go to B. of Ed. for physical exam.

Pauline M., pupil over a year ago, who transferred to parochial, in to get help in getting school record. Checked record and found age different from that she was claiming and if record we had was correct, girl would not have days attendance between 13th and 14th birthdays. Called counselor at central office and reported. Got instructions for girl and gave them to her. Claims she does not know name of church. Counselor told her to return home and get approximate location and we could then call the chancery office for the exact location of the New York church. Girl to return.

Talked to clerk in office about girls' cases for whom I gave her information yesterday. Parental School papers being filed.

George T. in to get my telephone number. Father can not come but will telephone me.

Josephine B. in to see about after-school job. Told her one woman had telephoned she needed no one. Another was to call Wednesday.

9:50–10:20 A.M.

John M. and mother in. New case—took record. Mother wants boy released. Consulted with dean of boys and Principal— decision boy should not be released. Mother difficult. Clerk in office did interpreting, tried to show need for more than 7th grade education. Older sister is making $7. Explained that we would help sister get better job and help John get after-school work so he could stay in school. After mother left, talked further to John about need for education. Explained about birth certificate and physical examination for after-school job. Telephoned central office to get exact age of older sister and name of continuation school. Called continuation school and asked them to put the girl in touch with the central placement department.

Mail received—

Book on Vocational Guidance for review for school journal. Supplies from central office.

11:05 A.M.

Elizabeth P. reported on list of clothing needed. Mother wants to wait a while before applying for pension—prefers to get along without it if she can. Mother to go to company doctor today and will talk about her sick relief. Mother wants me to report their case to County Agent for coal and food. Elizabeth asked me about job in lunchroom. This I discouraged—one job was enough. Checked on hour she returned from job last night, 8 P.M.

11:10 A.M.

Telephoned High School and asked counselor to mail back credit slip for Edward M.

George K. came to ask about clothes we had ordered for him from School Children's Aid. Sent boy to office to clerk who checks in the clothes.

Consulted dean about three boys:

Walter S., whose father has not yet come to school—special delivery letter being sent by principal.

John M. who was refused certificate yesterday.

John E.—problem case.

11:45 A.M.

Consulted with librarian about Paul R., who writes her from Camp about future placement of boy. Librarian see boy's mother.

George O. reported back from eye clinic—is to go tomorrow again.

Left time sheet in principal's office to be signed.

Consulted with clerk on parental school papers for two girls, Julia and Mary K. who failed to enroll at Farragut.

12:00 M.

John S. in to be excused to go to B. of Ed. Had boy excused. Wrote card for him to take and gave directions for going.

Mildred E., graduate Feb., brought in birth cert. Made out card for her to take to central office to get over age card. Mildred has promise of job at radio shop in neighborhood.

Sophie W., graduate of a year ago, Feb., drop-out of senior high school came to get help in getting records straightened out— had changed first name when in our school and mother had to sign affidavit. Called central office to get exact instruction of what they wanted done. Sophie is trying to get into Ill. Bell Telephone Co.

12:30–12:55 P.M.

Lunch

Talked to two teachers about John M. and John S.

12:55 P.M.

Started to make up weekly report, interrupted by following:

Truant officer came in and went over a number of cases.

1:15 P.M.

William L. came to be excused to go to dental clinic Wed. A.M.

Clerk returned records on cases of Julia and Mary K.

1:30 P.M.

Note from clerk asking for information about a case.

1:35 P.M.

Theresa S. and mother in. Had wanted girl to go to dressmaking school—could not afford it. Counselor explained that dressmaking schools were for older people—if girl could not go to high school and take dressmaking, best plan to enter as dressmaker's apprentice. Called central office to see if they would consider special placement at this time. Counselor explained about getting birth certificate and told girl to return, so that special record could be sent to Placement.

2:05 P.M.

Anna M. in with birth certificate—will plan to have physical exam. tomorrow.

Tony B. came in to be excused to apply for job Wednesday A.M. Checked out properly through office. Talked with Tony about applying.

Checked in supplies which arrived in A.M.

Finished weekly report—copy to principal and to director.

Reports made out for supplies and request for leave.

3:35 P.M.

Left.

8:00 P.M.

Father of George T. telephoned and said boy could be placed on job in early evening.

Wednesday, Feb. 27

8:30 A.M.

Checked in.

Talked to truant officer about several cases. Asked her if she would visit Antoinette D., graduate.

Joseph T. reported what he did yesterday—two firms took his application. Talked over places where he plans to apply today. Had Joseph excused.

Elizabeth P. reported mother talked to company doctor about sick relief—will get it in about a week. Mother would like me to ask if county agent could visit her—she is unable to go there.

Edmund K. and Chester L. in—sent home to bring back proof of age.

Homeroom teacher down to show me further excuses from Victor Z. Victor sent for—insists he is sick.

9:10–10:00 A.M.

Talked to dean about advisability of sending boy to Camp. (Victor's father died of T.B. this summer.) Approved greatly. Telephoned Dr. A. in charge of camp openings and will consider boy. But Victor must be oked by Dispensary for T.B. Victor not eager about whole plan. Took Victor to Principal and he instructed the boy to bring mother tomorrow A.M.

While I was handling this case, truant officer came in and reported that D. family is moving out of city—brought name of city.

Teacher down to talk over three cases in her homeroom—Adolph M. who needs glasses sent for. Explained and told boy to talk over with parent and see me tomorrow.

Frank H. misplaced teeth. Telephoned central office to find out best clinic for dental surgery. Gave boy card and told him to talk over at home.

Theresa J., very bad eyes—is being treated at clinic—checked to see if she was there this Monday.

Talked over with teacher advisability of transferring both Theresa and Joseph H. to special sight-saving room in other school.

10:30 A.M.

Genevieve S. and Anna M. brought notes to be excused to go to Bd. of Education for physical examination.

Howard T. reported he applied for job and he believes that man is considering him seriously.

Josephine B. stopped to see if I had heard from employer—will come in later in day.

10:45 A.M.

Telephoned county agent and reported family of Elizabeth P. Made out School Children's Aid card and turned into office.

10:50 A.M.

Josephine B. came back about job. Telephoned three women about employment and found one who wanted girl for week-ends. In calling one employer found out about girl released a couple of years ago (made entry on girl's record).

11:20 A.M.

Teacher stopped to report that girl who entered Harrison High School had already dropped out.

11:25 A.M.

Checked in registration of graduate at High School. Hunted up credit slip and left on principal's desk to be mailed.

Wrote letter to Cleveland librarian who requested occupational material. Wrote note to central office, forwarding letter.

Note from teacher, asking me to speak at Girl Reserve Meeting late in March.

Letter to Edward F., graduate, to come into see me.

12:30–1:00 P.M.

Consulted while at lunch with teacher of public speaking club about getting up special bibliography of books which president of club could use (president of club plans to be lawyer—mother had wanted boy to take lessons in public speaking. We advised in consultation with other specialist that boy engage in activities such as these and do extra reading on lines of his interests).

Dean called me in on case of Walter S.—father had brought him back. Boy finally met the school's requirements and was reinstated.

Interviewed two new cases about after-school work, Joseph K. and William J. Explained about getting birth cert. and physical examination.

Genevieve S. and Anna M. excused to be examined, proper cards made out requesting examination.

Sophie W., Feb. graduate, back. Did not pass examination at Ill. Bell Telephone. Wanted me to advise her about clinic where she could get glasses changed.

Paul S., drop-out, came in to see me—nothing in particular. Talked over family and his job, and leisure activities. Gave him card to leader of boy's club.

George T. in about after-school job. Called Central Placement, about usher job. Gave George card of introduction to Oriental Theatre.

Consulted Dean of Girls about two cases, Lillian K., nutrition case and Stella N., discipline case.

Elizabeth P. stopped and I reported that county agent would visit tomorrow.

Nurse from elementary school stopped to tell me about civil service examination for janitress—knew I had several mothers who might be interested.

Josephine B. stopped in. I called employer and made appointment for her to apply.

Teacher came in to talk over two boys.

Principal sent up letter for me to answer from Morgan Park Military Academy requesting information about boy who is making application.

Called Stella N. in—asked about family, older brother whom we placed. Asked her if she wanted week-end job. Stella reported girl who was not going to Continuation School (we have been refusing to release Stella for full-time job). Telephoned Continuation School and reported case of Mary K.

Melvin F. in to ask me to call Continuation School and get permission for him to come Friday instead of Thursday. He wanted to stay home to get message from prospective employer. I telephoned Continuation School and got permission.

3:00 P.M.

John S. reported he passed physical—will have mother come to school.

Teacher stopped to ask me if I knew anything about Marie J.

3:30 P.M.

Checked out.

Thursday, Feb. 28

8:20 A.M.

Checked in.

Joseph T. excused to apply for jobs.

George O. excused to go to eye clinic.

Edward M. excused to go to dental clinic.

Anna M. and Genevieve S. wanted to be excused to apply at printing company. Refused as I knew company does not hire girls under 16.

Mr. N. over—reported that Jennie left home last night and did not return—does not know where she might be. Will let us know as soon as he has any clues.

Henry S. came to ask about military academies. Wants go get into aviation—thought he might do it through army. Explained courses in engineering schools in aviation—asked him to have father and mother come over.

Matron brought me in several application blanks for women to apply for civil service examination as janitresses.

Mail arrived:

Book from employer on book binding.

Letter from employer requesting information on William V.

Report on physical examination for John S.

Notice from music school.

Two graduates, Edward K. and Chester L. in to report that they got their over age cards and assignments to continuation. Had been to placement. Talked over employment policies of specific firms where boys were going to put in applications.

Telephone call from counselor of neighboring junior high school wanting to come over for conference.

Telephone call from supervisor of counselors from Minneapolis, wanting to come out for consultation.

Telephone call from Director of Bureau wanting short report (oral) at staff meeting.

Counselor from junior high school arrived about 10:15 A.M. and stayed until 2 P.M. Minneapolis supervisor stayed from about 10:30 A.M. to 2:45 P.M. Counselor from junior high school wanted to learn about office workings and how counselor coördinated with it. Supervisor wanted to know about general policies and specific

plans of interviewing and guiding. During these conferences the
following persons were taken care of: (no entries were made until
at end of day and so some forgotten).

One boy in about after-school work.

One boy in about summer work.

Telephone call from local doctor, asking help on Mary S., former
pupil here, who had tried to commit suicide by taking iodine.
He felt girl should be taken into custody immediately—was
threatening suicide again. Girl was to return on following day
to him for complete physical—had been spending nights with
gang of boys. Wanted me to get word to court officer on case.
Counselor telephoned court and left word for probation officer to
call—asked it be marked emergency.

Dean brought Lillian H., nutrition case to me. Later new homeroom teacher much worried came to find out what we had done
and what she could do.

Institute for Juvenile Research called to consult about boy whose
mother refused to come to Institute. Tried to work out plan of
interviewing mother. Need for interpreter. I promised to call
next day telling her nationality.

Mother of John S. came in to give O.K. on his after-school employment.

Elizabeth P. excused to go to county agent—later returned and
checked in.

Employer called saying she would take girl for week-ends.

Edward F. came in in response to my letter. Uncle still does not
want to come to school. Made plans with truant officer to interpret and make visit tomorrow P.M.

Edward K., graduate, in to report—he has no work yet. Friend
sent word that he had job at Sears. Edward to return Tuesday
when I shall have more time.

Stella N. came to say she will have work week-ends to help earn
way in school.

Truant officer from Continuation School; later phoned about Mary
K. whom I reported yesterday and we consulted on another case,
Sigmund J.

Boy over from H. to get school record when he was in kindergarten.
Needed date of birth for some athletic contest. Hunted up
record, made out school record and had it properly checked out
by principal.

Homeroom teacher came twice to check up on Miles D., problem
case.

Before leaving building tried to get probation officer again. Reported main facts to office director, who promised she would get
message to Miss M., officer, tonight and have Miss M. call me.

3:45 P.M.

Left.

10:30 P.M.

Miss M. of Court called. Gave her facts. Will get in touch with doctor and will be in touch with me tomorrow.

Friday, March 1

8:25 A.M.

Joseph T. reported what he did yesterday and wants to apply today Had him excused.

Tony B. back in school—absent yesterday. Wrote note to Dean to be sure Tony had cleared absence—oked. Tony applied with father yesterday at Western Electric. Had not got job Wednesday. Wants to apply today. Had boy excused.

O. and J. (two boys who want full-time release) sent to me by dean to be sure they were following instructions. O. having work done on teeth. J. to get proof of age. Latter thinks he can get job with milkman. Questioned J. about friends at School. Visiting teacher over there reports that boys claim they stole for a J. boy at F. J. gave me some names and later in the morning stopped to leave a list of four or five more boys whom he knew.

K. in with note to go to Bd. of Educ. for examination. Reports he can not get after-school job he thought he had.

Matron in and brought me more civil service application blanks.

Elmer F. remembered that he was to be examined at Institute for Juvenile Research on Monday and came to get instructions. Gave them and had boy excused for Monday.

Note from Jennie N.'s mother explaining absence of yesterday. Said father had "kicked them out." Note sent down by homeroom teacher.

Elizabeth P. came in to get help about coal. County agent had given mother slip. They ordered coal and gave up slip to driver. Company wanted pay because they do not hold contract with county agent. Mother paid and company had not returned slip. Called Coal Company and they promised to return slip today.

Henry S. reported that mother and family are going to Hot Springs. When they return will consult with me about military academy.

9:20 A.M.

Hunted up Mary P. and told her I had after-school job. Called employer and made final arrangements. Had Mary excused for a longer time at noon to get clothes and to tell mother.

Mother of Frances K. over. Frances did not get job at Bell Telephone. Made out letter of recommendation for Frances to take to Placement Dept. on Monday. Frances at Continuation School today. Consulted homeroom teacher.

George P., graduate, in to get advice. Is laid off and wants to make change. Had him read part of pamphlet on printing, talked over his present job, his objections, etc. Gave him card of introduction to employment dept. of other printing firm. Discouraged change but told him he could investigate while he was laid off.

Mail arrived:

Report from central office on four pupils.

Credit slip from C. H. S.

Telephoned Social Service Dept. of Institute for Juvenile Research. Gave social worker nationality of family of Henry S.

Note to principal about sending out credit slip for Edward M. Made notations on personnel record.

Truant officer in—consulted on several cases, and made final plans for joint visit in afternoon.

Consulted with dean to be certain she would be around in P.M. in case Mrs. Z. came about Victor.

Teacher in to find out about family. Boy in her homeroom is refusing to buy school paper. My record showed economic need—will act accordingly.

Lillian H. in to report mother is going to take her to dental clinic on Saturday.

Max K. in to ask about X-ray—how much money he should take tomorrow when he goes to clinic. Gave him note reminding clinic about reducing fee.

George T. wanted to be excused to apply for after-school job. Refused as this can be done out of school hours.

11:20 A.M.

Teacher in—asked her for personal qualities of William V. about whom employer inquired.

Tried to start writing up some of record.

Clerk sent request for some of my supplies.

11:30 A.M.

Checked with counselor at Senior High School who had furnished me with name of employers of after-school girls, whom I had solicited for jobs.

Talked to teacher about Lillian H.

Did some more work on records.

Talked about Elizabeth P. to sewing teacher from whose class Elizabeth is excused in P.M.

12:10–12:40 P.M.

Lunch.

Talked to teacher about part-time job she had heard of.

Talked to teacher about boy absent.

Victor Z. met me in hall and reported mother was coming.

12:40 P.M.

Tried to locate Mary P. whom I had excused—not in homeroom and could not reach by telephone. Mary arrived—had had to iron a house dress to go this P.M. Had her write down exact directions of how to get to employer.

Josephine B. reported she got job. Is going to work tonight.

Boy stopped to see if sister had come in, graduate.

Telephoned Mrs. S. and asked her if she would be interested in civil service examination. Will be glad if I will send in application. Told her to have Clarence come in next week to see me. Boy still unemployed. Mailed application blank.

1:20–2:00 P.M.

Visit to home with truant officer. Explained need for Edward to have glasses before he got certificate. (Uncle who supports boy had failed to respond to my two requests to visit school.) Misunderstandings cleared up—uncle gave consent and will pay for glasses himself.

Mrs. Z. waiting for me on my return. Explained about Camp—not very eager for boy to go but gave consent for him to go to T.B. clinic Sat. (wrote note for boy to take). Will let him see Bd. of Educ. doctor and make application for camp after that.

Sent for William L. Explained about examination for janitress—boy will take application to mother and will see me Monday.

Howard T. says he expects job I sent him to will turn up—but will be interested in job at newspaper, which teacher told me about.

Miss M., probation officer, called to report what she had done. Asked my advice. Juvenile officer from police station to take girl to detention home Saturday.

Joseph H. came in to get card to nutrition clinic where he will go Saturday.

Teacher consulted on Victor Z. Reported conversation with mother.

Took some occupational material to a social science teacher.

3:35 P. M.

Left.

6:00–8:30 P. M.

Staff dinner meeting.

Write-up of this report made on Saturday. No time for write-up on case records this week.

ANALYSIS OF RECORD
Persons Seen

Pupils	92
Teachers	26
Former pupils	22
Deans	11
Truant officers	10
Mothers	7
Clerks	4
Principals	3
Fathers	2
Matrons	2
Librarians	2
Counselor from Jr. H. S.	1
Counselor from Sr. H. S.	1
Assistant principal	1
Nurse	1
Sister	1
Supervisor	1
Total	187

Contacts Made
Telephone and Office Calls

Employers	7
Central office	4
Court (probation officer)	3
Dispensary	3
Father	3
Counselor at other school	3
Doctor	2
Teacher	2
Continuation school	1
County agent	1
Coal company	1
Director of bureau	1
Medical department, central office	1
Mother	1
Supervisor of counselors	1
Principal	1

Letters Written or Received

Central office	5
Other schools	4
Employer	3
Clerk	2
Clinic	2
Principal	2
Assistant principal	1
Dean	1
Director of vocational guidance	1
Dispensary	1
Graduate	1
Librarian	1
Mother	1
Teacher	1

APPENDIX D

THE WORK OF CINCINNATI COUNSELORS[3]

The division of the Vocation Bureau which has now developed into the Occupational Research and Counseling Division, for eight years (1918–1926) included only occupational research in its program. However, in 1926–1927 the program was enlarged to meet a recognized need for educational and vocational counseling to be carried on by those who were in direct contact with a wide variety of occupational and educational opportunities in the community. The work in counseling began as a demonstration program in two down-town junior high schools and gradually extended its activities to a related school area. This gradual development has made possible a more thorough program than could have been undertaken had the services of the limited staff been extended immediately to the entire school system. The program at present is carried on in three six-year high schools, and three junior high schools and in nineteen eight-grade elementary schools which contribute to these, thus making possible a continuous program of counseling for pupils from the eighth through the twelfth grades in approximately one-half of the Cincinnati Public Schools, with a limited service available for special cases referred from any school or social agency.

The program carried on by the counselors consists of occupational research, classes in occupations, and counseling individual pupils.

1. *Occupational Research*

The Vocation Bureau believes that one essential of a counseling program is a solid foundation of accurate and up-to-date educational and occupational information which may be drawn upon by the counselors for their classes in occupations, and for conferences with individual pupils. In order to secure this information and to keep it at the maximum of accuracy, as well as to provide each counselor with contacts with business, industry and the professions and the point of view which such contacts make possible, the counselors spend approximately one day a week in the gathering and preparing of new and the revising of old data. In the process are included visits to schools and training centers and to industrial establishments; interviews with employers, managers, and workers, as well as with technical authorities in the various business and professional fields. The counselors study and analyze the information which they thus secure, and prepare it so that it may be used by other counselors, by teachers, and by pupils. This material now contains information concerning over 500 occupation and 89 training centers and is prepared in three forms: (1) printed pamphlets, (2) simple mimeo-

[3] From *Annual Report,* Occupational Research and Counseling Division, Vocation Bureau, Cincinnati Schools, 1933–34.

graphed descriptions, especially for the use of children, and (3) detailed occupational analyses filed in loose-leaf notebook form for the use of all counselors, who thus have in each school a definite fund of up-to-date information concerning occupations and the schools and special training centers which offer preparation for these. In addition the counselors' reference library contains over 3000 pamphlets and 200 books concerning some 1200 occupations.

It has been found that one of the most effective ways of helping the child to work out a satisfactory educational and vocational plan is to discuss with him frankly the definite facts concerning any occupation in which he may be interested, considering it in the light of its advantages and disadvantages, his special interests and abilities and the preparation required.

2. *Classes in Occupations*

Classes in occupations (or group conferences as they might be called) are taught by the counselors, who meet with each group of the eighth and ninth grade pupils for ten[4] lesson periods which are correlated with the classes in social studies. The aims of the classes in occupations are to help the child realize the importance and interrelation of all work, to broaden his concept of occupations, and to assist him in developing a method of thinking about occupations that will be of assistance in making his own educational and vocational plan as well as in helping him to understand the vocational problems of those upon whose work we depend. The classes in occupations are therefore of value both as a vocational and as a social study. In addition they provide an opportunity for the counselor and child to become acquainted and a helpful setting for the individual conference which follows.

3. *Counseling*

The conferences provide an opportunity for the counselor to discuss with each individual child the problems that directly affect him. They are of long enough duration to enable the counselor to gain the child's confidence and become acquainted with the various problems which may affect his future. The counselor is concerned not only with the child's future vocational plans and the ways in which he may secure the best possible preparation while he remains in school, but also with his educational and social adjustment, his leisure-time activities, his personality, and his family problems. The counselor is, moreover, concerned with *all* children—the slow child who is failing in school, and needs classes especially adjusted to his abilities; the bright child who needs help in selecting college entrance requirements; the child with special mechanical, artistic, or some other outstanding ability; the shy, unhappy child; the normal, average child. All these and many others come for counsel. The counseling is based on a knowledge of the child and of facts,

---

[4] In the senior high schools the periods are fewer.

made available through a careful system of record keeping, which lead to an understanding of each individual's problems and aim to reveal such problems as should be referred to specialists in various fields. Close coöperation with the social agencies of the city (such as the family case working agencies, the Juvenile Court, etc.) has resulted in many of these agencies' referring for counseling all children among their active cases who fall within certain age groups. In each case the agency sends a helpful record of information concerning the child whom they are thus referring.

Through the counseling program the counselor gives information to the child as it is needed, helps him to secure valuable experiences, assists him to interpret the information and experiences, and to discover his own interests and abilities. The counselor encourages the child to work out his own plans and make his own decisions, and never attempts to force another's decision upon him. Above all it should be emphasized that the counselor constantly strives to help the pupil develop a method of thinking which will assist him to meet his future as well as his present problems, including those which pertain to the preparation for, choice of, and adjustment of his part in the world's work.

4. *Statistical Summary of Cincinnati Counselors' Work, 1933–34*

COUNSELORS' ACTIVITIES	SEVEN COUNSELORS	AVERAGE PER COUNSELOR
Occupational Research (days)	148.5	21.2
Occupational and Related Outlines Prepared	79	11.3
Classes in Occupations	1,190	170
Individual Pupils Counseled	4,013	573
Total Conferences with Individual Pupils .	5,620	803
Conferences per Pupil—Average	. . . . .	1.4
Brief Contacts with Individual Pupils (shorter time than conference)	10,825	1,546
Group Conferences with Pupils	223	31.8
Trips for Pupils (to factories, places of business, schools, etc.)	126	18
Contacts with Social Agencies re Pupils . .	759	108
Contacts with Parents (visits from parents home visits, telephone contacts)	849	121
Letters to Parents	1,825	260
Conferences with Principals, Teachers, and Staff	4,436	634
Clerical Work Done by Counselors (hours)	451.5	64.5
Clerical Assistance to Counselors (hours) .	750.25	107
Special Assignments (hours)	484.5	69
Transportation on Job (hours)	158.75	23

The above table indicates that special counseling service was made available for 4,013 pupils. These pupils also benefited from the classes in occupations. Furthermore, a special service (a brief conference) was given to some 5,000 additional pupils. Another 1,593 pupils were members of the classes in occupations, but time did not permit their being included in the counseling program. All of the above benefited from the research concerning occupational and educational opportunities. It is, of course, impossible to estimate the number of pupils who made use of the results of this research through their own teachers as they were members of schools not included in the classes in occupations or in the counseling program.

Similar figures are available for comparable purposes for a number of years. The only significant change during the past year has been that the amount of work done with individual children (individual and group conferences, etc.) has increased and that the time for this has been taken from that spent in occupational research which has decreased by forty-six days for all counselors.

APPENDIX E

BLANK FORMS IN USE FOR THE PURPOSE OF RECORDING INFORMATION ABOUT PUPILS FOR THE USE OF THE COUNSELOR

The practice in Chicago was for the counselor to meet the seventh-grade pupils in groups, and to explain the different courses that the pupil might elect in junior high school. The following blank was filled out by the pupil under the direction of the counselor. Later these blanks were examined and, if there were obvious inconsistencies between selection of course and choice of occupation, the adviser arranged for an individual interview.

1. Name..
2. Address................................Phone..........Date..........Room..........Class..........
3. Junior High School................Grammar School................Birth date..............
4. Birthplace Father..............Mother.............Child.............Language..............
5.   HOME

6. Name	Occupa-tion	Educa-tion	
7. Father			16. Type of books enjoyed..........No. per week........
8. Mother			17. Magazines...
9.			18. Home Study..........................Time.....................
10.			19. Supplementary reading........Subjects..............
11.			20. Outside lessons (music dancing, art)................Time practice......
12.			21. Home duties.........................Time.....................
13.			22. Movies.....................................Times per week....
14.			23. Clubs..
15.			24. Leisure occupation..
			25. ....

26. Parent's plan, Education..
27. Occupation...
28.   SCHOOL
29. Studies enjoyed most...least..........................
30. School clubs..
31. Athletics..
32. Offices held..
33. Course chosen, dates..
34. Occupational choice or general tendency, dates................................

The card also contained space for school record during junior high school, employment record, and physical record, as well as counselors estimate with respect to an enumerated list of qualities.

In Cincinnati the first contact with the pupil is in the eighth grade in the class in occupations, which is taught by the counselor. At the initial session of the class the counselor obtains personal information about each pupil to be utilized later when individual conferences are held. Following are the Student Information and Teacher's Estimate blanks used in the Cincinnati schools.

CINCINNATI PUBLIC SCHOOLS

Student Information

Date...

Public School.........................Grade.........................Home Room.........................

School attended last year...

Student's Name...

| Last Name | First Name |

Address (1)...Telephone.................

(2).........................(3).........................(4).........................

Age......Date of Birth: month.................day......year........Place of Birth............

( ) Father $\begin{cases} \text{living} \\ \text{dead} \end{cases}$ Name.............Birthplace.............Occupation................

( ) Mother $\begin{cases} \text{living} \\ \text{dead} \end{cases}$ Name.............Birthplace.............Occupation................

( ) Step-parent   Name.............Birthplace.............Occupation................
    Guardian

BROTHERS AND SISTERS

NAME	AGE	EDUCATION	KIND OF WORK
( )			
( )			
( )			
( )			
( )			
( )			
( )			
( )			
( )			
( )			

(Now go back and place checks in front of the names of all those who live with you.)

OTHERS WHO LIVE WITH YOU

NAME	RELATIONSHIP	KIND OF WORK

Student Information—Continued

1. What languages are spoken in your home?..
2. What are your favorite school subjects?..
3. What school subjects have been easiest for you?................................
4. What school subjects have been hardest for you?.............................
5. What grades have you repeated?........................Skipped?............................
6. Check any of the following subjects that you have had:

Electricity	Printing	Cooking	Typing
Machine Shop	Sheet Metal	Sewing	Shorthand
Mechanical Drawing	Woodworking (Manual Training)		Bookkeeping

7. What outside lessons have you taken in the past?............For how long?........
8. What outside lessons are you taking now?........................For how long?........
9. What are your favorite interests or hobbies?................................

....

10. What other thing do you usually do outside of school?........................

....

11. Name the magazines and books you like best................................

....

12. How many hours at home do you study each day?................................
13. In what clubs and activities do you take part in school?........................

....

   Outside of school?........................

....

14. Name any jobs you may have had................................

....

15. If you have a job now, name it................................
16. Name the school you expect to be in next year and the subject in which you are most interested................................

....

17. How far are you planning to go through day school?........................

....

18. Name several kinds of work that you might like to do later on........................

....

19. If you have decided on one of these, name it................................
20. Write here any special questions you would like to ask the counselor about schools, occupations, etc........................

....

CINCINNATI PUBLIC SCHOOLS

Teacher's Estimate (*Confidential*)

........................White
........................Negro

Student........................School........................Grade and Section................
Teacher........................Date........................

Please check the traits listed below which you feel apply to this child. The position of the check on the sliding scale indicates your judgment.

Teacher's Estimate—Continued

PERSONALITY

very shy   strong but pleasing   too aggressive

☐ no opportunity to observe

Comments:

INTEGRITY

dishonest   doubtful   honest and dependable   unusually high sense of honor

☐ no opportunity to observe

Comments:

LEADERSHIP

follower—unable to lead others   satisfied to have others lead   sometimes leads others   exceptional leader marked ability

☐ no opportunity to observe

Comments:

COÖPERATION

antagonistic in a group   works well with others   very tactful and coöperative

☐ no opportunity to observe

Comments:

HEALTH

very poor   average   very good

☐ no opportunity to observe

Comments (Please note any physical handicaps):

WORK AND APPLICATION

needs much prodding to do ordinary work   needs occasional prodding to just "get by"   does work required of own accord   completes suggested supplementary work   uses initiative to do more than required tasks

☐ no opportunity to observe

Comments:

Note any facts you happen to know about the home and family of this child. For example, financial status of the family, family's interests in child, child's attitude toward family:

Note any special aptitudes or interests:

Would you like to have a conference with the counselor concerning this child? yes ( ) no ( )

If you have any suggestions as to this child's plans please note on other side.

APPENDIX F

VOCATIONAL GUIDANCE IN BOSTON

[Mimeographed statement issued by Vocational Guidance Department Boston Public Schools]

The Department of Vocational Guidance is one of the organized supervisory departments in the school system for the care of the child. Its work begins in the elementary school, and carries through the secondary school and beyond into the higher educational field of the commercial and industrial world.

Its reason for being is due to the many complexities in the social and economic life of the times. When one realizes that the home occupations and apprenticeship systems no longer predominate, and that the kinds of occupations today number in the hundreds, if not thousands, organized *vocational* guidance of some sort is absolutely necessary. The enrichment of our school curricula, in keeping pace with the above changes in our national life demands *educational* guidance.

OBJECTIVES

I. *Through Educational and Vocational Guidance.*

1. To assist pupils to a knowledge of educational and vocational possibilities.
2. To assist pupils to a knowledge of the common occupations and an understanding of the problems of the occupational world, so that they may prepare more fully for lives of usefulness in the community. Vocational and political citizenship go hand in hand.
3. To obtain for each pupil, as far as possible, every opportunity which it is the duty of the public schools to provide.
4. To aid pupils to realize their educational or vocational aims.

II. *Through Placement.*

1. To assist graduates and undergraduates, who must leave school to work, in finding suitable positions. Physical and mental fitness, school preparation, and vocational interests are the determining factors in placement.
2. To aid those who need readjustment in their work.
3. To aid those, who in order to continue their school work, must have after-school, Saturday, or summer work.

III. *Through Follow-up.*

1. To help young workers to a better understanding of their relationships to other workers in their own and other occupations and to society.

2. To insure better coöperation between the public schools on one hand, and the higher educational institutions or the various commercial and industrial pursuits on the other hand, in order that there may be no gap between the two groups.
3. To make scientific studies of the information gathered for the benefit of the child, the school, the employer and society.
4. To assist in adapting the schools to the needs of the pupils and the community, through modification of the curricula.

SPECIFIC ACCOMPLISHMENTS

I. *Through Educational and Vocational Guidance.*

1. *For Elementary and Intermediate Pupils.*

"A Guide to the Choice of a Secondary School" was prepared to furnish information on all of the courses in the secondary schools in Boston, and to serve as a basis of study for counselors, teachers, pupils and parents. These pamphlets are distributed to all the pupils of the eighth grades of the City, and become the personal property of the pupils.

2. *For Secondary School Pupils.*

(1) Talks to high school assemblies and smaller groups have been given by members of the department.

(2) Individual interviews with members of the senior and freshman classes and with those in need of educational or social adjustment.

(3) Coöperation with departments of English, Civics, and Economics, in the study of occupations.

(4) A file of college and special opportunities which have interested high school graduates of this community during the past ten years, is available for use of pupils, parents, counselors, teachers and all others interested.

3. *For Elementary, Intermediate, and Secondary School Pupils.*

(1) Besides the Director, six vocational instructors (men) and eleven vocational assistants (women) constituting the central office, the department has representation in each type of school through a vocational counselor. Meetings with these counselors have been held:
   a. For purposes of information.
   b. For discussion.

(2) The counselors, according to the time allowed, give careful guidance
   a. In the choice of a secondary school.
   b. In the study of occupations.

(3) In some schools specific work in the teaching of occupations is given by members of this department. A vocational

assistant has been assigned to one intermediate school for this purpose. The pupils in the seventh, eighth, and ninth grades receive instruction. One period a week has been set aside in the curriculum for this purpose and a course of study has been prepared by the department for use at that time. In the Boston Trade School and the Mechanic Arts High School vocational instructors are giving full time to guidance and classes in occupational civics. Vocational Assistants also do this work in the Girls' High School, the Memorial High School for Girls, and the Dorchester High School for Girls.

(4) Every undergraduate who appears at the office for work is carefully studied with the hope of returning him to some place in the school system where he may receive further instruction before entering the working field.

(5) The Boston Public Library has coöperated with the department in arranging for books on occupations on the shelves of all branch libraries.

(6) A careful study of all evening school opportunities (both public and private) for boys and girls in Boston, has been made by the department and the schools listed according to the subjects taught.

II. *Through Placement.*

1. The department functions throughout the year. The office is open daily (except Sundays and legal holidays) from 8:30 to 5 except Saturdays when the hours are 8:30 to 1 (summer 8:30 to 12).

2. Placement is made only when it is determined that this is the best thing to do.

3. A report is requested from the school covering the school accomplishment, physical characteristics, and personality traits. This, with our own interview of the child, gives the department a basis for placement. On the other hand the job is carefully investigated and recorded (see card forms) in order that we may properly select the one for the other.

4. Those who enter permanent work are urged at time of placement to continue further study evenings.

5. Much time is spent in obtaining after-school work and summer work for those who are compelled to work in order to continue schooling.

6. Great care is given in readjustment cases, due either to ability or temperament.

7. Handicapped children are given special attention. The department coöperates with medical and social agencies in aiding this group.

III. *Through Follow-up.*

1. In order to help young workers to a better understanding of relationships to other workers and to society as a whole, the department conducts for these workers a noon office hour and an evening office hour twice a month, the first and third Fridays, 5 to 8 P.M. The young people bring to us all sorts of problems, financial, home difficulties, and many that may be termed temperamental.

2. In the fall of the year after graduation the department checks up with the higher educational institutions which our high school graduates indicated they intended to enter. This often means that we are obliged to write to as many as eighty different institutions throughout the country. The records of these young people are kept in a separate file and followed up once a year until they have obtained a degree, or have withdrawn, when the reason for withdrawal is requested.

3. For those in commercial and industrial pursuits various methods are pursued. Some are visited on their job. Others are sent letters inquiring about their welfare. Telephone messages and letters are sent to employers, asking an expression of opinion regarding the quality of the young people's work. Constructive criticism is welcomed from both.

4. From time to time the department has made recommendations to committees in charge of the reorganization of the curricula.

5. Many scientific studies have already been made and charts and graphs prepared by the department.

6. Complete studies of the graduates of our high schools, both boys and girls, five years after high school graduation, have been made by the Department.

7. A study of the graduates of high schools, ten years after high school graduation, is under way. From the results of these investigations, it will be possible to check the product of our schools in many aspects. Follow-up work, carefully and thoroughly done, offers to the educational administrator a splendid opportunity for the evaluation of the work of the schools.

8. As a result of this follow-up work better and more effective coöperation between the school department and the business and industrial world has been brought about. Follow-up presents a real opportunity for both of these groups to learn much concerning the work of the schools and the work of business.

APPENDIX G

PLAN FOR COURSE IN OCCUPATIONAL INFORMATION DRAWN UP BY DEPARTMENT OF VOCATIONAL GUIDANCE, BOSTON

Below is a proposed plan for the study of occupations in the ninth grade, Boston, from Board of Superintendents' Circular No. 17, 1928–29, pp. 35–39:

LESSON SHEETS—GRADE IX

Unit III.—Occupational Information—A Survey of the Field of Occupations in Boston (See Board of Superintendents' Circular No. 2, 1928–29, page 10.) (Approximately 12 lessons.)

OBJECTIVES	SUGGESTED PROCEDURE	OUTCOMES
1. Detailed study of those occupations most commonly found in Boston.	1. The Geographic Survey. A. The Neighborhood. B. Municipal Boston. C. Metropolitan Boston. (Ten-mile circle.) Note:—This can be very brief if such a survey has already been made in civics. The purpose here is to give an idea of occupational Boston. 2. The Neighborhood. A. The local trade center. B. The local banks. C. The local manufacturing establishments. D. The local mechanical shops. Suggestions: (1) Have the children draw a simple map of the neighborhood and have them put on it by symbols: *a*) The local trade center. *b*) The local banks. *c*) The local manufacturing establishments. *d*) The local mechanical shops. *e*) The local professional centers. *f*) The local transportation companies. (2) Have children study the kind of	1. To enable pupils to know the occupational opportunities Boston offers.

OBJECTIVES	SUGGESTED PROCEDURE	OUTCOMES

work done in these various centers.

(3) Have pupils report on the different kinds of workers employed in these places and tell about the duties they perform. Select several typical occupations for detailed analysis.

(4) Have pupils discuss the need of skill in these lines of work.

(5) Have the pupils list the different ways in which the necessary training for these occupations may be secured.

(6) Have pupils discuss the opportunities offered by these places.

(7) Have pupils discuss the advantages and disadvantages of owning one's own business.

(8) Discuss the advantages and disadvantages of working in one's own neighborhood.

(9) Have pupils try to find out something about the story of occupational development of their own neighborhood.

(10) Have pupils try to list some of the occupational opportunities that the future may hold for their own neighborhood.

(11) Have pupils try to find famous characters who were workmen in their own neighborhood.

e.g., Donald McKay—East Boston.

3. Municipal Boston.
   A. The retail district.
      (1) The department stores.
      (2) The automobile district.
      (3) The market district.
   B. The wholesale district.
      (1) Wool   (4) Furniture
      (2) Shoe and   (5) Clothing
          leather   (6) Food: Fish,
      (3) Cotton   fruit, meat,
                            milk, candy
   C. The waterfront and railroad terminals.

D. Financial district.
E. Newspapers.
F. Manufacturing.
G. The professional center.
H. The educational center.
   Suggestions:
   (1) Have a large map of municipal Boston on the blackboard or have individual maps for pupils. Mark the great centers as they are discussed.
   (2) Study in detail each center to get an idea of the occupational groups within it, and the occupational opportunities it offers. e.g. The Occupational Study of a Department Store.
      a) The occupations.
         1. The office force:
            a. Stenographers.
            b. Bookkeepers.
            c. Accountants.
            d. Clerks.
            e. Office machine operators.
            f. Telephone operators.
            g. Messengers.
         2. The selling group:
            a. Salespeople.
            b. Buyers.
            c. Floormen.
            d. Cashiers.
            e. Stock girls.
            f. Examiners.
         3. The delivery group:
            a. Shippers.
            b. Chauffeurs.
            c. Expressmen.
         4. The store maintenance group:
            a. Carpenters.
            b. Painters.
            c. Electricians.
            d. Engineers.
            e. Watchmen.
            f. Janitors.
            g. Porters.
            h. Cleaners.

         i. Automobile mechanics.

5. Personnel group:
  a. Matron.
  b. Doctor.
  c. Nurse.
  d. Dentist.
  e. Recreation worker.
  f. Editor of the store paper.
  g. Educational director.
  h. Employment manager.
  i. Detective.

6. Executives:
  Officers, managers.

b) The occupations related to it.
  1. Manufacturers.
  2. Wholesalers.
  3. Banks.
  4. Insurance.
  5. Transportation:
    Railroads, steamships, aeroplanes, trucking.
  6. Public officials:
    Customs officers, consuls.
  7. Lawyers.

e.g., The Occupational Study of a Shoe Factory.
  Note:—Any type of large factory well known in the district may be substituted for the shoe factory.

a) The occupations.
  1. The clerical group:
    a. Bookkeepers.
    b. Stenographers.
    c. Clerks.
    d. Office machine operators.
    e. Telephone operators.
    f. Accountants.
    g. Messengers.
    h. Advertising force.

    2. Factory workers:
       a. Sorters. d. Stitchers.
       b. Cutters. e. Finishers.
       c. Machine operators.
    3. Selling group:
       Salesmen, buyers.
    4. Factory maintenance
       group:
       a. Machinists.
       b. Carpenters.
       c. Painters.
       d. Electricians.
       e. Plumbers.
       f. Janitors.
       g. Engineers.
       h. Cleaners.
       i. Watchmen.
    5. Delivery group:
       Shippers,   chauffeurs,
       teamsters.
    6. Personnel group:
       Nurse,   employment
       manager.
  b) The occupations related to
    it:
    1. Banks.
    2. Retail selling.
    3. Wholesale selling.
    4. Cattle raising.
    5. Tanning.
    6. Shoe findings:
       Cotton   Linings
       Thread   Buttons
       Buckles   Rubber
       Heels, etc.
    7. Transportation:
       Railroads, steamships,
       etc.
    8. Public officials:
       Customs officers, con-
       suls.
    9. Lawyers.
   10. Foreign salesmen:
       Retail stores.
(3) Have pupils give biographies of
    some of the great pioneers of
    industry in or around Boston.
    a) Merchants: Amos Law-

rence, Eben Jordan, Wil-
liam Filene, etc.

b) Shipbuilders: Donald Mc-
Kay, etc.

c) Sea captains.

d) The fishing industry: Stories of the Gloucester fishing fleets, etc.

e) Manufacturers: W.   L.
Douglas, etc.

f) Engineers: Gridley Bryant,
etc.

g) Inventors, mechanics, etc.

(4) Have children bring in stories of
the old businesses in the city.
e.g., The rope walks in the North
End. Shipbuilding in East
Boston.

4. Metropolitan Boston.
Typical industries of the surburban towns
and cities.
e.g., Woburn tanneries.
e.g., Lynn shoe and leather.
e.g., Waltham watches, etc.

Suggestions:

(1) On the map of Metropolitan
Boston have pupils indicate outstanding occupations.

(2) Study any occupations that
have not already been studied in
connection with municipal Boston.

(3) Have pupils bring in any stories
of historic interest in connection
with some of these industries.
e.g., The granite industry of
Quincy.

2. The growth of new in- dustries.	1. New Industries.
	A. Scientific.
	  (1) Engineers:
	    a) Sanitary.
	    b) Electrical.
	    c) Road builders.
	    d) Traffic.
	  (2) Laboratory workers:
	  Laboratory technicians.
	  Research workers in science, in mechanics.
		1. An appre- ciation of some of the newer opportuni- ties.

         (3) Radio-Engineers, mechanics, operators.

         (4) Aviation—Aviators, mechanics.

         (5) X-ray workers.

         (6) Mechanical dentistry.

     B. Business—Special executives.

     C. Clerical workers—Office machine operators.

     D. Store—Professional shoppers.

     E. Personal service—Beauty specialists.

  2. New Phases of Old Professions.

     A. Public Health Nurse.

     B. Factory nurse.

     C. Statistician.

     D. Domestic arts specialist.

     E. Forestry.

     F. Scientific agriculture.

     G. Advertising.

     H. Commercial artists.

     I. Interior decorators.

        Suggestions:

        Note: Material on these newer professions is not easily obtained. The newspapers and current magazines are the best sources.

        (1) Have the class keep a file or a scrapbook of all the materials they can find.

        (2) Have pupils who have information on some of the newer occupations write it out and leave it for succeeding classes.

        (3) Have pupils write to associations or to the advertising departments of some of the newer industries for printed material describing them.

OBJECTIVES	SUGGESTED PROCEDURE	OUTCOMES
3. The training necessary.	1. The qualities necessary. 2. The special skills necessary. Suggestions: This topic may be treated under 4, in the detailed study of some of the occupations. One or two occupations in which the class is particularly interested may be selected for definite study of these qualities.	1. An understanding of the demands of occupations.

READINGS—GRADE IX, UNIT III

For Teachers	*Pupils*
Chamber of Commerce Pamphlets. Massachusetts Department of Labor and Industries. Division of Statistics. Census of Manufacturers. Occupations. Gowin, Wheatley and Brewer.	Citizenship in Boston. Egan, Patton, Cloues. Vocational Civics. Giles. Occupations. Ziegler and Jacquette. Preparing for the World's Work. Isaac Doughton. Guidance for Youth. Davis.

APPENDIX H

NEW YORK STATE REQUIREMENTS FOR COUNSELORS[5]

The nature of guidance and counseling with young people in our schools demands the services of persons particularly qualified for the work by virtue of personality, maturity, experience and special training.

Personality—The counselor needs to have a personality which will gain and maintain the respect and confidence of young people; the ability to work with fellow teachers and to meet employers and others with whom he must make contacts outside the school.

These traits of personality are most essential for successful counseling with young people because the counselor is the one to whom the pupils should feel free to go for assistance when difficulties arise. The confidence which the pupil has in the counselor as a friend and adviser is all important.

Since the counselor must work in close harmony with all other teachers on the faculty he must be able to maintain cordial relations and a coöperative attitude. The success of the guidance program within a given school unit will be determined by the coördination of the activities of all concerned.

In all contacts with employers and others outside the school the counselor must create a feeling of good will and understanding. In this way the counselor can secure for pupils the consideration deserved.

Maturity—The exercise of good judgment is conditioned largely by a varied and extended experience. This may be expected from mature persons. Valuable as maturity is, counselors should not be appointed who are not physically active and who have advanced to an age when a sympathetic attitude toward the problems of young people has been lost. It does not seem probable that the desirable qualities will be possessed by persons under 30 or over 45 years of age.

Experience—The range of occupational experience is so great that no person may have all the desirable kinds. It is desirable that the counselor have experience in the school grades or type of school in which he expects to counsel. Since the greater number of our young people leave school at an early age and enter factory and commercial occupations, experience in these occupations will be valuable. Other experiences directly related to guidance problems are: social case work; visiting teacher service; participation in local surveys and report writing under direction; administrative work in the school grades in which the

[5] *Qualifications of Teachers of Vocational and Educational Guidance*, The State Education Department, Albany, L. A. Wilson, Asst. Commissioner for Vocational and Extension Education, August 1, 1930.

person expects to work; personnel work in large industrial or commercial establishments.

Education—In general, the education of counselors should be comparable with that required of other teachers with whom the counselor is to work. This is true, not only because the work demands adequate preparation, but because the qualifications for positions in the same school and on a similar salary schedule should be comparable.

Certification—. . . Teachers and other persons who devote half time or more to those activities commonly recognized as guidance functions in the full-time schools or those specially appointed for guidance work in the part-time schools are required to hold either a limited or permanent vocational and educational guidance certificate. The following duties are construed as guidance functions: teaching classes in the study of educational and occupational opportunity; counseling with pupils and parents relative to educational and vocational plans of pupils; assisting pupils to secure proper employment at the time of leaving school; engaging in follow-up of pupils who have left school to enter employment.

REGULATIONS OF THE COMMISSIONER OF EDUCATION

QUALIFICATIONS OF VOCATIONAL AND EDUCATIONAL GUIDANCE COUNSELORS

1. *Personality and maturity.* Candidates for certification should have: ability to work with men and women, particularly teachers, parents and employers, and to inspire and keep the confidence of boys and girls, and associates; ability to meet people, to take the initiative to deal with situations as they must be met in the counseling position.

Such persons should be mature in both years and judgment. (The ages of 30 and 45 are suggested as the limits for entrance to this work.)

2. *Experience.* Candidates must have satisfactory evidence of three years of approved experience. This experience must include teaching and such other experience as will enable the counselor to appreciate by contact the problems of young people both in school and in employment. The following kinds of experience are particularly valuable:

a) Industrial, commercial and professional, exclusive of teaching but inclusive of personnel work.

b) Classroom, shop or laboratory teaching or administrative work in the school grades in which the counselor expects to work. (This does not include student teaching.)

c) Social case work for social agencies and visiting teacher service.

d) Participation in local surveys and report writing under direction or in laboratory case work and reports on problems related to guidance.

3. *Education and special training.*

a) Graduation from an approved four-year high school course and the possession of a permanent certificate to teach, or *b*) Graduation from an approved four-year high school course and completion of at least three years (in 1934 four years) of approved college work.

c) In addition, all candidates for a certificate to perform guidance activities, must present evidence of having completed the following courses which may have formed a part of the previous professional training of the applicant:

General Courses

	CREDIT HOURS
Educational psychology (psychology of adolescence preferred) .	2
Principles of teaching	2
Educational measurements	2
Sociology	2
Economics	2
Principles of secondary education	2
Total	12

Special Courses

Educational and vocational guidance (advanced)	2
Analysis of the individual and counseling	2
Studies and research in educational and occupational opportunities	4
Principles and problems in vocational education (advanced) .	2
Labor problems, legislation and employment conditions . . .	2
Psychological tests in guidance	2
Total	14

Six credit hours to be elected from the following:

Social problems and case work	2
Seminar in occupational and educational information	4
The Junior high school	2
The high school curriculum	2
Personnel administration	2
Philosophy of education	2
Industrial history	2

Types of Certificates

1. The permanent vocational and educational guidance certificate is a life license. It is granted to applicants who meet the full requirements.

2. The limited vocational and educational guidance certificate is valid for three years. It is issued only upon request of a superintendent of schools after the applicant has been assured of a position to teach and

upon evidence that the requirements under paragraphs 1 and 2 have been met and that the applicant has completed at least six credit hours of work in the special courses required for the permanent certificate. The limited certificate may be renewed for three-year periods after the holder has had two years of successful counseling experience and has completed prior to each renewal 12 credit hours of work in the general and special courses required for the permanent certificate.

APPENDICES

Part Two: Placement

APPENDIX I

METHODS USED IN THE STUDY OF PLACEMENT

The data on which the placement section is based were secured by observation and interview in eight different cities, supplemented by a questionnaire sent out in the early part of 1933. Through the latter an attempt was made to secure information on a nation-wide basis in the following manner: Letters asking for lists of offices placing juniors or the handicapped were sent to the United States Employment Service, state directors of the United States Employment Service in every state, the United States Children's Bureau, all local branches of the National Vocational Guidance Association, the National Council of the Y.M.C.A., the National Board of the Y.W.C.A., and community chests and councils of social agencies in all cities with a population of 100,000 or more. The last-named were asked for lists of social agencies doing placement work of the sort indicated. Special lists of agencies for serving the handicapped were secured from Miss Louise Odencrantz of the Employment Center for the Handicapped, New York City, the American Federation of Organizations for the Hard of Hearing, and the American Foundation for the Blind.

Altogether letters were written to 166 different agencies or persons asking for lists. As a result questionnaires were mailed to 224 different employment offices with a letter explaining the purpose of the study. Fifty-nine completed questionnaires were returned by superintendents or directors of agencies. Ten of these had to be rejected for various reasons, thus leaving forty-nine which could be used. By sources of information the returns were as follows:

	QUESTIONNAIRES SENT	QUESTIONNAIRES RETURNED	QUESTIONNAIRES USED
Junior offices listed by U. S. Employment Service or Children's Bureau .	59	25	23
Offices listed by community chests . .	29	4	3
Y.W.C.A.	69	11	8
Y.M.C.A.	23	6	4
Agencies for the handicapped	44	13	11
	224	59	49

The forty-nine offices returning questionnaires that were used employed 146 persons on their placement-office staffs. One hundred two of these workers were employed full time, twenty-one half time, and twenty-three "part time." Altogether, in the twelve months or fiscal year reported on, forty-five of these offices interviewed 200,214 applicants and placed 27,920. Two offices failed to give any figures of interviews or placements and the replies of two are omitted because they were obviously inaccurate.[6] Few inferences can be drawn from these figures since there is no means of knowing whether all used the same definition of "interview" and of "placement." They merely reveal something as to the degree of activity of the agencies reporting.

In addition to the forty-nine questionnaires received from directors indicating the practices of their respective offices, ninety-four questionnaires were returned by individual placement workers giving personal information, ten of which were discarded for various reasons, leaving eighty-four which are used in this report. Sixty-seven of these were from persons placing juniors and seventeen were from workers in agencies for the handicapped.

The number of questionnaires returned by directors of offices was not as great as had been anticipated. The poorest returns appear to have been from the lists provided by executives of chests and councils of social agencies. Letters were written to the executives of ninety-three community chests and councils of social agencies. Seventy-nine of them replied, a remarkably complete return. Thirty-one reported that there were no social agencies in their cities doing any placement of either juniors or the handicapped. The other forty-eight gave a list of 137 agencies. Forty-three of these agencies were eliminated because they were on other lists, such as Y.M. or Y.W.C.A., offices for the handicapped, or junior offices connected with schools. Thirty-nine were crossed off because their names indicated that they were relief agencies rather than placement offices, and twenty-six had to be discarded either because they did not come within the definition, such as agencies placing normal adults, or because they were commercial agencies, or because their very names indicated rejection, such as "Grandma's Kitchen." This left twenty-nine agencies that seemed to meet the requirements and to them questionnaires were sent. As indicated above, four

[6] One office reported very nearly the same number placed as interviewed and the other gave a figure for placement that was very much larger than the number interviewed!

questionnaires were returned from this group, one of which had to be discarded since its function turned out to be that of placing children in foster homes instead of applicants in jobs.[7]

The relatively small number of returns from the Y.M. and Y.W.C.A.'s is due to the fact that most of the local branches doing employment work are serving adults, and only a few of those serving juniors have kept separate records.[8]

It is reasonable to assume that the questionnaires returned represent a fair sample of practice in agencies placing juniors. As for the handicapped, the number of agencies serving this class alone is small, and it is believed that replies have been received from a reasonable proportion of them.

The area covered by questionnaires and field visits included nineteen states and the District of Columbia. Altogether by both methods information was secured from fifty-four agencies in thirty-six cities. The geographical distribution was as follows:

California	*Louisiana*
Berkeley	New Orleans (2 agencies)
Fresno	
Glendale	*Maryland*
Long Branch	Baltimore (3 agencies)
Oakland	
Sacramento	*Massachusetts*
San Diego	Boston (2 agencies)
Colorado	*Michigan*
Denver	Detroit
	Grand Rapids
D. C.	
Washington	*Minnesota*
	Minneapolis (2 agencies)
Georgia	
Atlanta	*Missouri*
	Kansas City
Illinois	St. Louis
Chicago (2 agencies)	

[7] As a matter of fact the showing for the social agencies was better than this would indicate. As stated in the text 43 of the 137 agencies reported from this source were on other lists. All of these, the Y.M. and Y.W.C.A.'s and the agencies for the handicapped are social agencies. When grouped according to nature of agency it is evident that 23 of the 49 returns were from social agencies.

[8] Some of the returns from this group are somewhat vitiated by reason of the fact that they cover both junior and adult placement.

New York	*Rhode Island*
Brooklyn	Providence (2 agencies)
Buffalo	
New York (5 agencies)	*Tennessee*
Rochester	Chattanooga
Oklahoma	*Texas*
Oklahoma City (2 agencies)	Dallas
Ohio	*Washington*
Cleveland (3 agencies)	Seattle
Cincinnati (2 agencies)	
Dayton	*Wisconsin*
	Appleton
Pennsylvania	Milwaukee (3 agencies)
Philadelphia (2 agencies)	Sheboygan
Pittsburgh	

Following is the letter sent to the agencies together with the two questionnaires.

THE NEW YORK SCHOOL OF SOCIAL WORK

122 East Twenty-Second Street
New York

My dear Superintendent:

I am bringing to completion a study of vocational guidance which is to be published by the American Association of Social Workers. In order to make as complete as possible the part devoted to placement activities, I am trying to supplement my own observation by the use of questionnaires, which I am sending to agencies placing juniors and the handicapped.

Two types of questionnaire are enclosed. One covers the work of the agency and is sent in the hope that you as the person in charge will fill it out or see that it is correctly done. The other is intended for individual employees in placement offices from superintendent down.

I am enclosing two copies of the first, one of which may be kept for your files, if you wish. Not knowing how many employees there may be in your office, I am sending several copies of the second questionnaire. If more are needed to take care of your entire staff, I will gladly send them.

Please note that the information desired relates exclusively to the placement of juniors and the handicapped. If your office places other than these, please give information only for the divisions placing the types named. Also, the individual questionnaires should be filled out only by those dealing with juniors and the handicapped.

I shall deeply appreciate your help in making this study as complete as possible.

Yours very truly,

JOHN A. FITCH

JF:F

NEW YORK SCHOOL OF SOCIAL WORK

122 East Twenty-Second Street
New York, N. Y.

(Please return questionnaire to John A. Fitch at above address.)

The information asked for below is an individual record and is desired from each employee of placement offices handling juniors or the handicapped, from director or superintendent down.

City.............................State.............................Date...............................

1. Name of person answering...

2. Title or position of person answering...

3. Name of organization...

4. Type of placement done by organization:
   Junior...
   Handicapped...

5. Please give a list of your duties and indicate what proportion of your time is devoted to duties requiring ten percent or more of your total time:

6. Please indicate below, with a check, your educational experience:
   Grade school...
   High school..
   Attended college...............................Years..
   Graduated from college...
   Postgraduate study (other than School of Social Work)..................
   ....
   Attended School of Social Work..
   Graduated from School of Social Work..
   Master's degree...
   Doctor's degree...

7. Please indicate daily hours of work:
   Begin A.M...
   Lunch period (how long)...
   Stop P.M..

Saturday hours, if different...

How much overtime?

 a) Last week..

 b) On the average..

8. Please list all different jobs held since leaving school, including present position, together with length of time in each:

....

....

....

9. Length of annual vacation with pay.......................................

 Any without pay?...

10. Annual salary:

 Present salary...

 Maximum for your position...

NEW YORK SCHOOL OF SOCIAL WORK

122 East Twenty-Second Street
New York, N. Y.

(Please return questionnaire to John A. Fitch at above address.)

The information asked for below is desired from agencies, organizations, or departments or subdivisions of agencies, doing job placement for juniors or the handicapped and should be filled out by director of such placement or someone designated by him. (Where possible please answer questions with a check mark.)

City.............................State.............................Date.............................

Name of person answering...

Title or position of person answering...

Type of persons placed in jobs:

 Juniors: Minimum age.........................Maximum age.........................

 Handicapped...

Supervising Organization:

 State department of labor.........................School board.........................

 Social agency (give name)...

 Independent organization (give name)...

 Other (specify)...

A. Organization

I. Where is office located?

 School building.................Downtown office building.................

 Elsewhere (specify)..

II. Number of persons employed on placement office staff
  Full time..
  Half time...

III. Please give below (*a*) titles of all positions (if civil service designation differs from that ordinarily used, please give both); (*b*) number of persons in each position; (*c*) minimum and maximum salary for each; and (*e*) major duty for which each is responsible.

a) Title of Position	*b*) Number in each position	*c*) Minimum and Maximum Salary
(1)..........		
(2)..........		
(3)..........		
(4)..........		
(5)..........		
(6)..........		

e) Major Duty for Each Position

(1)..
(2)..
(3)..
(4)..
(5)..
(6)..
....

IV. How many of the staff members who interview applicants are
  a) College graduates ....
  b) High school graduates..
  c) Other (specify)...

V. What experience is required of new staff members who interview applicants?
....
....
....

VI. Are staff members
  Appointed from civil service lists?..
  Required to hold licenses or certificates?...
    If so, please indicate nature of license or certificate................
....
  Subjected to any other test?..
....
....
....

VII. Give number of applicants interviewed in last
Twelve months (or fiscal year)..

VIII. Number of placements in same period...............................

B. The Applicant

I. Recruiting
    1. Is there any recruiting of applicants?
        a) At present?..
        b) In good or prosperous times?...........................
    2. If so, what methods are used?

....

....

....

....

II. Receiving and registering applicant. (If there is any difference
between present practice and that of ordinary times, please indicate present practice here and usual practice on separate sheet.)
    1. Is applicant received
        a) By special reception clerk?...............................
        If so, what other duties does this worker have?

....

....

....

....

        b) By interviewer?..
        c) By some other worker (specify) ....
    2. Who fills out application blank?
        a) Applicant?..
        b) Clerk?..
        c) Interviewer?..

III. The interview. (If there is any difference between present practice and that of ordinary times, please indicate present practice
here and usual practice on separate sheet.)
    1. Is the interview conducted in private?
        Yes..
        No..
    2. About how long is the average first interview?..................
    3. What information is usually available about applicant other
        than what is on application blank?
        a) School record..

....

        b) Teachers' estimate ....
        c) Results of intelligence tests...............................

....

  d) Other (specify)..

  ....

  e) Are tests given in placement office
   (*a*) By interviewer?..
   (*b*) By someone else (specify)?................................
   (*c*) What kind?..

   ....

   ....

  f) Are applicants sent elsewhere for tests?........................
   What kind?..

  ....

4. Does interviewer advise applicant to return to school?
 Always?..
 Sometimes? (explain)..

 ....

5. Where it seems probable the applicant would profit from
 further school attendance, and the reason for leaving school
 seems to be economic, does the interviewer refer the applicant
  a) To scholarship fund? Yes................No................
  b) To social agency? Yes................No................

6. Does interviewer clear with social service exchange?
  a) Yes (all cases)..
  b) Yes (special cases)..
  c) No..

7. Does interviewer advise applicant about further training
 opportunities?
  Yes..
  No..

8. Does interviewer advise applicant about his vocational
 choice?
  Yes..
  No..

9. What is the primary purpose of the interview?
  a) Placement............ *b*) Vocational guidance................
  Remarks..

  ....

  ....

  ....

IV. Referrals. (If there is any difference between present practice
 and that of ordinary times, please indicate present practice here
 and usual practice on separate sheet.)
  1. Does interviewer refer more than one applicant to a job at
  the same time? Yes................No................
  Explain policy..

  ....

2. Is applicant required to furnish references?   Yes........No........
3. How is a placement verified?   (If more than one method is used, please number in order of frequency.)
  a) By return of introduction card...................................
  b) By letter of inquiry..
  c) By telegram..
  d) By telephoning employer...
  e) If the latter, how soon after referral is call made?
  ....

4. Are jobs investigated
  a) Before referral?...
  b) Shortly after referral?..
  c) Any other time?...
5. If no opening exists for which applicant is fitted, does interviewer solicit openings by telephone or otherwise?
  Yes...................................No.............................
6. If suitable opening comes in while applicant is absent, is he sent for?....................How?...........................
  ....
7. If applicant previously registered who is absent, and new applicant who is present are equally qualified for a job that has just come in, which is sent?...........................
  ....

V. Follow-up after Placement.   (If there is any difference between present practice and that of ordinary times, please indicate present practice here and usual practice on separate sheet.)
  1. Is contact made
    a) By letter?..
    b) By telephone?...
    c) Evening office hour?...
    d) Other means?...
  2. What is the purpose of follow-up...................................
    ....
    ....
    ....
    ....
  3. Please explain methods used in follow-up.
    ....
    ....
    ....
    ....

C. The Job

If there is any difference between present practice and that of ordinary times, please indicate present practice here and usual practice on separate sheet.

1. What methods are used in recruiting jobs?
   a) Phone calls................................   b) Ads..................................
   c) Visits to employers...
   d) Other publicity (specify)...
   ....

2. What proportion of employers' orders are received by
   a) Mail?...
   b) Telephone? (employer calling)...
   c) Telephone? (office calling employer)...
   d) Personal contact?..

3. When employers' orders are received over telephone, who receives them?
   a) Telephone operator..
   b) Special order clerk..
   c) Interviewer...
   d) Other worker (specify)...

4. Do interviewers visit places of employment? Yes.............No............

5. If so, for what purpose?
   a) Recruiting jobs..
   b) Investigating work places...
   c) Follow-up...
   d) Other purposes (specify)...
   ....
   ....

6. About what proportion of interviewers' time is devoted to such visits?...

7. Do you list all jobs offered?   Yes...........................No.........................

8. Would any of the following conditions lead you to refuse to list a job?
   a) Absence of educational content...
   b) Absence of promotional possibilities...
   c) Illegal conditions...
   d) Long hours...
   e) Low wages...
   f) Accident hazard..
   g) Health hazard...
   h) Moral hazard..
   i) Labor trouble..
   j) Other (specify)...

9. Do you clear unfilled orders with other offices?
   Yes...
   No...

D. Records

If there is any difference between present practice and that of ordinary times, please indicate present practice here and usual practice on separate sheet.

1. How long is applicant's registration card kept in active file?..................
....

2. How long is employer's order card kept in active file?.............................

3. Please send complete set of blanks and forms used, with explanation of use of each.

APPENDIX J

FUNCTIONAL ORGANIZATION IN AN EMPLOYMENT OFFICE

The following authoritative statement of the organization of an employment office is from the standard publication in this field. Chapter XV of Harrison's *Public Employment Offices* is entitled, "Departmental and Functional Organization in a General Office." The author of Chapter XV, is Mary La Dame, now with the U. S. Public Employment Service. Excerpts from Chapter XV are presented below with the permission of Mr. Harrison, Miss La Dame, and the Russell Sage Foundation.

The significant or distinguishing functions or operations of a local employment office . . . center around the employer's order for workers and the applicant who is seeking work. It is with the suitable organization into departments and by functions to be performed, the economical and effective alignment of duties in the bureaus, the adequate recording of these orders for workers and the registering of applicants for work, the exercise of judgment as to the suitability of particular applicants for particular vacancies, the ascertainment of the result when the former have been sent to positions, the securing of staff workers and their supervision, the maintenance of sufficient contacts with the public, the keeping of necessary records, and the choosing of proper office space and locations that the office is chiefly concerned . . .

The functions of an employment office may be classified broadly as those concerned with the placement process, and those with administration. It is but to promote and make as effective as possible the former that the latter exist.

The placement function of any local unit of a federal-state-local employment service is made up of various operations:

1. Recording orders received by telephone or mail.

   (An "order" is a request for a worker or workers with identical qualifications, the request being made by an employer to an employment office. It includes data as to the qualifications needed and conditions of employment.)

2. Soliciting orders.

3. Receiving applicants.

4. Registering applicants.

   (By "registration" is meant the recording upon the proper form in regard to an applicant some or all of the particulars which are necessary to intelligent referral. It is thus clear that a person can be interviewed without being registered. Or vice versa, the applicant may be registered after filling out a blank and mailing it to the office, without having been interviewed at all.

5. Interviewing and referring applicants to positions.
(By "interview" is meant the conversation which takes place between an applicant and the proper officer, in which the qualifications and desires of the applicant are brought out and in which a decision leading to referral may be made.)

6. Recruiting applicants.

7. Clearing unfilled orders and unplaced applicants.

8. Verifying referrals.
"Referral" is a term which has been coined spontaneously in employment offices throughout the country to avoid confusion with the word "reference" which has been used to designate the names of persons who will recommend an applicant. "Referral" is the process of arming an applicant with the proper credentials and sending him to an employer as a candidate for a position previously listed at the office.

9. Determining the activity of orders and applicants and notifying applicants to call in reference to a vacancy.

10. Filing order, registration, and verification forms.
(Verification is the process of determining the result of the referral of an applicant to an employer.)

11. Recording the performance of the office and gathering such other information concerning labor conditions as may be required.

In reality the primary operations of the placement process terminate, in the order in which we have listed them, with the first seven items. The referral of applicants to employers or of unfilled orders or unplaced applicants to the clearing house completes the initial process. All the subsequent operations, namely, 8, 9, 10 and 11, are record-keeping ones, but nevertheless essential to the proper functioning of the placement process.

Who Performs the Various Functions?

However limited or extensive a local unit of an employment service may be, all of the above functions . . . are inherent parts of it. Who performs each function and to what extent each admits of performance by one or more special workers will next be discussed.

Order-Taking. Orders received over the telephone are recorded either by interviewers or by a special worker. The small office admits of but one of these alternatives. The large office, of both. As to which person in the large office more satisfactorily performs the task there is considerable controversy.

Soliciting Orders. It has been the policy of most public employment offices to wait for orders rather than to go out and get them. In some of the more progressive offices, however, the superintendents themselves and the interviewers have visited employers periodically in order to secure their business and goodwill. But until the armistice was signed, very few offices employed special representatives to procure orders, and with varying results . . .

Some public employment office superintendents . . . are much averse to having orders solicited by one or more persons employed only for this purpose. They favor the performance of this function by interviewers.

Receiving Applicants. The duties entailed in receiving applicants is performed in most offices by the staff worker who is situated nearest the entrance. Simplicity of layout and signs aid considerably in properly routing the applicant. That these fail in the larger offices to prevent him from aimlessly wandering about or from interrogating several or the wrong interviewers, or from feeling altogether bewildered and timid, goes without saying. Much more satisfactory is the provision of a "floorman" in the men's division, or a reception clerk in the women's, junior, or other special divisions. The state employment office in Boston was the first to employ a floorman. In most of the larger offices of the wartime service they were also provided. In some offices, as in Columbus, Ohio, the superintendent acted in this capacity.

A floorman usually stands near the entrance, greets and directs each applicant; he also circulates about the floor, preventing congestion and maintaining discipline generally. The reception clerk . . . may occupy a desk near the entrance of the division to which she is assigned, there receiving and directing each applicant. She may provide for the dispatch of applicants to interviewers by the operation of a buzzer system, or by the distribution of colored discs on which numbers are printed, the color designating the interviewer and the number the sequence of the applicant. Through both the floorman and the reception clerk, though each may discharge certain additional duties, the function of receiving applicants is performed.

Registering Applicants. Registration may be performed either by the applicant himself or by a member of the employment office staff.

In favor of having the applicant fill out his own registration form, the following points are urged:

1. The intelligence of the applicant is indicated by the way in which he answers the form questions.

2. Certain personal characteristics, neatness, for example, are indicated that a clerk would not learn if he wrote out the registration form himself.

3. The applicant's clerical ability is directly demonstrated.

4. The time of writing out the card is saved to the office.

5. If the applicant reads the questions he will not resent them as much as if they are asked of him. He will see how they hang together and will appreciate their necessity.

On the other hand, a great many experienced employment officials take the opposite view and argue thus:

1. That all the ability that is shown in the filling out of a card is clerical, valuable only for workers in occupations which require this particular attainment. The great majority of positions do not require clerical ability.

2. That personality is not indicated in any way that we can safely interpret.

3. That it takes as much office time, first to give the applicant a card and to explain its use, and then to look over it in detail to make sure that it is complete, as it does for the office to fill it out in the first place.

4. That most of the cards would be partly illegible whether written by laborers or college graduates; whereas cards filled out by a member of the office staff would be in a concise and uniform hand.

5. That applicants do not answer questions satisfactorily nor give the information needed; whereas a member of the office staff would determine the data which would later be significant.

6. That a sample of the applicant's handwriting is obtained by simply having him sign his name at the bottom of the card.

In practice and by consensus of opinion the latter method seems to have proved more satisfactory . . .

Interviewing and Referring Applicants. In choosing the personnel of an employment service, probably the first function to be considered and provided for is interviewing. In an office of two persons, both are, or at least should be, chosen from the point of view of their ability to select applicants. Interviewing is not one of the functions which can be performed equally well by all members of the staff. It requires a greater degree of intelligence and a wider and deeper knowledge of human relations than do the other placement process operations. Yet in few if any offices is interviewing a man's sole duty; he usually performs at least three or four other functions. Obviously the freer he is to question and observe applicants and to weigh their replies about their occupational qualifications and desires, the greater his chance of judging them accurately both per se and in relation to specific vacancies. Particularly if the range of occupations which an interviewer covers is limited, the very repetition this involves, if practice counts for anything, makes for expertness of judgment.

Interviewing usually culminates with the decision of the interviewer to refer or not to refer an applicant to an employer. This decision is an integral part of the interview. A decision to refer the applicant, however, entails certain other operations not necessarily performed by the interviewer. These consist of making out an introduction form to the employer, presenting it to the applicant, and either clipping together the order form on which that employer's requisition has been noted and the registration card of the applicant referred for future record of the proper entries, or actually recording such entries immediately after referring the applicant.

In the great majority of offices the interviewer usually performs these operations. Otherwise any clerk who is not occupied in discharging other duties may perform all of them, or he may write only the introduction card. . . .

Recruiting Applicants. A few of the public employment bureaus, even before our entrance into the World War, gave some attention to the recruiting of applicants for war industries. The great majority, however, did not. Some of these latter operated on the assumption that available applicants would register if they desired the service of the office, and that if they did not the office was under no obligation to make any special effort to induce them to register. . . .

Only under very abnormal conditions would it be necessary to provide special workers to recruit men.

Clearing Unfilled Orders and Unplaced Applicants. Clearance consists of:

1. The assembling by the interviewer of unfilled orders and unplaced applicants for transmissal through the proper channels to other sections of the same office or to other offices not under the same roof.

2. The correct recording and transfer of the above.

3. The receipt of orders or applications from a clearance service within a local area or of clearance Bulletins from the State Clearing House and the distribution on the proper form of the items received for clearance to the proper interviewers.

4. The effort by interviewers to fill the vacancies or to place the applicants received for clearance orders on file or applications on file, or vice versa.

5. Communication by telephone, telegrams or letter with the proper clearing house, with other sections of the same Local Service or with other extra-local offices to effect clearances.

6. The cancellation of items.

7. The keeping of clearance records.

All the above operations, which involve any judgment concerning applicants or vacancies, must be performed by the interviewer who must also be responsible for some of the record keeping. The remaining operations may be delegated to those workers whose time best permits the performance of them.

Verifying. The recording of the result of the referral of applicants from the returned verification cards, and in the absence of these the ascertaining by telephone or letter of the result of an applicant's visit to an employer are fairly simple operations which in small offices are performed by interviewers themselves. In larger offices they are usually delegated to one or more of the workers who perform other functions. . . .

Determining the Activity of Orders and Applicants and Notifying Applicants to Call in Respect to Certain Vacancies. The above functions are such as not to require any very high order of ability; they can be performed by any of the clerical workers of the office trained to do so. In no offices are workers employed expressly to discharge these duties. In offices where there are assistants to the interviewers, they usually follow up unfilled orders and also notify applicants to call with respect to certain vacancies.

Filing. The filing directly related to the placement process is concerned with the active and inactive order and registration forms, with index, verification and employers' ledger cards, or any other forms utilized in the process.

Since it is desirable for an interviewer to take cognizance at the time of every new order received, he, rather than the order clerk, usually files it immediately. The filing of inactive order and registration forms, however, together with others that must be kept, is constant and in large offices is usually delegated to the order and registration clerks. Order-taking and registration give the clerks who perform these functions a familiarity with occupations which is helpful when occupational filing is required. Few public employment offices provide special file clerks. The fact that the staff of an office is much less engaged in the afternoon in the recording of orders and the registration of applicants, has made it possible for those performing these functions to do the filing.

Report Making. The daily reports of the work of a section are usually made out by an interviewer. The fact that these are required at the end of each day; that they can be made up only after the placement process is brought to a close; and that the volume of reporting is considerable and time consuming, militates against its complete specialization. . . .

The administrative functions of a centralized local service are many and diverse, but they entail a comparatively small volume of work.

Policy Making. Whatever policies and procedure are permitted the local service to determine or recommend will be decided upon by the superintendent in conference with his staff and the local employment committee.

Initial Organization. The initial organization of the office and subsequent adjustments not standardized by the state administrative office will devolve upon the local superintendent appointed to that office. He

to examiner. Referring all problem cases to psychiatric social worker. Referring all cases for other departments of the Association to department directors.

Taking telephone calls which come in her name or come from or for skilled or unskilled office workers.

Making order cards for all orders accepted from employers. When call is for kind of worker Bureau cannot supply, giving employer other sources which can help him.

Keeping in constant touch with employers to see what calls are still open and to see whether new jobs have developed. If applicants sent have been accepted, why, etc. Visiting employers for investigations and contacts.

During whole interviewing process with applicants and employers, keeping standards in mind—building up responsibilities in each group, helping to make the individual self-dependent and to think her problems through honestly—helping the employer to develop fair standards in which the individual is the important part. Talking over hours, wages, race, age, and religious discriminations, etc.

Matching abilities of applicants against requirements for which jobs are open, for filling specific orders promptly. (Carrying on matching process always during interviewing hours also. Telling applicants "what employers want" and how they must develop to be satisfactory for the jobs they are seeking.)

Referring applicant to employers, with proper introduction cards. Checking with employers later, to discover whether applicant was accepted. If not, why not, etc.

Telephoning applicants for particular jobs available or sending them postcards if not accessible by telephone. (Telegrams, when urgent.)

Telephoning employers for specific applicants—to interest them in granting an interview or in creating a job.

Pasting references, periodically, of skilled and unskilled applicants and keeping them in mind for particular jobs. Much "sorting of applicants" can be done in conjunction with this clerical process. Keeping track of badly filled references for further follow-up with employer— letter, telephone call, or something which will get the desired information.

Keeping current record on registrants' cards of every contact (call, telephone or letter—personal, school, employer, social agency, etc.) on current history card.

Keeping monthly report (current daily entries) of total interviews, individuals served (new and former) persons referred to jobs, referrals to jobs, persons placed, persons not registered who applied.

In special cases accepting payments from applicants, making receipts and checking payments on individuals' cards and in order book. Done only when it comes in naturally with regular interview. Making financial statement for Business Department on the night when conducting follow-up interviews.   (On other nights financial statement is prepared by clerk.)

Entering employers' orders in order book (required by law for all fee-charging agencies) and numbering them chronologically.

Referring all unfilled employers' orders to secretary in charge of clearance daily at 3:00 P.M.

Discussing special or problem cases with director and psychiatric social worker (often in department conference).

Sorting cards on current file for one month follow-up and turning them over to general office worker for sending.

Keeping list of:

1. All individuals referred to Social Coöperation Department.
2. All individuals under seventeen years of age, for Continuation School.
3. All individuals referred for scholarships.
4. All individuals under seventeen years of age.
5. Most desirable non-registered applicants (because our non-registered files cannot be made up in occupational classifications.)

Following up places to which individuals have been sent, for report of action.

Keeping in touch with changes in skilled and unskilled office workers' field, specific changes in particular business organizations and general changes in field as a whole.

Spending at least one day a week in the field, for soliciting jobs, and educating employers in the use of the Bureau.

Having one evening office hour a week for workers who have been placed and for workers who are facing problems on the job (whether placed by Bureau or not).   Talking over questions which are arising on the job, giving information about training, leisure-time activities, health, etc.—the regular placement and follow-up gamut.

Attending all department meetings, attending occasional Central Branch staff meetings, rotating with other members of department. Attending department committee meetings, rotating with other secretaries in department.   Attending special meetings in Branch or community (Welfare Council, Personnel Club, etc.), which deal with the problems of her particular group.

Representing director at meetings when director's presence is not possible.   Taking over executive responsibilities which are delegated by her.

APPENDIX L

FOLLOW-UP METHODS

Boston[9]

This summary of a study of the boys who were graduated from Boston English High School, Boston Suburban High Schools, and Mechanic Arts High School in 1920, 1921, 1922 was made ten years after graduation and is a continuation of a five-year study made five years previously.

1. Returns were received from 1,432 out of 2,007 graduates. This represents 71% of all the graduates.
2. The percentage of returns received from the English and Suburban High Schools combined, is 72% and for the Mechanic Arts High School 67%.
3. There were 1,213 graduates of the Boston English High School and Suburban High Schools included in this study.
4. The vocational interests of these graduates are very similar to those in the five-year follow-up study.
5. The occupational status of these boys ten years after high school graduation shows the following changes from the report of five years ago.

OCCUPATIONAL FIELD	FIVE YEARS LATER *percent*	TEN YEARS LATER *percent*
Skilled labor	7	7
Office clerical	22	17
Retail selling	7	5
Wholesale selling	6	8
Executive and administrative	15	15
Proprietors small businesses	4	6
Professional	36	39

6. Ten years after high school this study shows that approximately 2% of the cases reported were unemployed. This figure probably is too small to reveal the actual situation, but it is the best that can be arrived at with our present plan of reporting.
7. There were 219 graduates of the Mechanic Arts High School in this study.
8. The occupational status of these boys ten years after high school graduation shows the following changes from the report of five years ago.

[9] Result of ten-year follow-up study by Boston Department of Vocational Guidance. See also Chapter VI and Appendix F.

OCCUPATIONAL FIELD	FIVE YEARS LATER	TEN YEARS LATER
	percent	*percent*
Skilled labor	46	31
Office clerical	10	16
Retail selling	6	3
Executive and administrative	8	10
Professional	21	27

9. Out of 1,213 graduates of the English and Suburban High Schools reported in this study, 874 were engaged in the same occupational grouping both five and ten years after high school graduation. There is, therefore, 72% occupational stability from the five year to the ten year period after graduation.

10. Out of 219 graduates of the Mechanic Arts High School, 173 were engaged in the same occupational grouping both five and ten years after high school graduation. There is, therefore, 79% occupational stability among these graduates both five and ten years after high school graduation.

11. Table III shows in great detail the shifting of the graduates from occupational group to occupational group. One example as to how this table may be used is as follows:

    477 graduates of the English and Suburban High Schools were engaged in professional work ten years after high school graduation. Of this number 433 were already engaged in that type of work five years previously, the difference being accounted for by two boys who five years previously had been proprietors of small businesses; sixteen who were in executive work; sixteen in clerical work; and a scattering in other fields.

12. Out of 1,213 graduates of the English and Suburban High Schools 529 or 44% were actually following the vocational interest they expressed while in high school ten years later. At the time of the five-year study 48% were following their vocational interest.

    Some of the percentages for the various occupational groupings are as follows:

    Professional work—67% follow their vocational interest.

    Clerical work—45% follow their vocational interest.

13. Out of 219 graduates of the Mechanic Arts High School 102, or 46% were engaged in the type of work for which they expressed an interest while in high school ten years previously. It will be observed that the percentage of Mechanic Arts High School boys who followed their vocational interest is approximately the same as that of the English and Suburban High Schools. 50% of the boys of the Mechanic Arts High School who expressed an interest while in high school in skilled mechanical work were doing that form of work ten years later, while 42% of the boys who desired to enter professional work were engaged in professional work ten years later.

14. Information on the weekly salaries received by these graduates ten years after high school graduation was received from a total of 501 boys, or about 40% of the total number of cases studied. Weekly salaries range from $30 to $200 and the *median salary* is $53. The median salary five years previously for approximately the same percentage of boys was $32 per week. The present salary indicates an increase of $21 per week in a period of five years.

15. Salary information was received from 79 graduates of the Mechanic Arts High School out of a total of 219 graduates. The salaries range from $30 to $55 per week, with a *median salary* of $39. Five years previously these Mechanic Arts High School graduates received a median salary of $30 per week.

The median salaries for the various occupational groupings of the graduates of English and Suburban High Schools ten years after high school are as follows: professional work—$52; proprietors of small businesses—$60; executive—$53; wholesale sales—$63; retail sales—$42; clerical—$36; skilled mechanical work—$47.

16. Out of a total of 1,213 graduates of the English and Suburban High Schools who replied to this questionnaire, 110 or 9% were employed in states other than Massachusetts ten years after high school graduation. The three states which had the largest number of these graduates employed were New York, Pennsylvania, and Connecticut.

17. Only 5% of the graduates of the Mechanic Arts High School were employed in states other than Massachusetts ten years after graduation.

18. How many boys who were graduated from the English and Suburban High Schools worked their way through college? This study shows that out of a total of 308 graduates replying to this question 232 or 75% worked their way through college.

19. For the Mechanic Arts High School 34 out of 37 boys worked their way through college.

20. How do these high school graduates obtain their various positions? A total of 526 replies to this question were received from English High and Suburban High School graduates, showing the following results: individual effort, 339; assistance of friends, 75; employment agency, public, 15; school or college, 35; commercial, 9; advertisement, 19; relatives, 34.

21. Replies to the question as to how their various positions were obtained were received from 109 Mechanic Arts High School graduates, with the following results: individual effort, 56; assistance of friends, 24; employment agency, public, 3; school or college, 16; commercial, 5; advertisement, 0; relatives, 5.

22. What factors influenced these graduates in their choice of a life work? A total of 564 responses was made to this question from the English and Suburban High School graduates with the following

results: chance, 163; deliberate planning, 230; influence of teachers or other, 58; availability of a job, 70; necessity for any kind of work, 43.

23. 106 replies were received to the question as to what factors influenced them in a choice of their life work, from Mechanic Arts High School graduates, with the following results: chance, 21; deliberate planning, 49; influence of teachers or others, 10; availability of a job, 17; necessity for any kind of work, 9.

Philadelphia

The following statement by the Junior Employment Service of Philadelphia indicates the methods used in keeping in touch with the child, beginning with his decision to leave school to go to work.

Before a child over fourteen years of age leaves school for employment, arrangements are made for him to interview the school counselor who goes thoroughly into the question of school leaving. The counselors through their touch with Junior Employment Service, are informed regarding employment conditions for young workers and are usually able to keep children from absenting themselves needlessly while "looking for a job." Both the pupils and school benefit by this procedure. In special cases referred by the school, attendance officer or social worker, Junior Employment Service tries to secure positions for children of certificate age, but in general, placement is carried on only for those beyond the compulsory school age who have finished their school education. Through scholarships, and through adjustments of school work, and of misunderstandings with teachers and parents, etc., many more children are kept in school. If, however, school leaving seems inevitable, the school counselor gives the fourteen- or fifteen-year-old child a *preliminary blank*, and instructs him to have his prospective employer fill out the "promise of employment" before he brings it back to school. The "school record," which gives the grade completed, is not signed by the principal until after the pupil brings in the "promise of employment" signed by an employer.

If a pupil attending school applies to Junior Employment Service for the *preliminary blank*, he is invariably referred back to the school for it. In this way, the school always has a chance to make every effort to prevent school leaving.

The child and his parent then come to the local Junior Employment office for the child's physical examination and the fulfillment of all other requirements for the issuance of a certificate. A medical inspector from the Division of School Medical Inspection is assigned to each Junior Employment office daily from 9:00 A.M. to 12 M. for the purpose of making (without charge) physical examinations of applicants for employment certificates. Before an employment certificate can be issued, the medical inspector must certify that the child is physically fitted for the occupation specified in the employer's promise of employment.

In the afternoon, employment supervisors visit establishments to which employment certificates have been issued. These visits enable the supervisors to make sure that conditions under which children work conform with the requirements of the law. If they find that a child is no longer working for an employer, and that he has neglected to return the certificate, or if they find that the work is irregular, and merely an excuse for evading school attendance, the employment certificate is lifted and the employer informed of his responsibility under the Child Labor Law. Failure of the employer to return the certificate of the child who is no longer employed, may be reported to the Junior Employment Service by the child himself when he comes to Junior Employment Service for a new employment certificate or for help in securing a new job, or it may be reported by the continuation school when the teachers learn of the child's unemployment. As a result of these and other methods of checking juvenile employment, many children are re-assigned to school every year (approximately 3,500 in 1931–1932).

When it is learned that a child is no longer working for the employer to whom an employment certificate was issued:

1. *A letter* is sent to the employer asking him to mail back the employment certificate (if he has failed to do so).

> Dear Sir:
>
> It has been reported that. . . . . .is no longer in your employ. If this information is correct please return employment certificate #. . . . to this office at once by mail.
>
> If for any reason you do not have this certificate in your possession, please send a written statement to this office explaining what has become of the certificate.
>
> Yours very truly,
>
> EMPLOYMENT SUPERVISOR

2. *A letter—NP* (*notice to parents*) is sent to the parent asking him to come with his son or daughter to talk over and decide on a future plan now that the child is no longer employed.

> My dear. . . . .
>
> The employment certificate for your son. . . . . has been returned to this office informing us that he is no longer employed. Since he is under sixteen years of age, the school law requires that he
>
> 1. Secure another position and a new employment certificate; or
> 2. Return to class in a full-time day school and continue his education; or

3. Attend a full-time class of the vocational school, if such a class is available.

Please ask him to come in to this office to see me tomorrow morning between 9 A.M. and 12 M., so that we may talk over the three plans mentioned above, and he can decide which of the three is best for him at this time.

Very truly yours,

EMPLOYMENT SUPERVISOR

(If child does not respond, attendance officer is notified.)

At least once every two years, employment supervisors in each local office visit and revisit the firms located in their respective districts (a) to inquire into employment opportunities, (b) to learn working conditions, and (c) to advertise the service to employers. The information gained in each visit is recorded on duplicate cards, "Form C-160, Occupational Conditions," which are filed for consultation in the local employment and central administrative offices.

An analysis of the special personal qualifications, nature of work, opportunities for advancement and weekly wages in the occupations carried on in each firm visited is recorded on the reverse side of "Form C-160, Occupational Conditions."

If applicant is hired, he is sent "at regular intervals" "Form C-167, Placement Follow-up Three" (asking him to call at evening office hours).

If he did not get job "Form C-165, Placement Follow-up One" is sent, asking him to call at office.

Another form used in following up registrants who are working is "Form C-166, Placement Follow-Up Two" asking him to call at specific time.

Children 14 and 15 years old who require help in the matter of occupational adjustment or assistance in correction of physical handicaps are sent "Form C-154, Request to Call Two," asking them to call on continuation school day.

In selected cases, employment supervisors send letters to employers asking them to rate the young workers they have hired through Junior Employment Service, and inquiring whether they are still employed, whether they are giving satisfaction, what chances they have for advancement, and what suggestions for improvement the employers would make. If the employer is willing, this information is then used in advising the young workers. Employers have cooperated in this plan and the results have been excellent.

In its annual report for 1931–32 the Philadelphia Junior Employment Service gave the following statement of its follow-up practice in that year:

The plan tried out successfully with a group of older boys provides for a series of interviews with each boy placed and for a check-up with the employer upon the boy's progress. The interviews with the boys are arranged as follows:

1. Within a few days after accepting the position.
2. One month later.
3. Approximately three months later—planning if possible to have the interview during or just prior to the time of registration for evening school.
4. At the end of first year of work.
5. A minimum of one each year according to the needs of each case— until the boy becomes 21 years old.

The smooth operation of such a plan may, of course, be interrupted at any time by the boy leaving or losing the job. In general, the purpose of the follow-up is to help each one to realize the necessity of taking upon himself the responsibility of planning his own future.

No set program has been followed in these various interviews, and yet each one tends to serve a special purpose. The first contact is made as soon as possible after the position has been secured. Many young people experience difficulty in adjusting themselves to conditions which they meet in a new job—especially if it is their first one, and the counselor endeavors in the first interview to assist in this problem of adjustment.

In the second conference the emphasis shifts to a consideration of the duties of the job and the possibilities of advancement. Many of the positions, of course, offer little chance for promotion in the near future, but practically every job offers the boy, who is starting work, a better opportunity than he has ever had to learn about various occupations by direct observation. An effort is made to direct attention to a practical study of occupations through the material furnished by the position.

The third interview often appears to be the logical time to take up the consideration of further training, and, therefore, is usually arranged during or just prior to the organization of evening schools. At this time, the school records and reports of psychological examinations, which have been obtained for a small percentage of the boys, are of great assistance.

The fourth and subsequent contacts serve to check up on the progress of the individual. The normal boy will have developed considerably during a year at work, and many special problems are brought forward for discussion in these later interviews. In many cases interests have changed, and new planning is necessary.

The foregoing outline indicates that each interview tends to develop its own special emphasis, but the procedure is quite flexible and the guiding principle is to keep uppermost at all times the welfare of the boy in in all its aspects and to render such assistance as can be given to aid him in working out for himself the best solution of his problem.

Providence

The following statement of the procedure in follow-up in Providence is taken from pages 299–301 of *Organization and Supervision of Guidance in Public Education,* by Dr. Richard D. Allen, Assistant Superintendent of Schools of Providence. The statement following it, on benefits of follow-up studies is from pages 305–308 of the same book. See also Chapter VI, *Supra.*

1. In the orientation course of the eleventh and twelfth grades the pupils study the follow-up reports that have been made of previous classes. This fact tends to arouse their interest and to prepare them for the follow-up studies of their own class. The class counselor and the supervisor of placement, in their talks to the class, stress the import-ance of such studies, the need of promptness and accuracy, and the confidential nature of the facts given. Thus they do all in their power to ensure a favorable, coöperative attitude on the part of the pupils.

2. When the time for beginning the study approaches, the adviser usually invites the class officers to his home some evening to discuss plans for a class reunion. Sometimes they address the envelopes at this meeting and, together with the follow-up questionnaire, usually enclose a preliminary notice of the class reunion. An envelope addressed to the class adviser is also enclosed with a letter urging a prompt answer and full coöperation in the study. Usually from thirty to sixty per cent of the pupils will answer immediately.

3. After about two weeks, a second letter is sent to those who have not responded. It contains another copy of the questionnaire and a very urgent plea for coöperation. Usually this brings replies from twenty to thirty per cent more of the pupils.

4. The adviser calls the remaining pupils on the telephone—sometimes with the assistance of class officers. This brings replies from most of the delinquents.

5. The last five per cent of the pupils are the most difficult to reach. Some have moved away; some are discouraged and sensitive; and some are simply indifferent. Visits to the home by the counselor or by one of the home visitors are usually necessary in a very few cases.

6. Impossible as it may seem, many one-year studies show 100 per cent returns and the record is seldom below 97 or 98 per cent. Many three-year follow-up studies show 95 per cent of replies. The number is seldom less than 92 or 93 per cent. Five-year studies usually range between 85 and 90 per cent.

7. When the questionnaires are all accounted for the adviser treats them statistically, using previous studies as models. The assistance of the

supervisor of placement is always available and welcome, especially to new advisers.

8. Each study is then mimeographed by the central office and sent to all advisers, principals, and staff officers. Later the studies of all of the advisers of the grades in the different schools are combined to make available a picture of the city as a whole.

Benefits of the follow-up studies:

A. *For the graduates*

1. One of the ideals of vocational guidance is the preparation of an individual to meet the adjustment necessary in his vocational life with the maximum benefit to himself and to society. Everything possible is done in school to make the transition between the various school units harmonious. The transition between school and employment, or between high school and college is much more difficult than that between any two units of the public school system. The follow-up questionnaire invites the former pupil to register any of the difficulties he is having. If he is not employed, his returned questionnaire automatically registers him with the placement office. If he has inquiries concerning work in his particular field, and if the counselor, because of the size of the groups he has in school, finds it impossible to answer his questions, the placement office is glad to do so. . . .

B. *For the counselor*

1. The individual returns should help him to measure the effectiveness of his guidance. If Mary Smith has been aided in her selection of a stenographic course, has made an outstanding success of it, and has secured a raise in spite of the depression, the counselor may well feel that his guidance has been successful.

2. The returns serve to keep the counselor in touch with what is happening outside the school. Alice Jones who entered nurse's training reports that she wishes she had had Chemistry for example. Perhaps the subject is not required by the hospital she has entered. If her suggestion is seconded by several other girls who have entered the same institution, the counselor may well consider the advisability of planning the programs of those pupils still in school who are interested in this training in such a way that the subject is included therein.

3. Trends in business practices, in the types of work open to high school graduates, may be noted in the follow-up studies. It would be ideal if the counselor could have contact with the business houses into which his pupils go. Since time does not permit, the follow-up study will give some picture of the work these people are doing.

4. The follow-up studies may give the adviser first-hand information concerning occupations and occupational opportunities. He has a pupil interested in forestry. From his five-year follow-up study he remembers that Tom Adams went into this work and is now employed in the state. Tom would surely give this boy some of his time and tell him about the training and work in a manner more effective than a book.

5. The follow-up studies may furnish information to be used in his group guidance program. One counselor has used the most recent study as an introduction to the planning of the three-year program by the pupils.

C. *For the placement office*

1. The follow-up studies help to keep information about graduates up-to-date.

2. They furnish the office with the names of new companies employing graduates and with information about companies which are hiring graduates—methods of promotion, wage scales, etc.

D. *For the school administration*

1. Some of the suggestions made have pertinent food for thought in curriculum building. Consider the following recent one: "Bookkeeping should certainly be included in the last year of the stenographic course."

INDEX

INDEX

COLUMBIA UNIVERSITY PRESS
COLUMBIA UNIVERSITY
NEW YORK

FOREIGN AGENT
OXFORD UNIVERSITY PRESS
HUMPHREY MILFORD
AMEN HOUSE, LONDON, E.C. 4